A Nation Fragmented

JILL A. EDY AND PATRICK C. MEIRICK

A NATION FRAGMENTED
THE PUBLIC AGENDA IN THE INFORMATION AGE

TEMPLE UNIVERSITY PRESS
Philadelphia • *Rome* • *Tokyo*

TEMPLE UNIVERSITY PRESS
Philadelphia, Pennsylvania 19122
tupress.temple.edu

Copyright © 2019 by Temple University—Of The Commonwealth System of Higher Education
All rights reserved
Published 2019

Library of Congress Cataloging-in-Publication Data

Names: Edy, Jill A., 1966– author. | Meirick, Patrick C., 1966– author.
Title: A nation fragmented : the public agenda in the information age / Jill A. Edy and Patrick C. Meirick.
Description: Philadelphia : Temple University Press, 2019. | Includes bibliographical references and index. |
Identifiers: LCCN 2018037468 (print) | LCCN 2018038970 (ebook) | ISBN 9781439916018 (E-book) | ISBN 9781439915998 (cloth) | ISBN 9781439916001 (pbk.)
Subjects: LCSH: Mass media—Political aspects—United States—History—20th century. | Mass media—Political aspects—United States—History—21st century. | Press and politics—United States—History—20th century. | Press and politics—United States—History—21st century. | Political planning—United States—History—20th century. | Political planning—United States—History—21st century. | United States—Politics and government—1945–1989. | United States—Politics and government—1989-
Classification: LCC P95.82.U6 (ebook) | LCC P95.82.U6 E38 2019 (print) | DDC 302.23/0973—dc23
LC record available at https://lccn.loc.gov/2018037468

For Jill's Dad
For Michael Meirick and the memory of Lynda Meirick

Contents

List of Figures and Tables ... ix

Acknowledgments ... xiii

1 The Public Agenda in the Information Age ... 1

2 A History of the Public Agenda, 1975–2014 ... 18

3 The Character of the Public Agenda, 1975–2014 ... 61

4 Broadcast News and the Public Agenda, 1968–2010 ... 86

5 Media Choice, News Agendas, and the Public Agenda ... 115

6 Building Consensus on Public Priorities: Can the Public Agenda Be Focused? ... 148

7 Political Responsiveness and the Public Agenda ... 174

8 What Happened to *Us*? ... 199

Appendix A: Coding the "Most Important Problem" Question ... 209

Appendix B: Computing Diversity and Volatility in the Public Agenda ... 215

Appendix C: Measuring Agenda-Setting and Alternate Time Series Models	219
Appendix D: Collecting Data on the Media System and Using Ridge Regression	225
Appendix E: Analyzing the Pew Excellence in Journalism News Coverage Index	229
Appendix F: Coding Major Presidential Addresses	231
Appendix G: Public Agenda and House Hearings Data of the Policy Agendas Project	233
References	237
Index	249

Figures and Tables

Figures

Figure 2.1. Public concern about economic issues, 1975–2014	25
Figure 2.2. Public concern about domestic issues, 1975–2014	36
Figure 2.3. Public concern about international issues, 1975–2014	46
Figure 2.4. Public concern about terrorism, 1975–2014	52
Figure 2.5. Public concern about government and politics, 1975–2014	53
Figure 3.1. Public concern about issues during different historical eras	65
Figure 3.2. Public concern about issues during different media eras	67
Figure 3.3. Number of issues named as most important per poll respondent, 1975–2014	71
Figure 3.4. Number of issues "on the agenda" (named in 10 percent of Gallup poll responses), 1975–2014	73
Figure 3.5. Public agenda diversity measured across twenty categories, 1975–2014	74

Figure 3.6. Public agenda diversity measured across five broad
categories, 1975–2014   78

Figure 3.7. Public agenda volatility (the proportion of issues no
longer being named in 10 percent of responses after four to six
months), 1975–2014   81

Figure 4.1. Public agenda diversity over time as measured by
the authors' twenty-category H and nineteen-category coding
of the same data from the Policy Agendas Project   97

Figure 4.2. Agenda-setting relationship (Pearson's r) between
broadcast news and public agendas, 1968–2010   99

Figure 4.3. Path analysis model for issue coverage, news agenda
diversity, agenda setting, and public agenda diversity, 1968–2010   107

Figure 5.1. News agenda diversity by outlet, 2007–2012   139

Figure 6.1. The relationship between news consistency (mean
Pearson's correlation between outlet agendas) and combined
cable news ratings in points, 2007–2012   161

Figure 6.2. The relationship between news consistency (mean
Pearson's correlation between outlet agendas) and agenda-
setting effect of the overall news agenda, 2007–2012   162

Figure 6.3. The relationship between combined cable news ratings
in points and public agenda diversity, 2007–2012   162

Figure 6.4. The relationship between the agenda-setting effect
of the overall news agenda and public agenda diversity,
2007–2012   163

Figure 6.5. The relationships between social reality, news, and
public concern about the economy, 1968–2010   167

Figure 6.6. The relationships between social reality, news, and
public concern about crime, 1968–2010   167

Figure 7.1. Path model predicting whether the president speaks
about the public's top issue   185

Figure 7.2. Predicted values of public/House agenda match and
the interaction of lagged public agenda diversity and public
concern about defense, 1969–2013   196

Tables

Table 4.1. Issue-specific agenda-setting relationships between news coverage and public concern across the entire time span and three time periods	101
Table 4.2. Correlations between news coverage of issues and time, agenda setting, news agenda diversity, and public agenda diversity	103
Table 4.3. Linear regression predicting agenda-setting relationship and public agenda diversity from time, news agenda diversity, and news coverage of issues	105
Table 5.1. Zero-order correlations between public agenda diversity measures and their predictors	124
Table 5.2. Ridge regression models for news attention predicting public agenda diversity	128
Table 5.3. Top five topics by news attention in September 2008, a low agenda diversity month	136
Table 5.4. Top five topics by news attention in May 2009, a high agenda diversity month	136
Table 5.5. Mean correlations between issue agendas of news outlets	137
Table 6.1. Consolidated agenda categories for news and public agendas	156
Table 6.2. News agenda predictors of public agenda diversity, by outlet	158
Table 7.1. Predictors of response speeches in a year	183
Table 7.2. Public-congressional hearing agenda confluence	191
Table 7.3. Correspondence between public agenda and House of Representatives agenda	194
Table C.1. Original and alternate models for predicting agenda setting	221
Table C.2. Original and alternate models for predicting public agenda diversity	222

Acknowledgments

All book projects are group projects, and we are grateful to the many people who helped see this one through. Abby Peter and Madison Payton, who were University of Oklahoma undergraduates at the time, coded the Gallup "most important problem" data into consistent categories, and fellow undergraduate Travis Thompson hunted down data on how the media system expanded from the 1970s through the 2010s. Former graduate students Jackie Eckstein and Eryn Bostwick did preliminary statistical work to get data sets ready for analysis. Glenn Hansen offered invaluable advice for dealing with some of the more statistically exotic challenges the data presented. Rebecca Eissler helped us navigate the Policy Agendas Project data.

We acknowledge our debt to the many nameless coders who generated the data sets that made this project possible. They worked for Gallup, the Policy Agendas Project, and the Pew Research Center. The only one whose name we know is Joseph Uscinski. We are also grateful to the project directors who set out to gather this information and make it publicly available.

Many scholars offered constructive advice on parts of the manuscript, including Lance Bennett, Lori Bougher, Matthew Eshbaugh-Soha, Charlie Gee, Lindsey Harvell-Bowman, Jonathan Klingler, Max McCombs, Ashley Muddiman, and Josh Scacco. There were as many or more anonymous reviewers who gave of their time to read and critique both manuscript sections and the book as a whole. A host of patient people allowed us to bore them over lunch, including Talia Stroud and Rod Hart.

Susan Herbst and Bob Entman offered sage advice on the book publishing process, and the people at Temple University Press were a joy to work with. Editor-in-chief Aaron Javsicas was endlessly encouraging and patient, pushing us to create the best possible version of the book we envisioned. Nikki Miller helped us sort through the complexities of contracts and production. All along the way, they helped us realize what we hoped to achieve.

Lots of folks gave us moral support as the project grew and we obsessed over it. Amy Johnson, Ioana Cionea, and Makana Chock celebrated milestones and commiserated over setbacks with Jill. Patrick's wife, Christina McDougall, listened patiently to his descriptions of analyses and to his side of phone conversations about the project for four years.

Any remaining errors can only be our own.

A Nation Fragmented

1

The Public Agenda in the Information Age

> When we turn on each other, bankers can run our economy for Wall Street, oil companies can fight off clean energy, and giant corporations can ship the last good jobs overseas.
> When we turn on each other, rich guys . . . can push through more tax breaks for themselves and then we'll never have enough money to support our schools, or rebuild our highways, or invest in our kids' future.
> When we turn on each other, we can't unite to fight back against a rigged system.
>
> —**Senator Elizabeth Warren,** speech to the Democratic National Convention, July 25, 2016

> Understand, democracy does not require uniformity. Our founders argued. They quarreled. Eventually they compromised. They expected us to do the same. But they knew that democracy does require a basic sense of solidarity—the idea that for all our outward differences, we're all in this together; that we rise or fall as one. . . .
> For too many of us, it's become safer to retreat into our own bubbles, whether in our neighborhoods or on college campuses, or places of worship, or especially our social media feeds, surrounded by people who look like us and share the same political outlook and never challenge our assumptions. The rise of naked partisanship, and increasing economic and regional stratification, the splintering of our media into a channel for every taste—all this makes this great sorting seem natural, even inevitable.
>
> —**President Barack Obama,** farewell address, January 10, 2017

The phrase *American public* seems downright archaic in the twenty-first century. We have become a nation of groups: African Americans, born-again Christians, working mothers, LGBTQ people, Mexican Americans, Cuban Americans, low-wage workers, pro-lifers, anti-vaxxers, indebted college students, people with disabilities, environmentalists. As we have come to articulate and celebrate our diversity, ideas of the public as a united, undifferentiated mass have come to seem oversimplistic, even disrespectful. And each group has its central cause: climate change, marriage equality, immigration reform, police-community relations, family values, college affordability, the right to life, equal access to public places, paid family leave, minimum wage reform.

The potent tradition of American two-party politics has encouraged many to see this transformation from undifferentiated public to a surfeit of interest groups as a feature of the increasing polarization of American politics. Yet polarization into two increasingly homogenous political parties is quite a different phenomenon from fragmentation into more and more interests, and it has different implications for political processes. In the United States, party polarization is essentially framed as "the government should do more" (liberals) or "the government should do less" (conservatives), although some might effectively argue that it amounts to government supporting individuals versus government supporting businesses. Polarization could result in gridlock—the absence of policy making—or in large swings in public policy resulting from any change in the composition of the government. U.S. immigration policy is an example of the former; the passage and attempted repeal of the Affordable Care Act (Obamacare) are examples of the latter.

Fragmentation, on the other hand, suggests the kinds of outcomes that Senator Elizabeth Warren describes in her speech to the 2016 Democratic National Convention (quoted in the first epigraph). Although Warren is speaking out against the race-baiting rhetoric of Donald Trump, the pattern she describes has broader implications. Policy making may come to favor the few because no general public rises up to oppose it. When that policy making involves the expansion of rights to oppressed minorities, the lack of general public opposition may be of benefit in creating a more fair and equal society, but the pattern may extend beyond those cases. As Warren suggests, fragmentation may also clear the way for policies that favor the economically privileged and politically connected at the expense of everyone else because no widespread public opposition to it emerges. Our division from one another may have eroded the power of average people in democracy. Where once the sheer numbers of average people who recognized a shared problem might have counterbalanced the political influence of the wealthy or the connected, today the multiplicity of our concerns undermines our ability to, as Warren puts it, "fight back against a rigged system."

In his farewell address (quoted in the second epigraph), President Barack Obama, too, recognizes the problems of a fragmented public. Acknowledging our diversity, he nevertheless recognizes the importance of sharing common causes. Expressing concerns about unalloyed partisanship, he has as much to say about how people fragment into communities of interest, insulating themselves from those with different concerns and priorities. Obama expresses particular concern about how contemporary communication media foster those divisions, even to the point of undermining our shared understanding of social reality—of the facts.

Public fragmentation is not simply an aspect of partisan polarization, although each party has come to represent a coalition of causes. Thinking about American politics in terms of polarization continues to emphasize the role of political majorities, even as it recognizes the increasing distance between the two major groups. In contrast, thinking about American politics in terms of fragmentation reveals how the diversity of public priorities undermines the importance of majorities, potentially opening the door for adept interests to advance their causes at the expense of a general public that no longer recognizes its shared concerns.

This book examines how public interests have fractured over the course of the later twentieth and early twenty-first centuries and the role the media have played in their fragmentation. Between 1975, when three major networks still dominated television and the vast majority of Americans received a daily paper, and 2014, when most Americans had a Facebook account and could receive nearly two hundred cable channels, both the content and the character of the public's list of policy priorities, its issue agenda, have substantially changed. Today, even in moments of national crisis, the public agenda lacks the focus it had in the mass media era, and its fragmentation has implications for understanding media influence, political power, and, ultimately, how contemporary democracy works.

Fragmentation: The Public Agenda and the Public Forum

A lot of contemporary discussion about the state of American politics does not distinguish between fragmentation and polarization, but they are in fact conceptually distinct phenomena. Fragmentation involves a lack of consensus on issue priorities. Some people may see health care as the most important issue, while others see police-community relations as the most important issue. Where public concern is scattered across many issues, fragmentation has occurred. Polarization describes differently valenced opinions about a particular issue. One might support or oppose a single-payer system for health care. Where two groups are diametrically opposed on an issue or on a series of issues, polarization has occurred. Polarization can be observed in the context of particular issues;

fragmentation becomes visible when observing the public agenda, the ordered list of public issue priorities. Although a public agenda always exists, that list may be long or short, and public concern may be spread relatively evenly over many issues or focused on just a few. A more fragmented public is concerned with many issues simultaneously, producing greater agenda diversity—longer lists with less focus.

As Obama observes in his farewell address, democracy does not require uniformity or agreement among the public, so differences of opinion on particular issues are not necessarily troubling. Democracy does, however, require some degree of "solidarity," of common interests and a sense of shared fate, so what he calls the "splintering" of the public into "our own bubbles . . . surrounded by people who look like us and share the same political outlook" is deeply problematic. More fundamental than disagreeing about what to do about a problem (polarization) is disagreement about how to prioritize problems or about whether a problem even exists (fragmentation). When there is no agreement about what problems or issues we face, substantive debate about an issue becomes impossible. Rather than arguing to find a solution for any particular problem, we argue about what to argue about. If we cannot agree on whether police-community relations is a problem worthy of discussion and decision making, we will not be able to debate policies to address it. Developing a shared agenda is crucial for arguing to resolution.

In a geographically vast and demographically diverse nation like the United States, developing a sense of shared priorities is no mean feat. Normative theories of democracy usually imply the need for some sort of public forum, a shared communicative space for the public to collectively consider the community's issues, problems, and leadership. It is difficult to imagine a participatory democracy without such a space for identifying and prioritizing public issues and problems. A public forum also enables communication between leaders and citizens, for not only can citizens learn about the policy initiatives of leaders, leaders can learn about the concerns of citizens. Exactly how such a forum should function and whether a given forum functions well have been topics of scholarly debate, but those debates typically take for granted the necessity of the forum itself (e.g., Calhoun 1992).

Since the nineteenth century, the media have acted as a public forum, making people aware of incidents and circumstances beyond their immediate experience. A great deal of theory developed regarding the role of mass media, particularly mass circulation newspapers and broadcast television, in shaping the public agenda and the implications of their role for the ways that political power functioned in democracy. The vast audiences and small number of media outlets made using media a communal experience, but many scholars worried that powerful political leaders would use the mass media to manipulate public opinion and thus undermine democracy. In the later years of the twentieth and the early twenty-first centuries, the media system has been transformed with concomitant implications for the public forum, public priorities, and democracy. Now, scholars worried that the vastly varied media system, particularly cable television, would undermine democracy by dividing citizens who would no longer have media sources in common. A multitude of media outlets might either foster irreconcilable differences among people or enable people to opt out of even the most basic public affairs knowledge. As the media system changed, what became of the public agenda and, by extension, of the public itself? Did the media still serve as a public forum? And what were the implications for the way political power worked?

Mass Media, Mass Democracy, and the Public: The Rise and Fall of Mass Audiences

In the twentieth century, the role of the mass media as a public forum for mass democracy seemed obvious. Indeed, U.S. mass democracy and U.S. mass media grew up together. As voting rights expanded, so did the mass media. In 1833, the *New York Sun* ushered in the era of the penny press as the first mass circulation newspaper, so cheap nearly anyone could afford it. By 1850, virtually every white man in the country could vote. In 1920, the first commercially licensed radio station signed on the air (Douglas 2001), and the Nineteenth Amendment gave women the right to vote. In 1963, coverage of President John F. Kennedy's assassination marked television's ascension as a primary news source for Americans (Zelizer 1992), and, in 1965, the Voting Rights Act restored voting rights to African Americans. During this parallel development of mass media and mass democracy in the twentieth century, theories about the media's role as a public forum in democracy described and critiqued that role, articulating theories of media power that presumed the characteristics of mass media: a large, undifferentiated audience that received messages from a small number of outlets.

The idea of mass media as a national living room for political ceremony and spectacle emerged from ritual models of communication (Carey 1989; Katz and Dayan 1988; Peters 1995), but the idea of media as a public forum for establishing shared priorities was most clearly articulated in agenda-setting theory. In its earliest incarnation, the oft-quoted central tenet of news media agenda setting was that "the press may not be successful much of the time in telling people what to think, but it is stunningly successful in telling its readers what to think about" (Cohen 1963, 13). In other words, the news media were thought to focus public attention and concern on a limited set of public priorities, to set the public agenda. Media scholars Max McCombs and Donald Shaw (1972) demonstrated the news media's agenda-setting effects in the late 1960s. Although it was difficult to find evidence that campaign communication altered vote choice (Berelson, Lazarsfeld, and McPhee 1954), study after study would demonstrate that if news paid attention to an issue or a person, people thought the issue or person was important (Lazarsfeld and Merton 1948; McCombs and Shaw 1972). Evidence of a consensus-building effect also emerged: members of disparate groups who paid more attention to news had more similar issue priorities than did those who did not (Lopez-Escobar, Llamas, and McCombs 1998; Shaw and Martin 1992). Although the effects were pronounced, scholars distinguished between the news media agenda and the public agenda, in part because agenda-setting effects were not necessarily the same across issues (Neuman 1990). They also distinguished the media and public agendas from the policy agenda pursued by Congress and the president, who commonly sought to influence the media agenda and, through it, the public agenda.

Some scholars offered eloquent tributes to the role of the mass media in establishing a public forum. Elihu Katz says, "If one were designing a participatory democracy, one would make provision for a central space in which all citizens could gather together and . . . [i]deally the agenda would be agreed upon in the central space. . . . In the era of mass society and mass communication, these spaces would be served, even cloned, by generalized media devoted to the polity as a whole" (1996, 23). However, many recognized that the mass media's public forum manifested types of political power incompatible with normative theories of participatory democracy.

The idea of agenda setting as a form of political power emerged in roughly the same decade mass media agenda-setting effects were first documented. In the early 1960s, political theorists Peter Bachrach and Morton Baratz (1962) made the case that pluralism offered an inadequate explanation of political power. Pluralist analyses focused on decision-making processes and thus on open political conflict between opposing groups: Democrats arguing with Republicans, farmers arguing with ranchers, environmentalists arguing with developers. The decisions made illuminated the power structure. Bachrach and Baratz argued managing or controlling which decisions got made—that is, setting the political agenda—represented an even more fundamental form of political power.

If one could manage the agenda of decisions, one could limit the range of choices to those that did not threaten one's power and status. In this representation of power, overt political conflict was a kind of fig leaf. Relatively unimportant choices were vociferously argued, while the more fundamental issues that threatened existing power structures never came to the fore. In other words, Bachrach and Baratz distinguished between polarized debate on particular issues and crafting an agenda in which certain public problems were never debated at all.

Insights about agenda setting from political science and communication were blended to generate important theories about how political power worked in mass democracy. To the extent one could manage or control mass-mediated depictions of social reality, one could manage or control political outcomes. Control the issue agenda in a political campaign so it focuses on issues your party is perceived as handling better, and you win the election (Petrocik 1995). Manage the decision-making environment represented in the media, and you limit the range of choices to ones that do not threaten your power and status (Bennett 1990; Entman 1989; Hallin 1986). Manage the representation of the social world, and you manage public perception of something as a social or political problem in the first place (Lukes 1974; Spector and Kitsuse 2001). Pitch your policy directly to the masses via mass media's public forum, and you can avoid having to negotiate with your political opposition (Kernell 2007). Distract the public from your mistakes, and you escape accountability (Bennett, Lawrence, and Livingston, 2007; Entman 1991). The more effectively one controlled the public agenda, via the mass media's public forum, the more political power one had.

From the perspective of normative democratic theory, the concern was that the public would be convinced to focus on the wrong issues, trivial issues, or worse. Instead of debating regulatory reform of the financial industry to protect investors, the public could be distracted to debate criminal justice: How long should a particular con artist spend in jail for bilking his investors? The commercial incentives of the U.S. mass media just made the problems worse, for a commercially funded public forum was likely to give the public what it wanted rather than what it needed with regard to public affairs information. Many might prefer sensation and entertainment to the drudgery of policy discussion (Prior 2007), and commercially driven media that did not give it to them might risk financial failure (Uscinski 2014). Moreover, a medium without an audience would not be a public forum.

In the later part of the twentieth century, scholars found evidence that the public forum could be manipulated not only in terms of topics, or issues, but also in which aspects of the issues were most publicly prominent (McCombs 2004).[1] This possibility seemed even scarier, for here debate might never materialize. The right answer to a policy problem or issue would seem obvious to a public presented a selective view of it. If the media consistently depicted public aid recipients as irresponsible cheats, cutting welfare benefits seemed unproblematic (Gilens 1999). Thus, any political actor who could effectively manage the aspect agenda could sway public policy with little meaningful public contestation. In light of this, for many of the scholars who developed these theories, the idea of an elite-managed, unified public agenda was at best antidemocratic and at worst terrifying. Perhaps it brought to mind a technologically and culturally advanced nation persuaded to support a dictator who influenced its citizens to assist in, tolerate, or ignore industrialized genocide. Echoes of such persuasion might be perceived in media coverage of the U.S. downing of an Iranian passenger jet (Entman 1991) or of prisoner torture at Abu Ghraib (Bennett, Lawrence, and Livingston 2007). Where such research engaged in critical advocacy, breaking the hold of political and social elites over mass media, and thus over public opinion, was the goal. Could the public agenda be liberated from the control of political and social elites?

Theories of political power grounded in the agenda-setting tradition all suggested that if the media system changed, political power would work differently. While the psychological mechanisms underlying agenda-setting effects might not change, both the power of elites to influence and the nature of the public agenda would be transformed in the absence of mass audiences. By the late twentieth century, it was apparent that changes in the media landscape were reshaping the mass audiences that had developed over the previous 150 years, as the analog era of mass media gave way to the digital revolution and the information age.

Some scholars saw important benefits to the new media environment that was being created, first by cable, with its virtually unlimited number of channels, and subsequently by the internet, with its even larger capacity for unique content. The perspectives and problems of groups whose concerns were not typically reported in national media could find an outlet in the more fragmented and user-driven communication environment that was emerging (Chaffee and Metzger 2001). Scholars who argued that the objective style of news presentation, which began to develop in mid-

---

1. This phenomenon is distinct from framing, which relies on narrative (Edy and Meirick 2007) and argument (Druckman 2004) to move public opinion about a policy issue.

nineteenth-century mass media, offered little fodder for public discussion (e.g., Carey 1987) might see hopeful prospects in the politically partisan news the expanding media environment made viable (Chaffee and Metzger 2001). Bruce Williams and Michael Delli Carpini (2011) argued that the evolving system undermined the traditional media's control over information presented to the public, putting issues that might previously have been ignored onto the public agenda. This might trivialize public debate in some cases but could also liberate it from elite control. Lance Bennett and Shanto Iyengar (2008) suggested the type of self-selection possible in the expanded media environment had resulted in a new era of minimal media effects. Opinions would be reinforced rather than changed by media exposure, which in turn might suggest that the ability of political elites to shape public opinion had deteriorated. Those who worried about the potential for tyranny and demagoguery inherent in a unified national forum largely managed by political elites might applaud advances in communications technology that undermined their control. Hitlers and Stalins should be impossible in a media system that allowed users to elude the influence of a univocal media.

Other scholars saw cause for concern in the expansion of media choice and the fragmentation of media audiences. Katz mourned, "Yet, from the point of participatory democracy, television is dead, almost everywhere. It no longer serves as the central civic space . . . and the here-and-now of current affairs is being minimized, ghettoized and overwhelmed by entertainment" (1996, 24). In this early critique, he blended the two central concerns that have shaped research on how the public forum has been transformed, perhaps eliminated, by the growth in media choice. His concerns about the temptations of entertainment television overpowering the appeal of public affairs information were well founded (Prior 2007). Although some people are news junkies and took advantage of increased media choice to acquire even more public affairs information, more people used the expansion of choice to abandon news in favor of entertainment programming. Katz's implied norm of watching current affairs programming together—of knowing that one's neighbors watch and thus of feeling social pressure to watch oneself—has clearly faded. A second aspect of his elegy about watching together involves the fragmentation of audiences by political ideology. Where once citizens shared a common public forum, they can now choose sources of public affairs information they find ideologically congenial. There was evidence that they would do so if given the choice (e.g., Arceneaux and Johnson 2013; Iyengar and Hahn 2009) and that people who used different media had different issue priorities (Stroud 2011). Moreover, people surrounded by others who share their opinions tend to become more politically extreme and make riskier decisions (Sunstein 2009).

Still other scholars suggested the change was not as dramatic as many had argued, that the media continued to generate and address what were functionally mass audiences (Leccese 2009; Neuman 1991; Pew Research Center 2010; Uscinski 2014; Webster 2014).

The Public Agenda in the Information Age

As the mass audience fragmented, most scholars investigated the impacts of the evolving media system on individuals, divining its implications for the public by aggregating individual behaviors. Yet changing the nature of the public forum had consequences for the public as well. How might the absence of shared media sources affect public priorities? By what mechanism or mechanisms might the character of the public agenda be affected by the changing media ecosystem? And with what consequences for democratic governance?

Theories of media agenda setting and media choice at the individual level suggest two paths by which a shared sense of public priorities might be eroded by media that could be personalized to reflect individual preferences. To the extent that people avoid news and public affairs information, geographic and demographic differences in personal experiences might reassert themselves. Problems beyond the scope of one's immediate experience might become invisible, and the issue concerns of different communities could compete for priority on the agenda of a public that lacks a sense of shared concerns. African Americans might worry about crime, while LGBTQ Americans worry about civil rights and working class white Americans worry about jobs. In the absence of media cues to hold it together, the public agenda would *fall apart*. A second possibility emerges from the tendency of audiences to no longer watch news together but rather select news to match their interests. News media might promote different issue priorities that would in turn fragment the public agenda. Audiences for one news organization would come to have different issue concerns than audiences for another news organization, and the public agenda would be *driven apart* by media cueing. That is, differences in news content would lead to greater diversity in the public agenda.

Dwindling public consensus on which issues are the most important has consequences for democratic governance, too, and theories of political power distinguish its impact from that of polarization on a particular issue or issues. Polarization may undermine traditional sources of political power by making it hard to offer a one-sided perspective on an issue but generate uncivil and acrimonious public debate. Exposure to partisan news may lead different segments of the public to perceive a particular public problem differently. Those repeatedly reminded that large numbers of undocumented immigrants enter the country each year might view immigration reform very differently from those repeatedly reminded of how slow-moving and capricious the current immigration process is. People who see an issue in fundamentally different ways may be unwilling or unable to find a middle ground and compromise, and the result may be dysfunctional stalemate. This may seem an apt description of contemporary American politics, but there is another dimension beyond the pluralist political strife.

Theories of power that move beyond pluralism suggest that if fragmented publics are exposed to different issue agendas or to no issue agendas, debates on public issues may lack meaningful clash, since there would be little agreement on which issues the political system should address. Under these sorts of circumstances, instead of a stalemate in which nothing happens, there is a vacuum in which anything could happen. Well-intentioned political leaders seeking to represent the public would receive little public guidance about where to direct the limited resources of a legislature in addressing issues. Moreover, if people could no longer come together to make concerted policy demands on leaders with the threat of electoral punishment for failure ("Fix this problem or you're out of a job!"), the power of average voters, which depends on their numbers, could wane.

In the mass media era, managing the public agenda was a source of political power. In the information age, the increasingly fragmented audience could diversify the public agenda, resulting in political power derived from the ability of leaders to pick and choose among issues to address. Leaders could act on their own priorities with impunity, knowing a critical mass of public concern about another issue would never coalesce. Well-organized interests, recognized as more influential than the general public in the mass media era (Schattschneider 1975), could become even more powerful in a fragmented media environment, where the masses fail to come together.

Studying the Public Agenda

The analysis that follows reveals how the content and character of the public's issue agenda have transformed as the media environment evolved from the mass mediated world of the late 1960s to the personalized media world of 2014. Since 1935, Gallup has been measuring the public agenda by asking people, "What do you think is the most important problem facing this country today?" Compiling the answers generates a public agenda, a rank-ordered list of the problems most commonly named by individual respondents. It is a public agenda in the sense that it is not reducible to a person's priorities—it makes sense only as a measure of the public's concerns. There are unique benefits to using this measure of the public agenda. The Gallup measure has been in use the longest (Smith 1980, 1985) and it is the most consistently coded (McCombs and Zhu 1995). Moreover, it is an open-ended question—respondents can answer anything they want. Scholars have pointed out the subtle and not-so-subtle ways the perspectives of the political and media elite can shape questions on public opinion polls (e.g., Ginsberg 1986; Jacobs and Shapiro 1995). Under those circumstances, public opinion is confounded and limited by the mind-set of the pollsters. The "most important problem" question, however, allows respondents to nominate any issue that concerns them. If a person said "Martian invasion," the interviewer would write it down.

Although the Gallup measure of the public agenda has numerous advantages, it is not flawless and must be assessed with some subtlety. First, our analysis is focused on the public's issue agenda, but sometimes it can be difficult to distinguish between issues and aspects of issues in the Gallup data. For example, are jobs an aspect of the economy in general, or are jobs and the economy each separate issues? Where it is difficult to distinguish between issues and aspects of issues, it can be difficult to distinguish between fragmentation (a difference in issue priorities) and polarization (a difference in issue positions). Second, because Gallup's question constructs an agenda of "problems," connecting the news agenda to the public agenda can be tricky. Although similar measures are commonly used in studies of news agendas, agenda setting involves the transfer of salience, or awareness, between the media and the public. An issue's salience and the extent to which it is perceived as problematic are not quite the same thing (Wlezien 2005). For example, political campaigns dominate the news every four years and can be highly salient for the public but may not be perceived as a "problem." Moving through the analysis, we describe how the limitations of this measure of the public agenda were addressed to take advantage of the rich and unique insights it provides.

After documenting how the public issue agenda changed, we consider to what extent it has *fallen apart* as the public has paid less attention to news and to what extent it has been *driven apart* by changes in the issue agendas of news. We also consider how political representation in democratic institutions has changed as the public's issue agenda has become more diverse. Our goal is not to generate predictive theory or a formal model but rather to document and understand what happened as the public's sense of shared priorities deteriorated.

Essentially, there are two ways to think about the analysis. In one sense, it presents a *history* of the public agenda. None of the data come from laboratory experiments on individual or collective attitudes or behavior. Instead, the data document what actually happened as the United States transitioned from a mass-mediated communication environment, dominated by three broadcast television networks, to a fragmented, networked communication environment. In another sense, the analysis is an *explanation* of how the public agenda has evolved. Existing theory and research about the evolving media environment's impact on the public and on political processes suggest several potential explanations for an increasingly fragmented American public as well as a number of potential political consequences. Statistical relationships between the public agenda and public attention to the news media, news content, social reality, and government performance show us which factors seem to play bigger and smaller roles in shaping the public agenda and how the relationships among media, public, and government have changed as the public communication environment has changed. Like DNA tests, they help us identify culprits and clear suspects in explaining what happened to the public as the media environment was transformed. In this analysis, the statistics help us sort out whether the public's issue agenda has fallen apart as public attention to news media declined or been driven apart by the changing nature of the news environment and the news agenda itself, or some combination of the two. They also help us see what the consequences have been for democratic representation, particularly how political institutions have responded to an eroding consensus on issue priorities.

Like most scholarly analyses, this one simplifies the vast complexities of real life to generate useful insights. The focus is on the role of the media in shaping the public agenda and the relationship between the public agenda and political representation as they unfold over the course of forty years, but history rarely offers airtight evidence to explain its meandering. It would be a mistake to attribute everything that has happened to the public agenda in the late twentieth and early twenty-first centuries to changes in the structure and content of media. The end of the Cold War, the September 11 terrorist attacks, the rise of global trade, and the transformation of civil rights, along with dozens of other important historical events and trends, changed the content of the public agenda and might have played a role in changing its character. The relationships between media, public, and leadership have been altered by structural changes such as the increasingly rationalized redrawing of congressional districts that reduces electoral competitiveness and the growing influence of money in elections at all levels. Since the 1960s, the political system has also been altered to give determined individuals and organized interest groups greater ability to influence policy outcomes (Schudson 2015). These factors are not, and in many cases cannot be, accounted for statistically, but we remain open to them as we evaluate and contextualize our findings. Further, the concept of a public forum vastly oversimplifies what is known about the interactions between political leaders, the news media, and the public. There is no straightforward pathway between the public agenda and electoral or policy outcomes. However, public attention is an important component of many processes in participatory democracy, and the concepts of the public forum and the public agenda offer leverage for understanding how relationships between the news media and the public, and thus some key aspects of political power, have evolved.

Ultimately, the data reveal that public consensus on issue priorities has eroded over the course of the past four decades. Although there is support for both the *driven apart* and the *fallen apart* models suggested by individual-level theories of media use and media influence, neither works in quite the ways existing theory suggests. Instead, a subtle dance emerges between the news agenda's tendency to drive diversity in the public's issue agenda and the tendency of the public agenda to fall apart as the public pays less attention to news. Since there is virtually no difference between the issue agendas of the various news outlets, it is not disparate news agendas that account for public agenda diversity. Instead, changes in the overall news agenda result in more coverage of issues that tend to make the public's issue agenda more diverse. In this sense, media cueing drives the diversity of the public agenda. However, the moments when the news agenda tends to be most diverse are also the moments in which the fewest people are paying attention. Since the public pays more attention to news in moments of crisis, when news coverage tends to be more focused, the potential of everyday news coverage to de-focus the public agenda is not realized. Although there is evidence that the public agenda grows more diverse in the absence of news cues, the evidence also suggests that were the public more attentive to media outside moments of national crisis, there would be even less agreement on issue priorities.

Regardless of the mechanisms by which public consensus on issue priorities breaks down, a less focused public agenda undermines democratic representation. Political leaders pay less attention to a more diverse public agenda. This may be because the public sends less clear signals to its representatives about which issues it finds most concerning, but it occurs regardless of an institution's capacity to take up the public's issue concerns. Today's political leaders may be able to avoid those issues that are difficult or threaten their hold on power to a greater extent than representatives from earlier eras, even as the contemporary media system has undermined their ability to shape public opinion.

Overview of the Chapters

Chapter 2 presents a history of the public agenda from 1975 through 2014, a task not undertaken since Tom Smith (1980, 1985) published histories of the public agenda in the 1980s. The chapter examines the ups and downs of public concerns regarding twenty issue categories and what makes people care about them, providing context for the more abstract statistical analyses that follow. For some issues, historical events are the main driver, while others show signs that public concerns are propelled by political actors, particularly the president. Some are chronic sources of worry, some never raise much concern, some have risen and fallen over time, and some have grown more prominent through the years.

Chapter 3 employs statistical analysis to document changes in the character of the public agenda over time. Three key characteristics can help us see how the public agenda has changed: capacity (the number of issues on the agenda), diversity (how evenly concern is spread over issues), and volatility (how quickly issues cycle on and off the agenda). The results show the public agenda has become more diverse over time. They also suggest that although public attention is surely limited, previous assumptions about the capacity of the public agenda may be wrong: public concern could be much more thinly spread than previously believed.

Chapter 4 examines the relationship between traditional broadcast network news and the public agenda. It tracks the strength of the agenda-setting relationship between broadcast news and the public from 1968 through 2010. Far fewer people watched broadcast news by the twenty-first century, but the agenda-setting relationship between news and the public has not faded. This agenda-setting influence, however, does not generate consensus about public priorities. Instead, the news agenda has changed since the end of the Cold War, and attention to news increases awareness of issues beyond personal experience, expanding the public agenda.

Chapter 5 considers the impact of cable news on the public agenda. First, it explores how the expansion in the range of media options and the increasing public attention to cable news have influenced the character of the public agenda. Then it examines the uniqueness of cable news channels' agendas compared to that of broadcast news. Public attention to broadcast and cable news does not have straightforward effects on the public agenda. Although there is some evidence that attention to Fox News increases the diversity of the public agenda, attention to MSNBC tends to focus it, and CNN's relationship with the public agenda changes depending on the time frame. The agendas of cable news are not especially different from those of broadcast news and are less diverse than the broadcast news agenda. Thus, cable news does not appear to be the main driver of public agenda diversity.

Chapter 6 explores whether it is still possible to focus the public agenda and which social entities might have the power to do so. Attention and news agendas often move together: in moments when the public pays more attention to news, news agendas tend to be more similar across networks. Yet a test of what has been referred to as the "burglar alarm" model of news reveals that while a highly consistent news agenda can provoke a more focused public agenda, conditions have to be relatively extreme to make it likely. Then it turns to whether social reality and political leadership can shape public priorities. Changes in the media environment have not significantly altered the relative power of news media to shape public concerns compared to social reality. When the public has direct experience of a social condition (like unemployment or inflation), the news is less influential. If the public is less likely to have direct experience (violent crime), the news is more influential. Recent research on presidential leadership suggests presidents confronted with a fragmented public tend to lean into it by giving targeted speeches to specific groups rather than attempting to influence the public as a whole through major addresses. All of this suggests there is little hope of reconciling the fragmented public.

Chapter 7 makes an effort to assess some of the effects of public fragmentation on the political process. Presidents make fewer major public addresses responding to public concerns than they once did, not because such addresses are less successful than they once were but because public concerns rarely rise to such a level that presidents feel obligated to respond. Even the U.S. House of Representatives, the governing body with the greatest institutional capacity to address a long list of public concerns, becomes less responsive to the public agenda as the public agenda becomes more diverse. Consequently, a fragmented public agenda interferes with the processes of democratic representation.

Chapter 8 describes the implications of our analysis of media power, political power, and democratic processes. The fragmentation of the public agenda marks a transformation from "the public" to a multitude of "publics" that coincides with a decline in the importance of majority public opinion in American politics. The fragmented public agenda enables leaders to selectively address public concerns, potentially favoring those of their supporters or of wealthy donors. In such a climate, the power of organized interest groups further expands, while public dissatisfaction with a government that does not appear to do anything to address its concerns grows.

2

A History of the Public Agenda, 1975–2014

Common sense might suggest the public agenda is a reflection of the relative importance of real-world events and conditions, but as far back as the 1920s, scholars knew that this is not what actually happens. First, it simply is not possible to determine the relative importance of specific events and conditions. Which was more important in 1918, World War I or the flu pandemic? The war is better remembered, but the flu killed more people. Second, as Walter Lippmann wrote in 1922, "The world that we have to deal with politically is out of reach, out of sight, out of mind" (7). Most people do not experience public events directly but rather through communication processes—in Lippmann's time, newspapers and, possibly, letters and telegrams from family and friends. Today, the channels of communication may have changed—television and the internet—but our experience of the world is no less indirect. What he said still applies today: "The analyst of public opinion must begin then, by recognizing the triangular relationship between the scene of action, the human picture of that scene, and the human response to that picture working itself out upon the scene of action" (4). In short, there is no straightforward relationship between real-world events and the public agenda because so little of social reality is experienced and so much of it is constructed by communication.

Two crucial communicators of public events are political leaders and news media. Both respond to events—one thinks of President Franklin Roosevelt's address to Congress after the Japanese attack on Pearl Harbor and broadcast studios turning their rooftop cameras toward southern Manhattan as the World Trade Center burned on September 11. Yet both also exercise judgment and implement strategy in representing events and conditions. Consequently, it is important to distinguish between events, like Pearl Harbor, and political leaders' responses to them, like Roosevelt's address to Congress. Moreover, political leaders sometimes generate events—for example, by introducing policy or making speeches. News media sometimes highlight issues in feature stories or through investigative reporting. Because it is not objectively possible to identify their relative importance, there is no independent standard for judging the "right" amount of attention to give an event or a condition. Nevertheless, agenda setting research shows that how much attention news media pay to particular events and issues influences public perceptions of their importance (e.g., McCombs and Shaw 1972), and political communication research documents that the amount of news media attention can be influenced by political leaders (e.g., Bennett, Lawrence, and Livingston 2007).

The complex alchemy of these relationships makes the content of the public agenda unpredictable. Neither reality nor media representations of that reality can fully account for what is on the public agenda at any given point in time or how the content of the public agenda changes over time. Nevertheless, it is important to document the impact of history on the public agenda, for history is the opportunity structure on which representation processes play themselves out. Moreover, as this book demonstrates, complex relationships exist between the content of the public agenda and its degree of fragmentation. These relationships are sometimes inflected by social conditions and sometimes inflected by news media representations. This chapter presents a history of the public agenda from 1975 through 2014, offering a detailed look at the data that form the basis for the rest of the analysis.

History, Representation, and the Public Agenda

The last histories of the public agenda, published by Tom Smith in the 1980s (1980, 1985), appear at the beginning of the constructionist turn in social research. Smith describes the public agenda as driven by personal experience and historical events. Concern about the economy followed the business cycle, rising during economic downturns and fading during recoveries. Concern about foreign affairs peaked during World War II and the Vietnam War. Smith's relatively modernist perspective means that, for the most part, he does not consider how political leaders and news coverage might have managed or shaped the public agenda. In updating his histories, we enrich his conceptualization, first by considering the difference between personal and mediated experience and second by articulating the difference between events and the actions of political leaders.

Obtrusiveness (Zucker 1978) conceptualizes how people experience public problems and illuminates the fact that some issues are more susceptible to representational processes than others. Some problems, such as high gas prices, inflation, or unemployment, are apparent to people in their everyday lives: they are obtrusive. Other problems, such as foreign wars, national debt, or government scandal, are not directly experienced by average people but instead conveyed to them by public officials and media: they are unobtrusive. Many issues, like terrorism, are somewhere in between. Americans' experience of September 11 was mediated, while their experience of airport security is direct. Russell Neuman (1990) and Samuel Popkin (1991) argue that when issues are more obtrusive, the public is less susceptible to mediated representations, and agenda setting research has generally borne this out, showing that news media have greater agenda setting power for less obtrusive issues than for more obtrusive ones (Weaver et al. 1981; Winter, Eyal, and Rogers 1982; Zucker 1978). Obtrusiveness may help explain why public concern about some issues seems more tightly bound to real-world conditions, while concern about others seems shaped by political elites. On occasion, media attention can raise the salience of obtrusive issues (Behr and Iyengar 1985), and it may be that personal experience sensitizes people to media coverage of an obtrusive issue (Demers et al. 1989), but there is no evidence that unobtrusive issues can reach the public agenda without substantial attention from media, elites, or both.

Regina Lawrence (2000) distinguishes between institutionally driven and event-driven news—that is, news generated by official activities versus news generated by unexpected events. Institutionally driven news, like a fight over raising the U.S. debt limit, is typically managed by political elites engaged in ritual combat. Event-driven news, like a credit crisis, can spiral out of their control. Unexpected twists and turns, together with the inability to distract the public from the problem, create a situation much more open to influence from nonelite actors who may become meaningful members of the group that ultimately negotiates a policy solution before a watchful public. Lawrence's concepts of event-driven and institutionally driven news can easily be transposed to public issues. Public concern about some issues may be more affected by events (which should be conceptualized not only as sudden events but also as trends, such as rising unemployment or inflation). Concern about others may be more affected by elites who, for example, seek public attention and support for a new policy initiative. Many issues will have a complex blend of elite-driven and event-driven components. Watergate was filled with events: unexpected twists, turns, and revelations. It also had characteristics of an elite-driven partisan fight. Moreover, where something is placed on a continuum between elite-driven and event-driven can, in some cases, be subjective. Crack cocaine was a growing problem in the United States in the 1980s, but, as several scholars have pointed out, politicians made a lot of hay with it.

These concepts, obtrusiveness and whether issues are elite- or event-driven, help demonstrate why the content of the public agenda is so unpredictable. Although the public agenda is clearly shaped by social reality, that reality is highly dynamic over time and filtered in complicated and inconsistent ways. Reality is neither perfectly represented in the media nor consistently linked to public perceptions of issue importance, but that does not mean the public agenda is unaffected by the events and conditions of the time.

Documenting the Public Agenda: The "Most Important Problem" Question

Traditionally, the public agenda has been measured using Gallup's classic open-ended question, "What do you think is the most important problem facing this country today?" Gallup has been asking Americans this question since 1935 (Smith 1980, 1985), and survey respondents are free to name anything. Since they are asked about problems facing the country, their responses usually identify national issues, rather than personal or local ones. Gallup codes responses into categories, and the percentage of responses in each category creates an ordered list of "most important problems," providing a measure of the public agenda.

Over the forty years covered here, Gallup has asked that "most important problem" question 254 times. In the early years of the time frame, Gallup asked the question sporadically, so sometimes, historic moments that might have influenced the public agenda do not have a corresponding poll. For example, there is no poll to tell us whether the specter of the Y2K bug, a computer glitch that was scheduled to hit at the turn of the millennium, increased public concerns about technology issues. The largest gap between questions in the forty years included here is seventeen months. However, in 2004, Gallup began asking the "most important problem" question more or less monthly. Therefore, as is the case with most historical archives, more recent times are better documented than the distant past.

People's answers to the question are coded into categories at the time the poll is taken, and there is evidence that the categories vary quite a bit over the forty-year span. In some years, they were highly detailed, in others more rudimentary. They also vary with the topics of the day. Vietnam and Watergate are big in the 1970s. Monica Lewinsky appears in the 1990s. Afghanistan means something different in 1980 than it does in 2001. Smith (1980, 1985) recognizes this problem in his histories and addresses it by grouping responses into a few larger categories, but his coding scheme is not well documented. A better specified coding scheme for generating more consistent categorization of responses was created by Max McCombs and Jian-Hua Zhu (1995) in their study documenting changes in the character of the public agenda. The history that follows employs their categories, adapted to reflect changes in the public agenda since 1994, the last year included in their study.

A complete explanation of how the archival data were recoded appears in Appendix A. A brief overview of some of the issues the procedures deal with offers a sense of how the recoding worked. Broader categories were used to manage historical fluctuations associated with specific events. For example, Monica Lewinsky, Watergate, and other political scandals were recoded under "Government/Political," to reveal how concerns about the government have evolved over time. However, not all historical fluctuations can be managed this way. Sometimes, Gallup coders created new categories over the course of the time frame that represented not historical moments but lasting changes. The Gallup category "Economy in general" began appearing in the early 1980s and has never disappeared. For the kinds of changes occurring after McCombs and Zhu's (1995) study, new categories were needed. The media began appearing as a "most important problem" in the mid-1990s, so a category was created for it. In some cases, the meaning of categories likely changed over time. Sometimes, coders could be given instructions about how to cope with changes. For example, mentions of Afghanistan were coded as "Soviet/Europe" during the Cold War era and as "Middle East" after 2000. However, the meaning of terrorism underwent such profound change between 1975 and 2014 that a new category was created for it. In the end, Gallup's initial coding was recoded into twenty categories, largely derived from McCombs and Zhu's study, to illuminate trends in public concern over time.

A second issue affecting Gallup's coding was that, in some cases, interviewers coded multiple responses from a single subject. Smith (1980) suggests that Gallup's own documentation about which surveys allowed multiple responses and which did not is unclear. The data imply it was typical. Most of the percentage totals of responses to the survey are greater than

100, but the range is quite large, from 85 (which suggests not everyone gave an answer) to 215 (which suggests respondents averaged more than two answers each). This makes comparing relative levels of public concern across surveys complicated. If 30 percent of the answers mention international affairs on a survey in which the total percentage of all answers is 85, it suggests something different from 30 percent of answers out of a total percentage of 215. Smith's solution for this problem is to convert Gallup's raw data, the percentage of respondents giving a particular answer, to the percentage of responses in a particular category as a function of the total number of responses. In the above example, the level of public concern in the first survey is slightly more than 35 percent (30/85) and not quite 14 percent in the second (30/215). Because the time frame is so long and the variance in total responses is so large, the history presented here is based on the percentage of responses in a category. It is also worth noting, as Smith does, that the "most important problem" question does not tell us how concerned the public is about an issue. Every agenda the question generates takes the form of a list of public priorities, but how worried people are about the most important problem at one point in time (like the depths of the Great Recession) is not necessarily comparable to how worried they are about the most important problem at another point in time (like the month the Berlin Wall fell). Eighteen of the twenty coding categories are explored in detail here.

The excluded categories are "Other," which does not offer much insight into public perceptions, and "Media." It is intriguing that beginning in 1998, enough responses named the media as the most important problem facing the country today for the Gallup coders to include it as a category. However, since it never garners more than 1 percent of responses, it is difficult to say much about the social influences that shape it beyond, perhaps, the introduction of partisan cable news in 1997. The eighteen other categories are organized into five major domains: economic issues, domestic issues, foreign affairs, terrorism, and government. For each of the eighteen categories, we begin with a brief overview of what it includes and some of its general characteristics, such as whether concern is chronic or sporadic; whether and how often it has led the public agenda; and what constitutes extremely high or low levels of public concern. Then we present a more detailed history of how events and political activities correspond with changes in public concern about the issue.

In keeping with the traditions of agenda setting research, we assume that if citizens encounter a social problem both directly and via media, it is more likely direct observation or experience rather than the media's coverage that affects public opinion. For example, we assume the public's direct experience of job losses, eroding retirement portfolios, and home foreclosures was more influential than media coverage of investment firm bankruptcies and bailouts during the Great Recession. Similarly, reports that conditions were improving would be less influential than successfully selling one's house. One exception is concern about crime, where research shows that media effects on public perceptions tend to overshadow actual conditions (Dixon 2008; Funkhouser 1973; Morgan and Shanahan 1997; see also Chapter 6).

Economic Issues

Economic issues are among the most obtrusive. Despite the complexity of the U.S. economy, many of its characteristics are immediately observable to average people. Gas prices, inflation, interest rates, taxes, the job market, and public benefits like welfare and Social Security are part of people's everyday experience. At the same time, other aspects of the U.S. economy sometimes mentioned as most important problems are much less directly observable. It is through media and public officials that the public is more likely to hear about debts and deficits and allocation of government money. In the following discussion of public concerns about the economy, specific issues are arranged from the most obtrusive to the least obtrusive.

Concern about economic issues is more likely to be event-driven than elite-driven, although events in this issue domain tend to take the form of trends, such as rising unemployment or rising prices. Still, as in other areas of public concern, there is some evidence that political elites influence the public agenda. Figure 2.1 depicts changes in public concern about economic issues and some of the historical events associated with them.

Money. This category includes inflation, wages, taxes, cost of living, gasoline prices, corporate corruption, and the gap between rich and poor, making it a very obtrusive issue that can be directly experienced at gas pumps and grocery stores. Money generated the highest level of concern recorded for any issue, accounting for 67 percent of responses in October 1978. It has topped the public agenda in twenty-nine polls, more than any other issue, except the economy in general and the Middle East. In nine polls, more than 50 percent of responses named money as the most important problem; in thirty-three polls, money accounted for more than 20 percent of responses, and in seventy-seven polls, it accounted for more than 10 percent. Almost all the polls recording very high levels of concern were taken before 1982. In only two polls since 1982 has concern topped 20 percent. All the polls where money accounts for more than 50 percent of

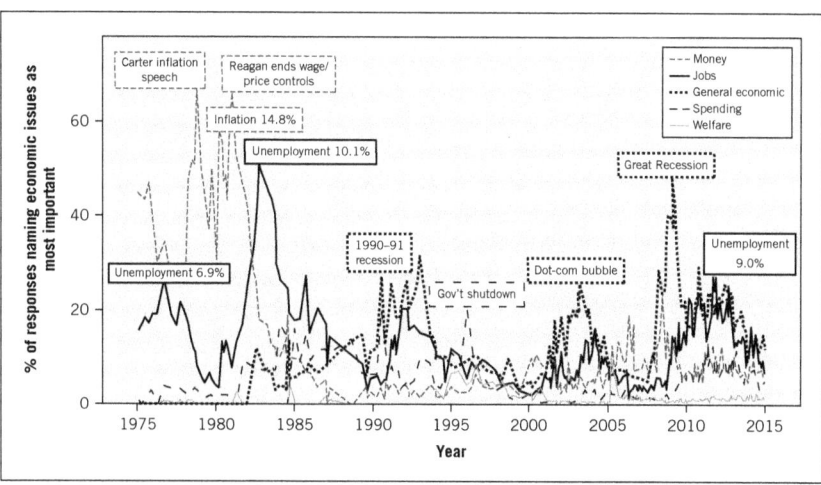

Figure 2.1. Public concern about economic issues, 1975–2014.

responses were taken between July 1978 and May 1981. Money is also a chronic concern: there are only two polls in which no one mentions money as a most important problem.

Money concerns topped 20 percent of responses in every poll taken between 1975 and August 1982, and it was the top issue on the public agenda from 1975 until June 1982. The inflation rate exceeded 10 percent for all of 1974 and the first four months of 1975, and concerns about money accounted for 43 to 47 percent of responses in polls taken in 1975. However, the fit between inflation rates and levels of concern is not perfect. Levels of concern rose between July and October 1975, even though the inflation rate declined by two points over the period and concern was more than 30 percent through 1976, when inflation rates were relatively low for the period (ranging from 4.9 to 6.7 percent). However, starting in April 1978, U.S. inflation rates increased steadily for twenty-four months, getting as high as 14.8 percent in March 1980, and as one might expect for an obtrusive issue, public concern was more than 30 percent in every poll taken between April 1978 and January 1982, with inflation in double digits virtually every month. Public concern ebbed to less than 28 percent in June 1982, following six months of marginally lower inflation rates.

Although real increases in inflation almost certainly raised its profile on the public agenda, there is evidence political leaders and media coverage did as well. Between February and April 1978, public concerns about money rose from 29 percent of responses to nearly 48 percent, although the inflation rate, relatively low at 6.5 percent, had barely changed. Shortly before Gallup interviewers began their April poll, President Jimmy Carter gave a nationally televised speech and press conference about inflation, and both his administration and the news media expressed deep, and ultimately justified, concerns about potential inflation. In October 1978, public concern about inflation reached the highest level recorded, although the peak inflation rate would not occur for another eighteen months. Days before that poll began, Carter delivered a nationally televised speech on inflation. Similarly, concern rose from 37 percent to more than 50 percent between August and October 1979, following a presidential news conference in which Carter declared war on inflation. Between January and March 1980, money concerns nearly doubled from slightly more than 30 percent of responses to nearly 60 percent as the media told of an OPEC oil summit that threatened to raise gasoline prices even as high inflation dragged on. Concern was chronically high, but it reached another peak of nearly two-thirds of responses immediately after Ronald Reagan ended wage and price controls.

In January 1982, the inflation rate dropped to less than 10 percent, signaling the beginning of the end of this inflationary period. Only once since that June has money led the public agenda: in May 2006, it tied with concerns about the Middle East. However, public confidence was slow to recover. The inflation rate in 1983 never exceeded 3.9 percent, but concern about money did not dip to less than 10 percent of responses until September 1984, even though the inflation rate that year had been higher than in the previous year. From that month until June 2000, public concern remained less than 10 percent.

Energy prices seemed to move public concerns about money in the 2000s. A wave of concern from April through June 2001 likely had multiple sources, as Congress was debating the proposed George W. Bush tax cuts and the price of energy soared in California (due, it would later be discovered, to market manipulations by Enron and other energy companies). A similar wave of concern in late summer 2005 seems to have been connected to gas prices. In the three weeks before the August poll, gas prices surged, and, the following month, Hurricane Katrina decimated the oil-producing Gulf coast. From August until December, concerns about money topped 10 percent of responses. Rising gas prices may also have been behind the wave of concern lasting from April through August 2006, which produced the highest levels of concern since the 1980s, almost 19 percent in May and more than 17 percent in August. This represents a complex conflation of agenda influences. Stories about high gas prices were ubiquitous in the media, but consumers also had direct experiences of these high prices at the pump or when they paid their utility bills.

A wave of concern in November and December 2007 may have had multiple causes. Oil and gas prices were up, but troubling news was also beginning to emerge about the housing market. From March 2008 until April 2009, a large wave of worry appeared. Concern about money dipped to less than 10 percent of responses for only one month and topped 20 percent in June and July, nearly missing 20 percent in May. The combination of high oil and gas prices and a housing market in disarray made Americans more worried about money than at any point since the inflationary 1980s.

In general, taxation has not greatly influenced public concern about money. For example, in the month President George H. W. Bush reneged on his "Read my lips: no new taxes" pledge, public concern about money accounted for less than 4 percent of responses. The Clinton tax increases in 1993 provoked no response, either. However, the final instance when public concern about money exceeded 10 percent, in January 2013, may have been generated by tax policy. It followed the last-minute tax deal President Barack Obama and Republican congressional leaders reached to avert a "fiscal cliff," which some experts expected would send the economy back into recession. The deal allowed President George W. Bush's tax cuts to become permanent for all but the wealthiest Americans, and the compromise was a bitter pill for both Republicans, who opposed any tax increase, and Democrats, many of whom wanted the Bush tax cuts to expire. More obtrusively, it also ended a payroll tax break so that 77 percent of Americans would pay higher taxes.

A complex conflation of real events and elite leadership seems to shape public concerns about money. Particularly in the 1970s and 1980s, it would seem that political leaders like Presidents Carter and Reagan could attract public attention to and generate concern for the issue but had a harder time assuaging public alarm once it was aroused. The public reacts relatively quickly to rising prices and inflation but is slow to be reassured.

Jobs. This category includes unemployment, recession, the loss of American jobs to overseas competitors, and trade deficits. Although trade no doubt seems somewhat unobtrusive, the polls reveal that the jobs category is driven by obtrusive concerns about unemployment. Notably, it appears to be the trend in employment rather than the unemployment rate itself that moves public opinion, and while the public typically registers even small shifts in the unemployment rate, public concern usually lags about six months behind a rise in unemployment. Moreover, it can be slow to fade.

Public concern about jobs is chronic: there are no polls in which someone did not name it as a most important problem. The greatest level of concern occurred in October 1982, when the category accounted for almost 51 percent of responses. It has represented more than one-third of responses in six polls, has topped 20 percent of responses in thirty-five polls, and has represented more than 10 percent of responses in more than half of all the Gallup "most important problem" polls taken from 1975 through 2014. Of the thirty-five polls where more than 20 percent of responses mentioned jobs, fourteen occurred while Reagan was in office, and seventeen were from Obama's administration, during the only two time periods since the Great Depression when unemployment reached or exceeded 10 percent. The nine polls registering the most public concern about jobs all come during Reagan's administration, and the greatest eight of these occur consecutively (June 1982 through November 1983), during the worst period of unemployment since the Great Depression.

Although there are 134 polls where public concern about jobs has topped 10 percent, jobs has led the public agenda only twenty-four times, fewer times than money, the economy in general, or the Middle East. Indeed, there are several examples in which very high levels of public concern about jobs do not propel it to the top of the public agenda. In November 1983, concern about jobs hovered at 30 percent of responses, but the public expressed more concern about the international situation. In 1976 and 1982, with concern about jobs at nearly a quarter of responses, the public was more concerned about money (inflation). In more recent years, concern about the economy in general has sometimes eclipsed concern about jobs, even when concern about jobs represented considerably more than 20 percent of responses.

Concern about jobs was quite high in the late 1970s, rising from slightly more than 15 percent of responses in February 1975 to more than one-quarter of responses by July 1976, although the unemployment rate actually fell slightly from 9 percent in May 1975 to 6.9 percent in July 1976. Not until the jobless rate had fallen to about 6 percent in October 1977 did public concern about the issue drop to less than 10 percent.

In January 1980, unemployment rates began to rise again, but public concern lagged behind. Polls taken in January and March showed fewer than 4 percent of responses mentioning jobs as the unemployment rate crept up from 6 percent in December to 6.3 percent in March. By June, the unemployment rate was 7.5 percent, and public concern was back in double digits. As the jobless rate stabilized, so did public concern, but when the jobless rate rose by a percentage point between September 1981 and January 1982, public concern increased sharply, from 17 percent to nearly 25 percent. By June 1982, unemployment was up another point, and public concern had reached one-third of responses. When joblessness hit double digits in September, public concern topped 50 percent. The four highest levels of public concern recorded in the series occurred in this time period as unemployment hovered around 10 percent from September 1982 until June 1983. Public concern declined along with the unemployment rate, but it was a slow process. By August 1984, unemployment was back at 7.5 percent and public concern had dipped to less than 25 percent of responses, but this was still a much higher level of concern than had been expressed when unemployment had been 7.5 percent back in June 1980. Although unemployment rates stayed steady through 1984 and 1985, public concern remained near 20 percent of responses, spiking to more than 27 percent of responses in October 1985. Not until May 1989, when the unemployment rate had been less than 6 percent for more than a year, did public concern drop to less than 10 percent of responses for an extended period of time.

In January 1991, the public agenda began to register a rise in unemployment that had begun in July 1990. The unemployment rate was up a percentage point, from 5.5 percent to 6.5 percent. Both the unemployment rate and public concern rose throughout the year. However, this unemployment cycle does not follow the typical pattern in which public concern remains high even after unemployment begins to fall. Public concern peaked at slightly more than 20 percent of responses in November 1991 and January 1992. Unemployment rates peaked at 7.8 percent in June 1992, by which time public concern had begun to fall, ebbing to less than 10 percent as unemployment rates reached 6 percent.[1]

In nineteen polls taken between 1996 and 2001, concern about jobs never reached 10 percent. Polls in August and September 2001 showed levels of concern of more than 10 percent for the first time in four years as the unemployment rate, which had begun to rise about six months earlier, reached nearly 5 percent for the first time since summer 1997. A similar brief increase in concern accompanied rising unemployment in late 2001 and early 2002; however, as unemployment continued a slow rise through that year, public concern about jobs ebbed, perhaps because so much attention was focused on the terrorist attacks. A wave of concern about jobs, with eight of ten polls registering more than 10 percent ran from May 2003 to May 2004. Unemployment had begun rising in November of the previous year, from 5.7 percent to 5.9 percent. It peaked at 6.3 percent in July 2003 but had dropped back to 5.6 percent by the following May.

---

1. The May 1992 poll has some anomalies that may help explain the early decline in public concern. It has a low total number of responses and an unusually large Miscellaneous category, which suggest some coding irregularities at Gallup.

By December 2004, concerns about unemployment dipped to less than 10 percent and did not rise to that level for the next four years. During much of that period, the U.S. unemployment rate hovered between 4.4 and 5.4 percent. However, in May 2008, unemployment rates began to rise, and, right on cue, about six months later (December 2008), public concern began to rise, topping 10 percent of responses by February 2009. It would remain at more than 10 percent for the next six and a half years as the Great Recession took its toll. In all fifty-five polls taken from February 2009 through September 2013, concern about jobs exceeded 10 percent. It topped 20 percent of responses sixteen times. This is the most sustained concern about jobs recorded in the series. However, concern did not peak when the unemployment rate peaked at 10 percent in October 2009. Instead, after a year of unemployment rates in excess of 9 percent, concern topped 20 percent of responses in March and April 2010. Another period of sustained concern, more than 20 percent, occurred from August 2010 until February 2011, as unemployment stubbornly persisted at between 9.2 percent and 9.5 percent. Ironically, the highest level of concern about jobs during the Great Recession occurred just as the unemployment rate began to recover. In August 2011, concern was more than 20 percent, and from September to November it would consistently account for about a quarter of responses. Yet the unemployment rate, after thirty months at 9 percent or more, turned a corner in October and dropped half a percentage point by December. Concern rose to more than 20 percent again in June and July 2012, although the unemployment rate had continued to fall to 8.2 percent. Another peak to about a quarter of responses appeared in September 2012 as the unemployment rate dipped to less than 8 percent. These late peaks may have been elite-driven, a product of the GOP strategy for defeating Obama's reelection bid, a possibility we explore in more detail in our analysis of the "General Economic Issues" category.

Public concern about jobs during the Great Recession never spiked as high as it had during the early 1980s recession, perhaps because unemployment never remained as high for as long. Moreover, job concerns ebbed more quickly in the 2010s than they had in the 1980s, dropping to less than 10 percent just two years after the unemployment rate sank to less than 8 percent. Concerns about jobs remained high for about four years following the 1980 recession. Unemployment rates had to drop to near 5 percent to assuage public concern about jobs during the Reagan years, while during Obama's administration, recovery to a jobless rate of 6 percent was enough. Nevertheless, as with concerns about money, the public is only slowly reassured following bad economic times.

Welfare. Although this category, which includes Social Security, is an obtrusive issue for many, it is a consistently low-ranking issue on the public agenda, and concern about it tends to be elite-driven rather than event-driven, responsive to proposed policy changes rather than to economic conditions. Concern reached its highest and third highest points (9.5 percent and 7.6 percent) in March and May 2005, as the George W. Bush administration proposed privatizing Social Security. Similar expressions of public concern emerged as a Republican congressional majority took office promising a major overhaul of welfare in January 1995 (about 7 percent of responses), as proposals to do so were debated that summer (about 7 percent), and right before President Bill Clinton signed sweeping welfare reform legislation in August 1996 (almost 9 percent). In almost a quarter of the polls, no one mentions welfare as a concern, and it never tops the public agenda.

Spending. This category includes government spending in general, the federal budget deficit, the national debt, government budget cuts, and several aspects of spending particular to the military. It is an unobtrusive issue, for the public cannot know much about government spending without mediated information. In a confluence of event-driven and elite-driven concern, it tends to rise on the public agenda when it is the subject of political conflict. More than 20 percent of responses have named spending as the most important problem twice, and it has accounted for more than 10 percent of responses twenty-five times. It has led the public agenda only twice, in October 1990 and January 1996. Democrats are commonly accused of spending more freely than Republicans, but the twenty-five polls registering the greatest public concern are split evenly between Republican and Democratic administrations. However, the six polls where no one mentioned spending as a most important problem were all taken during Republican administrations.

From 1975 until 1981, public concern about government spending never reached 5 percent of responses. Much of President Ronald Reagan's rhetoric invoked government spending as a primary cause of the nation's economic problems. About half of his major addresses[2] during his first term of office (1981–1985) discussed government spending, and it was during his presidency that elevated levels of public concern about government spending first emerged. Public concern about government spending first approached 10 percent in October 1981, after a late September

---

2. Here we use the classification of a Major Address from the Presidency Project at the University of California, Santa Barbara.

televised presidential address on the economy, which attributed the rising deficits and debt to government spending, and a sixteen-hour filibuster by Senator William Proxmire (D-WI), who opposed raising the U.S. debt ceiling to more than $1 trillion.

Concern about spending hovered at almost 10 percent until February 1984, when it jumped to more than 17 percent as stocks declined when Reagan's budget plan called for even more deficit spending. Of the dozen polls taken from February 1984 until the end of Reagan's second term, only three registered public concern about government spending at less than 10 percent. As deficit cutting and tax legislation moved through Congress in the summer of 1984, concern registered at more than 14 percent in June. In the October 1985 poll, which began the day after the Gramm-Rudman-Hollings Deficit Reduction Act passed the Senate, spending accounted for 15 percent of responses to the "most important problem" question.

During the first two years of George H. W. Bush's presidency, concern about spending stayed low, at 5 to 7 percent of responses. But in July 1990, it topped 20 percent of responses for the first of only two times. Negotiations with Congressional Democrats on deficit reductions forced Bush to break his campaign promise and raise taxes, resulting in the highest level of public concern about government spending recorded in the series. It also topped the public agenda for the first of only two times in October 1990, as stalled budget negotiations were blamed on Bush's changed stance on taxes.

Clinton presided over some very good economic times, and concern about government spending topped 10 percent only three times in the twenty-two polls taken during his presidency, including the month he took office. It reached its second highest level recorded, 20 percent of responses, and topped the agenda for the second and last time in January 1996, after stalled budget negotiations resulted in two government shutdowns totaling twenty-seven days in late 1995 and early 1996. It was at 10 percent in May 1996, the month after the final sections of that contentious budget had passed. It is worth noting that a central part of this budget struggle involved Speaker of the House Newt Gingrich refusing to raise the U.S. debt ceiling if Clinton did not accede to Republican demands for budget cuts.

Concern over government spending never reached 4 percent of responses throughout George W. Bush's presidency, even as the budget surpluses of 1998 through 2001 became then-record deficits in 2003, 2004, and 2008. It was only marginally higher in the early years of Obama's presidency, even as the record deficit of 2008 tripled in fiscal 2009 with federal bailouts and economic stimulus spending. It did not approach 10 percent of responses until 2011, rising to slightly more than 12 percent of responses that April. A series of polls showed levels of concern ranging from 8.1 percent to 12.5 percent from April through August of that year, as Congress and the president struggled over raising the debt ceiling. A second debt-ceiling crisis in late December 2012 and early 2013 coincides with another spike in public concern about government spending, with more than 10 percent of the public mentioning it as the most important problem from December 2012 through March of 2013 (peaking at nearly 15 percent in January).

It is intriguing that virtually all the largest spikes in public concern about government spending coincide with fights over raising the nation's debt ceiling but have little relationship with either the size of the deficit or whether the deficit grows or shrinks. Moreover, not every rise of the debt ceiling provokes public concern—every president in our time frame has raised it, and all have raised it more than once. Instead, concern increases when political leaders clash over deficit spending and government debt.

General economic issues. Gallup created this category in June 1982, and every poll since has included at least some mentions of the economy as the most important problem. The generality of the category makes it difficult to define as obtrusive or unobtrusive, event-driven or elite-driven. Evidence of both event-driven and elite-driven patterns appears in the polling series, and both obtrusive and unobtrusive aspects of the economy appear to move public concern in this category. At its highest peaks, concern about the economy accounts for 50 percent of responses, and it has been the top issue on the public agenda more times than any other, in more than seventy polls taken from 1975 through 2014. It has accounted for more than one-third of responses in eight polls and more than 20 percent of responses in sixty polls. In 152 polls (nearly 70 percent of the polls in which it has been available as a category), more than 10 percent of responses have named the economy as the most important problem. The nine months with the highest recorded levels of concern are September 2008 through May 2009, and eighteen of the twenty-two polls in which concern about the issue exceeds a quarter of responses appear between March 2008 and October 2012.

During Reagan's two terms of office, concerns about the economy in general were typically dwarfed by concerns about specific aspects of it (money or jobs). It was not until George H. W. Bush took office that these more specific public concerns tended to pale in comparison with concerns about the economy in general.

Concerns about the economy persisted throughout George H. W. Bush's presidency. In the first "most important problem" poll taken during his presidency, in May 1989, concern about the economy approached 15 percent of responses. It climbed after that. By July 1990, the economy topped one-quarter of responses, the highest level of concern recorded up to that time. Concern exceeded 13 percent of responses for the rest of the polls taken during his presidency, topping 20 percent in ten of sixteen polls taken between July 1990 and the end of his term. This concern may have been tied to struggles over government deficits and debt, an aspect of the economy both unobtrusive and, as noted earlier, elite-driven. Many observers suggest that public concern about the economy lost him a second term as president, with Bill Clinton's campaign famously stressing, "It's the economy, stupid." Only three "most important problem" polls were taken during the 1992 election year, making it hard to gauge. Gross domestic product was rising that year, but unemployment was for much of it as well. Nevertheless, the steep fall in public concern about the economy once Clinton took office lends some credence to the conventional wisdom.

Clinton's trajectory was just the opposite of Bush's. Shortly after Clinton took office, public concerns about the economy declined by half, from 31 percent of responses in the last poll of Bush's presidency (January 1993) to less than 16 percent of responses by September. By the time he left office in January 2001, public concern about the economy was less than 6 percent. The good economic times over which he presided had both obtrusive and unobtrusive aspects, and both economic conditions and the administration's news management practices probably played a role in keeping the economy off the public agenda.

During George W. Bush's first term in office, public concern about the economy seems shaped by some relatively unobtrusive events. By August 2001, concern about the economy was back to more than 15 percent as the bursting dot-com bubble produced a wave of internet company failures and a brief recession. Concern about the economy exceeded 10 percent until November 2004, reaching 20 percent of responses in six of thirty-five polls conducted in that time frame. Peak levels of concern during this wave last from July 2002 through November 2003, apparently sparked by a sharp decline in the stock market. By September 2002, the Dow Jones Industrial Average had lost more than a quarter of its value and the NASDAQ more than 40 percent. They would not bottom out until March 2003. Although public concern about the economy fell from more than 20 percent of responses in November 2003 to about 12 percent of responses in January 2004, it would not dip below 10 percent until the last month of George W. Bush's first term. During Bush's second term of office, more obtrusive economic events moved public concern about the economy. Concern remained low until late 2007 but began to rise in November. From January 2008 through the end of the time frame, concern surpassed 10 percent of responses in every poll.

In Obama's first term, obtrusive events kept the economy at or near the top of the public agenda. In all the polls taken in 2008 and 2009, the economy was the top issue on the public agenda. From February 2008 to August 2009, general economic concerns topped 20 percent in every poll. They accounted for one-third or more of responses in all polls taken between September 2008 and May 2009. Events happened so fast and public concern rose so rapidly that there is no way to know which specific events of the recession triggered public concern. Concern fell gradually starting in May 2009, one month before the official end of the Great Recession, and was consistently less than 20 percent of responses from December 2009 until June 2010, ranging from 15 to 19 percent of responses. It rose to more than 20 percent of responses again from July through December of 2010, a period that included the less obtrusive passage of the Dodd-Frank Wall Street Reform and Consumer Protection Act but also the more obtrusive peak in home foreclosures. Spikes of more than 20 percent appeared from May through November 2011, though concern was not consistently greater than 20 percent.

Evidence of elite-driven public concern about the economy appears in 2012. As the Republicans made the economy a key campaign issue, public concern about the economy remained at more than 20 percent of responses, and the economy was the top issue on the public agenda in all polls except one. This trend, like the increasing concern about jobs, stands out as likely elite-driven, since the unemployment rate was slowly improving, even though growth in the gross domestic product slowed throughout the year. Concern about the economy reached 25 percent for the last time in the poll taken the month before the election and had declined to 17.5 percent by the end of the year, though it led the public agenda in seven of the monthly polls taken in 2013. Economic concern declined and did not top the public agenda after September 2013, but it remained in double digits through the end of the series.

Domestic Issues

Like economic issues, domestic issues range from relatively obtrusive ones to relatively unobtrusive ones. People with school-age children have direct experience of the education system, and most of us have experienced the health care system, making them relatively obtrusive issues. In contrast, issues like space travel or the environment, whose subtle changes affect everyday life but are not always immediately apparent, are less obtrusive. Some domestic concerns, like law and order, may be largely driven by spectacular events, while others, like education, may be more driven by elite policy struggles. Here, issues are once again arranged by obtrusiveness, and Figure 2.2 depicts the changing levels of public concern about these issues and some of the historical events associated with them.

Health. This category includes the cost of care, care for the elderly, Medicare, poor quality care, lack of insurance, and specific illnesses, such as cancer and acquired immunodeficiency syndrome (AIDS). It is a chronic topic of concern, appearing in more than 85 percent of the polls, but widespread public concern about it has emerged relatively recently. July 1991 was the first time more than five percent of responses mentioned health care. Although the U.S. population is aging and public concern about health has been rising since 1991, evidence from the public agenda shows peaks and valleys of concern about health aligning with elite-driven policy initiatives. When Bill Clinton announced his health care task force in January 1993, public concern about health hit a new peak at more than 9 percent of responses. In September, when he gave a major public speech about health care reform, concern reached the highest level recorded in the series, more than 20 percent of responses. This was also the first of two occasions when health topped the public agenda. In the five polls

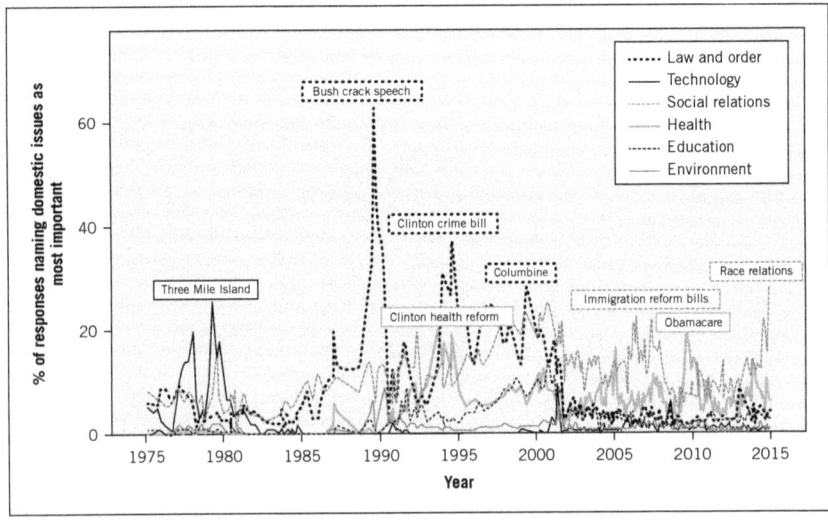

Figure 2.2. Public concern about domestic issues, 1975–2014.

taken between September 1993 and August 1994, when Clinton's health care reform bill was declared dead, between 12 and 20 percent of responses named health as the most important problem facing the nation. Over the rest of the decade, concern did not exceed 10 percent of responses, although it stabilized at higher levels than had been recorded in the 1970s and 1980s. In March and June 2000, public concern about health rose to more than 10 percent of responses as Clinton worked to include prescription drug benefits with Medicare, the federal health insurance program for the elderly. However, a major overhaul of Medicare in 2003, in which George W. Bush managed to get such a benefit through Congress, seems not to have drawn much public attention, either during the debate itself or when the law was implemented in January 2006.

The 2004 election season saw several months where health accounted for more than 10 percent of responses to the "most important problem" question, with concern rising from 8.6 percent in July to 11.5 in November. Concern rose to more than 16 percent in February 2005, as the Bush administration sought to freeze some Medicare payments and state governors clashed with the administration over how to cover the costs of care. From July 2007 until January 2008, concern about health care hovered between 9 and 11 percent of responses in all but one month. Candidates in the presidential primaries, most notably Obama, were speaking out about health care, and a fight had broken out over reauthorization of a program designed to provide health insurance to children, resulting in two presidential vetoes before the program was reauthorized.

Perhaps owing to the scale of the economic collapse that began in late 2007, health remained low on the public agenda until the Obama administration took up health care reform in 2009. In June 2009, a month before the administration's bill was introduced in Congress, concern rose to nearly 11 percent of responses and remained well above that level until the April 2010 poll, taken two weeks after the president signed the Affordable Care Act into law. It peaked in August 2009, as town hall meetings about the plan were disrupted by conservatives and Tea Party members, and a rumor arose that the new law would include "death panels" deciding whether elderly and disabled people merited continued care. Concern rose to more than 10 percent in November 2010, as Republicans ran against Obamacare in the midterm elections, and in January and February of 2011, as the new Republican House majority took office and planned a vote to repeal the law. A June 2012 Supreme Court decision that the law was constitutional did not attract much public concern, but the deeply problematic launch of the federal health care exchange website in October 2013 explains the sudden spike in concern to about 14 percent of responses in the November 2013 poll. This is the only other time when health topped the public agenda, and public concern remained at more than 10 percent until February of the following year.

An exception to this generally elite-driven pattern of public concern about health may be the sudden spike in public concern from about 4 percent to more than 10 percent in October 2014, days after the first case of Ebola was diagnosed on U.S. soil, in Dallas, Texas.

Education. Although education is a chronic topic of concern, appearing in more than 85 percent of the polls taken over the past forty years, it has never been a leading one, and it shows signs of being elite-driven. The highest level of public concern, not quite 14 percent of responses, was recorded in October 2000, as George W. Bush campaigned on a platform of education reform. Of the six polls recording the highest levels of public concern about education, five appear between March 2000 and September 2001. Peaks of more than 10 percent appear in the poll taken just after the Super Tuesday primaries, the poll taken just before the general election, and the one just before Bush's No Child Left Behind Act was introduced in Congress in March 2001. The only other time when education drew more than 10 percent of responses as the most important problem was in September 1998, when Clinton pushed for education reforms that included hiring one hundred thousand new teachers.

Environment. The environment is also a low-ranking issue on the public agenda, accounting for only a little more than 5 percent of responses in only two polls. Unlike health and education, concerns about the environment seem event-driven rather than elite-driven. Although environmental problems have direct effects on large numbers of people, the event producing the greatest spike in concern was unobtrusive. Public concern peaked in April 1990 at not quite 9 percent of responses, shortly after *Exxon Valdez* captain Joseph Hazelwood was convicted of negligence near the first anniversary of the tanker's spill of more than 10 million gallons of oil into Alaska's Prince William Sound. Other major environmental disasters have provoked little public concern. In the six months following BP's 2010 oil spill in the Gulf of Mexico, estimated at more than 100 million gallons (Trott 2015), less than 2 percent of responses to the "most important problem" question named the environment. In July 1986, two months after the nuclear accident at Chernobyl, survey respondents did not mention the environment or technology as a concern. Although the environment has never come close to topping the list of public concerns, it does typically appear on the public agenda. Only thirty-nine polls register no public concern.

Technology. This category, which includes energy, space travel, mass transit, computers, and the Y2K bug, has never topped the public agenda, but it garnered its highest levels of public concern during the late 1970s. In 20 percent of the "most important problem" polls, no one refers to technological issues. Concerns about technological issues are associated both with obtrusive issues, like the late 1970s energy crisis, and relatively unobtrusive issues, like nuclear energy safety. They are associated with events, though in several cases President Carter's public statements on the energy crisis probably accentuated public concerns.

The single highest level of concern about technology, 25 percent of responses, was recorded in May 1979, following the March 28 accident at the Three Mile Island nuclear power plant. Even in this month, however, concerns about money were more commonly named as the most important problem. Most of the other high levels of public concern about technology appear in conjunction with energy and oil crises of the late 1970s. The second highest level of concern, almost 20 percent of responses in February 1978, followed a coal strike and the fall of Mohammed Reza Pahlavi, shah of the oil-rich nation of Iran. These events were further compounded by the crash of a Russian satellite in Canada that was said to be leaking radiation. In July 1979, energy concerns were joined by news that the United States had developed a neutron bomb, and technological concerns approached 14 percent. Concerns about nuclear plants; protests at the Seabrook, New Hampshire, plant; and an energy crisis resulting in rising prices and the possibility of rationing were associated with elevated levels of concern about technology in August and October 1979. However, since October 1979, concern about technological issues has never exceeded 10 percent of responses.

Law and order. This category includes concerns about drugs, guns, espionage, and the court system as well as criminal violence. Although average people are sometimes crime victims, media research suggests concern about the issue may be driven by media coverage of crime rather than crime itself (e.g. Dixon 2008; Funkhouser 1973; Reeves and Campbell 1994; Reinerman and Levine 1997). Consequently, for this issue, unobtrusive factors (media coverage) may have more impact on public opinion than obtrusive ones (victimhood). Similarly, although public concern about crime appears event-driven, it may be that political and media institutions capitalize on the steady supply of criminal activity to promote preferred policies and attract large audiences (Reeves and Campbell 1994; Reinerman and Levine 1997).

Law and order draws some of the highest levels of public concern registered in the polls. At its peak in September 1989, it accounted for nearly 63 percent of responses. It is also a chronic concern, appearing in all but two of the polls. In eighteen polls, more than 20 percent of responses refer to law and order, and in forty-six polls, more than 10 percent do. It has been the top issue on the public agenda in at least sixteen polls.

Some scholars argue public concern about drugs and drug-related crime, both of which would appear within the category of "Law and Order" in the "most important problem" coding, were largely manufactured by politicians and the news media (e.g., Reeves and Campbell 1994; Reinerman and Levine 1997). Although there are definite signs that concerns about drugs drove this issue during the 1980s and some signs that public concerns about law and order in this time frame were elevated as a result of elites' activities, the relationship is not entirely straightforward. Reagan's war on drugs, declared in 1982, did not raise the law and order issue on the public agenda; nor did the start of first lady Nancy Reagan's "Just Say No" campaign in 1984. Events did not necessarily move the public agenda, either. The death of star college basketball player Len Bias in 1986 from a cocaine overdose had a marginal impact on public concern. However, as the number of cocaine-related arrests rose and more and more crime news featured crack-related crime (Fryer et al. 2013), public concern about law and order increased from 1986 through the end of the decade.

Although not all elite actions provoked rising public concern, there are some clear connections. Public concern was rising when Reagan signed the Anti–Drug Abuse Act, which created mandatory minimum sentences for drug possession and harsher penalties for possession of crack, as opposed to powder, cocaine. Craig Reinerman and Harry Levine (1997) note that during 1986, an election year, media attention to crime was also high, with numerous television magazine programs devoted to the "crack epidemic." Public concern reached the highest levels recorded in the series in 1989, as the George H. W. Bush administration created the Office of National Drug Control Policy, making its director, William Bennett, colloquially referred to as the "drug czar," a member of the cabinet. Media attention to crack cocaine also hit a peak in 1989 (Fryer et al. 2013), and public concern about law and order, fueled mainly by worries about drugs, exceeded 30 percent all year. Concern reached its peak, nearly 63 percent of responses, in September 1989, days after Bush gave a nationally televised speech announcing Bennett's drug plan. During the speech, the president held up a bag of crack cocaine that he said had been purchased across the street from the White House. The third highest level of concern ever recorded, slightly more than 37 percent of responses, came in August 1994, just before Clinton signed the largest crime bill in U.S. history.

There is also evidence that public concern is at odds with social reality when it comes to crime. When U.S. violent crime rates peaked in 1991, public concern was not as high as it had been during the 1980s or as high as it would become later in the 1990s. Moreover, as violent crime rates steadily fell, public concern did not. From September 1993 until September 2001, the poll taken just before the terrorist attacks, concern about crime ranged from 10 percent to more than 30 percent, suggesting that it had become chronically elevated. It surpassed 20 percent in all but one of the twelve polls taken between 1994 and 1997. It was the top issue on the public agenda from January 1994 until July 1995 and topped the public agenda again from July 1996 until August 1997.

With intermittent polling and chronically high levels of public concern, it is difficult to persuasively link public concerns to specific incidents. It is possible in virtually any month to find a high profile case that might raise public concern about crime. For instance, two months after the Oklahoma City bombing, law and order accounted for more than 22 percent of responses. Following the 1996 murder of child beauty queen JonBenét Ramsey, it accounted for more than a quarter of responses. After the Long Island Rail Road massacre in 1993, it reached 31 percent of responses. However, a clearer link emerges with the mass shootings at Columbine High School in April 1999. Public concern about law and order jumped from 13 percent of responses in January 1999 to almost 29 percent of responses the month following the deaths of thirteen high school students.

Concerns about law and order have not accounted for more than 10 percent of responses since the September 11 terrorist attacks. Recent high-profile crimes and mass shootings have not had much impact on public concerns about law and order. It garnered 4.5 percent of responses following the 2007 Virginia Tech shootings, up from 2.9 percent of responses the month before. After a mass shooting in a Colorado movie theater in July 2012, concern about law and order fell from 2.7 percent of responses to 1.9 percent. Casey Anthony's acquittal for the murder of her daughter in 2011 and the shooting of unarmed African American teenager Trayvon Martin in 2012 similarly had no effect on public concern about law and order, each event associated with a change of less than 1 percent. The only crime between September 11 and the end of 2014 to have a noticeable and lasting effect on public concerns about law and order was the mass shooting at Sandy Hook Elementary School in December 2012. Public concern rose from about 3 percent in the month before the shootings to nearly 7 percent in the poll that began on the day the shootings occurred, reaching a peak of more than 9 percent in February 2013 and remaining at more than 6 percent for four months before subsiding. Nevertheless, the two deadliest mass shootings in U.S. history through 2014, Virginia Tech and Sandy Hook, have not drawn nearly as much public concern about law and order as Gallup documented in the 1990s.

The low levels of public concern following such devastating events offer an intriguing counterpoint to the concerns of scholars writing in the 1990s of how the government used media and managed public concern to support the passage of "tough on crime" laws. Selecting spectacular incidents and crafting narratives about them may offer leaders an opportunity to build public support for their preferred policies, but recent public concern about law and order reveals that events themselves, even when terrible and unprecedented, do not necessarily arouse public concern. The public's ability to demand change may hinge on more than media attention to spectacular events. For good or for ill, elite leadership—a willingness to expend political capital to constitute the event as an issue and the issue as a priority—may be needed to spark public demands for change in democratic contexts. This raises the question of whether such leadership is still possible in modern media environments.

Social relations. This is an omnibus category encompassing a wide variety of topics, including poverty, family problems, ethics, and teen pregnancy. It also includes both immigration and racism, although gay rights, like other forms of civil rights, are part of the government/political category. The concerns on the list are potentially obtrusive parts of everyday life, but like problems related to law and order, there is the potential for media and government attention to shape public concern about unobtrusive aspects of social life. Social relations are similarly complex when one considers whether they are event-driven or elite-driven. Spectacular events may raise public concern about a particular issue, but many of these issues represent smoldering problems that may rise on the public agenda when media or government turn attention to them.

The extensive list of issues included under social relations and the durability of the problems it includes contribute to making social relations a chronic concern on the public agenda, peaking at almost 28 percent of responses in December 2014 and never falling below the 1 percent of responses recorded in November 1980. Ten percent or more of responses to the "most important problem" question have listed social relations in over half the polls in the series. It has been a particularly prominent category relatively recently. Of the eighteen times it has accounted for more than 20 percent of responses, fourteen of them have been since 2000. The earliest recorded instance of it topping 20 percent of responses was August 1997. In comparison, the highest values recorded in the 1970s and 1980s were slightly more than 14 percent. Perhaps unsurprisingly, social relations is also a more prominent public concern under Democratic rather than Republican presidents. Of the twenty polls recording the highest levels of concern about social relations, only five were taken while a Republican was president (George W. Bush in all five cases). Only six of the twenty lowest levels of public concern were recorded while Democrats were president (Carter in five cases, Obama in one).

From 1975 until 1984, social relations drew more than 10 percent of responses in only one poll, but beginning in 1985, concerns about social relations topped 10 percent of responses more often than not. In the eighteen polls taken during Reagan's first term in office (1981–1985), concern about social relations never reached 10 percent of responses. However, it accounted for more than 10 percent of responses in five of nine polls taken during his second term in office. Only six of twenty polls taken during George H. W. Bush's term of office (1989–1993) recorded levels of concern about social relations at less than 10 percent of responses. During Clinton's eight-year presidency (1993–2001), concern about social relations failed to reach 10 percent only twice in twenty-two polls, and in his second term, social relations accounted for more than 20 percent of responses for the first time in the series. Although concern about social relations is typically higher under Democratic presidents, it received the most consistent public attention during George W. Bush's presidency (2001–2009). The "most important problem" question was asked eighty-nine times, and concern about social relations was more than 10 percent about 75 percent of the time. In seven polls, it exceeded 20 percent. Public concern about social relations was somewhat lower during Obama's presidency, with only twenty-eight out of seventy polls registering levels of concern of more than 10 percent, but the highest level of concern recorded in the forty-year series appears in the very last poll, December 2014.

The breadth of the category and chronically high levels of concern about social relations later in the time frame make reasons for public concern somewhat difficult to identify, though patterns of elevated concern offer some clues about what might underlie them. In several instances, high-profile events involving race relations are associated with elevated levels of public concern about social relations. In May 1992, after the outbreak of riots in Los Angeles following the acquittal of four white police officers for beating African American motorist Rodney King, concern about social relations rose to nearly 20 percent of responses, from slightly more than 12 percent in the previous poll in March. In July 1994, the month after O. J. Simpson's arrest for his ex-wife's murder, concern about social relations increased to more than 15 percent of responses, up from less than 9 percent of responses in the previous poll in January. In August 1997, concern rose to about 20 percent from 15 percent in January following Haitian immigrant Abner Louima's beating and sodomization by New York City police. However, not all racial incidents raise public concern about social relations. Neither Trayvon Martin's death in 2012 nor George Zimmerman's acquittal for his killing in 2013 spiked public concern.

Incidents involving immigration are also associated with public concern about social relations, although not always in straightforward ways. Public concern about social relations reached its third highest peak, more than 23 percent of responses, in April 2000, during the struggle over whether six-year-old Cuban refugee Elian Gonzales would remain in the United States or be returned to his father in Cuba. Following a final court decision in June 2000, which, in essence, returned the boy to his father, concern again rose to more than 21 percent of responses. Public concern was greater than 20 percent in April 2006, as comprehensive immigration reform was introduced in the Senate, and again in June, just after the reform package passed in that chamber. The House and Senate could not agree on their respective versions, so the Senate tried again in 2007, and public concern about social relations again topped 20 percent in May (when it was introduced) and June (when the final cloture vote failed). Public concern about social relations reached its zenith in the December 2014 poll, the last in the series. Although one might associate this with a series of high-profile incidents of police violence against African Americans, a closer look at the polling data shows concern about immigration producing much of the spike. In July, Obama announced he would take executive action on immigration policy, and concern about social relations grew to more than 20 percent of responses. Immigration continued to be the major factor driving concern about social relations until December, when lingering concerns about immigration and a sharp spike in concern about race relations propelled social relations to the highest level recorded in the series, almost 28 percent.

School shootings also seem to provoke concerns about social relations. High levels of concern in May 1999 (23 percent of responses) might have been a response to Russell Henderson's guilty plea in the murder of Matthew Shepard, an antigay hate crime, but are more likely a response to the Columbine school shootings. Concern about crime also doubled from the previous poll. A similar spike appears in April 1998, following a school shooting in Jonesboro, Arkansas, and high levels of concern were recorded in March 2001, when a school shooting in Santee, California, occurred on the day interviewing for the poll began. That these acts of violence generated concern about social relations as well as (and in some cases instead of) law and order or terrorism is telling. The perpetrators of the violence were young white American men, and viewing their acts as reflecting on social relations absolves the actors of responsibility. In only one of these three polls did concern about law and order outweigh concern about social relations, although this may be in part a product of the omnibus nature of the social relations category.

A few spikes in concern about social relations fit none of these patterns. The only poll before 1985 in which social relations accounted for more than 10 percent of responses was in August 1979, as the U.S. government considered bailing out Chrysler, which seemed poised for bankruptcy. In May 1989, a sudden rise to a bit more than 14 percent of responses, the highest recorded in the 1980s, reflected concern about poverty and homelessness, although poverty had been declining since 1983. An apparent rise in concern in October 2000 may be a methodological artifact.

Foreign Affairs

Foreign affairs are typically the least obtrusive type of issue. The United States has not seen conventional war on its own soil since the Civil War, so although many families are touched by policy decisions to go to war abroad, its everyday impact on most Americans has been negligible since the end of World War II. Similarly, most Americans have no direct experience of foreign affairs. Foreign affairs also occupy an odd limbo between event-driven and elite-driven issues, and how they are perceived depends largely on whether one interprets American foreign policy, and particularly recent U.S. wars, as a matter of necessity or a matter of choice. Murray Edelman (1988) points out the strange, intimate relationship between political enemies who, in some respects, depend on each other as sources of power and legitimacy. A president facing domestic political scandal may order missile strikes against an enemy state, and a president facing recession may ramp up missile testing. However, the actions of other nations, such as test-firing missiles or supporting terrorist incursions, may also represent a real threat to U.S. security that needs to be addressed. For any given instance where foreign policy emerges on the public agenda, it may be unclear whether it is event-driven or elite-driven.

Categorizing responses related to foreign affairs may have given Gallup's coders some problems. During the Cold War, regional conflicts were typically seen as having international dimensions. Following the Cold War, the language citizens used to express their concerns about regional conflict may have been less formulaic, causing coders to have trouble consistently coding responses. For example, a sudden shift in public concern between general international issues in April 2004 and the Middle East in May 2004 may have been the product of changing patterns of public discourse, or it may have been a coding artifact. Figure 2.3 depicts how public concern about foreign affairs has evolved over the forty years from 1975 through 2014 and some of the historical events that are associated with the changes.

General international issues. This category, including generic concerns about war, foreign policy, foreign aid, national security, nuclear weapons, summit failures, military preparedness, and national prestige, is a topic of chronic concern to Americans. Every poll in the series includes some mention of international issues as the most important problem, and the topic tops the public agenda at least fourteen times. The percentage of responses naming international issues peaks at almost 35 percent in November 1983. In about 17 percent of polls taken from 1975 through 2014,

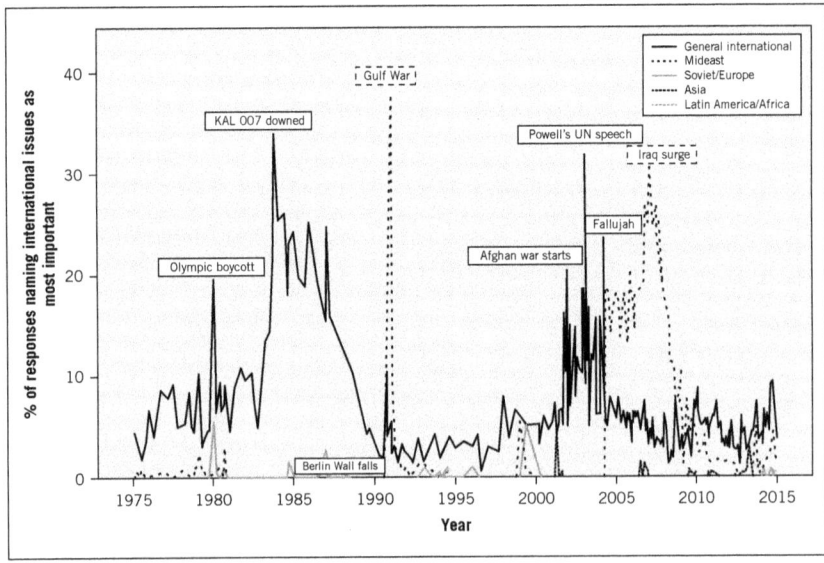

Figure 2.3. Public concern about international issues, 1975–2014.

general international issues account for more than 10 percent of responses to the "most important problem" question.

High levels of concern about general international issues are much more typical in the 1980s than at any other point in the polling series. The two highest values recorded in the 1970s appear in February 1979 (slightly more than 10 percent of responses), as China and the Soviet Union faced off over China's invasion of Vietnam and the U.S. began evacuating Americans from Iran following the fall of the shah, and January 1980 (nearly 20 percent of responses), days after Carter announced the United States would boycott the 1980 Summer Olympics in Moscow to protest the Soviet invasion of Afghanistan. Most polls in which more than 20 percent of responses named general international issues were taken during Reagan's administration. Of the fourteen polls where concern rises above 20 percent, eleven were taken between October 1983 (shortly after the Soviets downed a Korean passenger jet) and February 1987. In all twenty polls taken between April 1983 and September 1988, concern about international issues accounted for more than 10 percent of responses, and it rose to the top of the public agenda in ten of those polls. In the next poll taken, in May 1989, concern had dropped to near 5 percent of responses. Between that poll and the one taken in October 2001, concern about general international issues would rise to more than 10 percent only once, in October 1990, as an international coalition formed to oust Iraq from Kuwait.

Prior to the fall of the Berlin Wall in November 1989, the lowest level of concern about general international issues registered in the 1980s had been 4.4 percent of responses. This may seem low, but more than one-third of all the polls in the series record lower levels of concern. The long series of low values recorded between autumn 1989 and autumn 2001 might be expected, but a similarly long series of low values appeared from May 2004 until the end of 2014.

Since the close of the Cold War, concerns about general international issues have risen above 20 percent of responses three times, all in the wake of the September 11 attacks: December 2001 (as the war in Afghanistan began), February 2003 (following Secretary of State Colin Powell's UN address advocating war with Iraq), and April 2004 (days after the killing and mutilation of four U.S. military contractors during the first battle of Fallujah). In all three of those polls as well as the February 2004 poll, general international issues topped the public agenda. There was sustained public concern about this topic from October 2001 to April 2004.

During the Cold War, international issues were commonly presented as East–West confrontations waged by proxy in places like Central America and Asia, so public concern about such issues may have emerged as general international concerns instead of regional ones. This may help explain why regional concerns in much of the world are so rarely mentioned as a most important problem, although American self-absorption probably plays a key role as well.

Latin America/Africa. Public concern about this category peaked at 2.5 percent of responses in January 1987, and respondents mentioned this region in only eight of the 254 polls included here. Concern about other world regions is similarly low throughout the time frame.

Soviet/Europe. Public concern about this category peaked at slightly more than 5 percent of responses in January 1980.

Asia. The peak level of concern about this category was also slightly more than 5 percent, in April 2001. For Asia, the Soviet Union, and Europe, the polls register no public concern in about 85 percent of the surveys.

Middle East. By contrast, 65 percent of polls mention this category as the most important problem for the United States, and there have been ten polls in which it accounted for more than a quarter of responses. It has been the top issue on the public agenda forty-two times between 1975 and 2014, more than any other issue except the economy. Public concern first spiked to about 10 percent of responses in October 1990, a little more than a month after Iraq invaded Kuwait, and climbed to slightly more than 17 percent in November. In a poll taken at the end of January 1991, during the height of the first U.S. war in Iraq, nearly 38 percent of responses named the Middle East as the most important problem. In three polls taken during the 1990–1991 Gulf War, it topped the public agenda. By March 1991, however, concern had dropped to less than 5 percent. There was no spike for the Middle East following the September 11 terrorist attacks, perhaps because respondents mentioned terrorism as the problem rather than the region. The U.S. war in Afghanistan similarly produced no mentions of the Middle East as a most important problem.

A sudden spike from no responses in April to more than 18 percent of responses in May 2004 suggests potential problems with Gallup's coding: in the same month, mentions of general international issues plummet. However, the Middle East topped the public agenda in thirty-nine of forty-five polls taken between May 2004 and January 2008. Between May 2004, the month after U.S. media began consistently reporting on prisoner torture at Abu Ghraib, and September 2008, public concern about the Middle East generated more than 11 percent of responses in every poll. In the fifty-three polls taken during that time frame, the Middle East accounted for more than 20 percent of responses fifteen times, including all thirteen monthly polls taken from October 2006 through October 2007, as Defense Secretary Donald Rumsfeld resigned, Saddam Hussein was tried and hanged, and Iraq descended into civil war. In February 2007, following Bush's announcement of a "surge" strategy that would send twenty thousand additional troops to Iraq, public concern topped 30 percent of responses. Virtually all these moments could be interpreted to a greater or lesser extent as being event-driven or elite-driven triggers of public reaction. When the U.S. economy collapsed in the fall of 2008, the Middle East's relative importance on the public agenda plummeted to single digits in every month but one. Although the Middle East has accounted for only a small percentage of responses in recent years, it was mentioned in every poll between May 2004 and December 2014.

Terrorism

Terrorism is a separate category in this analysis because hijackings, bombings, hostage-takings, assassinations, and other terrorist acts have been thought of differently in different eras. When the coding scheme adapted for this analysis was created in the mid-1990s (McCombs and Zhu 1995), terrorism was a component of the "Law and Order" category, suggesting it was a particular type of crime. In this era, hijackers and bombers were typically brought to trial for their crimes (such as hijacking the cruise ship *Achille Lauro* or blowing up the Alfred P. Murrah Federal Building in Oklahoma City). Hijacking and hostage-taking were sometimes political acts but were also committed by criminals and seemed similar to kidnapping for ransom. In 1971, D. B. Cooper famously hijacked a Boeing 727 and demanded a $200,000 ransom for the plane and its passengers. Thus, this categorization seemed to fit. Yet the terrorist attacks of September 11 have changed the tenor of U.S. discourse about terrorism to include not just talk of how to protect individual citizens but how to enhance national security. Like the Oklahoma City bombing, the hostage-taking at the Tehran embassy and the bombing of the U.S. Marine barracks in Beirut, the attacks were an assault on the government. Moreover, many recent acts of terrorism have left no living assailants to face criminal prosecution. To cope with the dynamic ways in which citizens, media, and government have thought and talked about terrorism in the past forty years, it is placed in a category of its own.

Terrorism is typically an unobtrusive issue in the sense that most citizens acquire knowledge about it through media. Although it does have direct impacts on people (for example, airport security measures have commonly been altered as what was once called "air piracy" changed), the terrorist act itself is typically remote from most citizens. News of terrorism is typically event-driven, although it is not entirely free of elite-driven influences, as the ebb and flow of public concern demonstrate.

Public concern about terrorism has been recorded at more than 10 percent only twenty-five times in 254 polls, and in ninety polls, no one mentioned it. It has topped the public agenda six times. Of the twenty-five polls in which concern registered more than 10 percent, only one occurred before October 2001. In November 1979, Iranian revolutionaries took hostage employees of the U.S. embassy in Tehran, and in January 1980, more than 14 percent of responses named terrorism as the most important problem (placing it third behind money and general international issues). July 1996 marked the next greatest expression of public concern prior to the September 11 terrorist attacks, when somewhat less than 7 percent of responses mentioned terrorism as the most important problem. New information had emerged that a bomb might have brought down TWA Flight 800 off the coast of New York, and Unabomber Ted Kaczynski was indicted on federal charges. The April 1995 Oklahoma City bombing, the most devastating act of terrorism on U.S. soil prior to September 11, evoked no public concern about terrorism in the poll taken that June.[3]

The highest levels of public concern were measured in the immediate aftermath of the September 11 attacks—more than 37 percent of responses in October 2001 and nearly 41 percent in November. In eleven of twenty-three polls taken from October 2001 through January 2004, more than 20 percent of responses named terrorism, and all the polls where concern registered as more than 10 percent of responses (save the January 1980 poll) were taken between October 2001 and July 2005. Concerns about terrorism topped the public agenda six times between October 2001 and June 2002.

A blend of event-driven and elite-driven public concern about terrorism emerges in the mixture of dips and spikes appearing after 2002. Some spikes are clearly event-driven, though not all major terrorist attacks substantially increase public concern. The last time in the series public concern about terrorism accounted for more than 10 percent of responses was in July 2005. The London bombings coincided with the first day of Gallup's interviews, so they seem a likely reason. In contrast, although concern

---

3. No measures of the public agenda are available near the time of another horrendous act of terrorism, the bombing of Pan Am Flight 103 over Lockerbie, Scotland, in December 1988.

about terrorism spiked to more than 15 percent of responses in March 2004, it is unlikely that this was due to the Madrid bombings—which killed 191 people—since this event took place on the last day of Gallup's March interviews. The April 2004 poll showed public concern about terrorism at a little more than 9 percent of responses, and other major terrorist attacks in geographically and culturally distant parts of the world similarly provoked little increased concern. An appalling attack in Mumbai, India, that killed more than 170 people in November 2008 did not increase U.S. public concerns about terrorism.

Whether other spikes are elite- or event-driven is harder to discern. The third and fourth highest recorded levels of public concern about terrorism appeared in 2003, in January (nearly 29 percent of responses) and March (28 percent of responses). These peaks could be event-driven, for in January, the deadly toxin ricin was discovered in a London apartment, and six suspected terrorists were arrested in Buffalo, New York. On the day interviews for the March poll began, September 11 mastermind Khalid Shaikh Mohammed was arrested. However, this was also a moment in time when the George W. Bush administration sought world support for war with Iraq, and the news was filled with stories of manhunts and investigations of suspected terrorists that might have been driven by elite interests rather than the events themselves. In both those months, terrorism once again topped the public agenda while the Bush administration developed an argument that Iraqi dictator Saddam Hussein possessed weapons of mass destruction and might have been involved in the September 11 attacks.

Between the September 11 attacks and the U.S. invasion of Iraq, concern about terrorism persisted at more than 12 percent of responses for all but one month, February 2003, when Colin Powell laid out the U.S. case for war before the United Nations. The sudden shift may be a coding error on Gallup's part, but it may also register public concern about both the possibility of war and international opposition to it. Following the invasion, concern about terrorism remained at less than 11 percent, until November of 2003, when it rose to more than 19 percent of responses after the revelation of a memo by Secretary of Defense Donald Rumsfeld suggesting lack of progress in the war on terrorism. It increased to more than 20 percent for the last time in our series in January 2004, following Hussein's capture.

The only other sustained wave of concern about terrorism, though much milder than that of the early Iraq war, occurred between July and October 2004 (between 10 and 12 percent of responses). This increase in public concern was likely elite-driven, since it occurred during the general

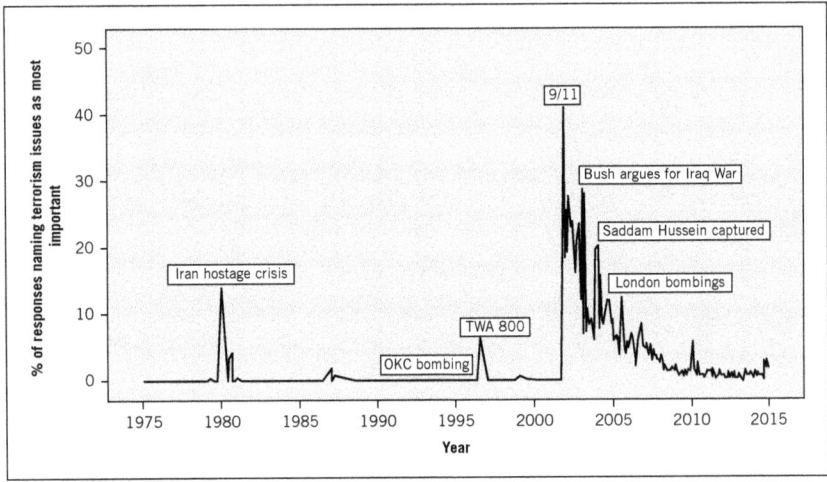

Figure 2.4. Public concern about terrorism, 1975–2014.

election campaign, when Bush, seeking reelection, emphasized the war on terror and national security (ICPSR, n.d.). The evidence here suggests the campaign was successful in moving the public agenda toward greater concern about terrorism, though it also suggests presidential persuasion is less powerful than what might be termed "actual events." Figure 2.4 depicts how public concern about terrorism has changed over the past forty years and presents some of the terrorist attacks, consequential events, and political responses that occurred during the time frame.

Government/Political

The Government/Political category is relatively broad and includes concepts associated with government corruption and incompetence but also a few "hot button" policy issues, such as school prayer, abortion, and gay marriage. These issues appear under Government/Political rather than Social Relations because the *policy* rather than the *issue* itself is named as a most important problem. The category is relatively unobtrusive, since most people do not directly experience the effects of scandalous behavior by government officials. However, for some social groups and in cases of extraordinary government incompetence, such as the federal response to Hurricane Katrina, it can become very obtrusive. It can be either elite-driven or event-driven. Sudden disclosures of scandalous behavior commonly generate event-driven routines for both news media and officials. However, government scandals are typically uncovered by enterprise, often by the opposition, and in this sense, the timing of revelations and the trajectory of investigations can be strategic and elite-driven.

Smith (1980) notes that naming the government itself as an important problem facing the nation was rare before the Watergate scandal. Just before Richard Nixon resigned, 23 percent of responses named government as the most important problem, but after the immediate crisis passed, concerns about government remained much higher than they had been before Watergate (Smith 1980). From 1975 through 2014, public concern about government continued to grow. It peaked at about 28 percent of responses in October 2013. Of the twenty polls showing the highest level of concern about government, sixteen were in 2013 and 2014, and all appeared after August 2005. Of the eleven times concerns about government have led the public agenda, nine were in 2013 or 2014, and all the polls taken between October 2013 and December 2014 were among the top twenty-five. Concern exceeded 10 percent of responses in 71 of 254 polls (28 percent). Figure 2.5 shows the changing levels of public concern about government as a problem and identifies some key events across the forty-year time span.

Four of six polls taken during the time frame when Gerald Ford was president (1975–1977) showed concern of more than 10 percent, which is perhaps unsurprising. In the first poll in the series, taken in February 1975, almost 12 percent of responses named government as the most important problem. As interviews for the poll were being conducted, leading Watergate figures H. R. Haldeman, John Ehrlichman, and John Mitchell

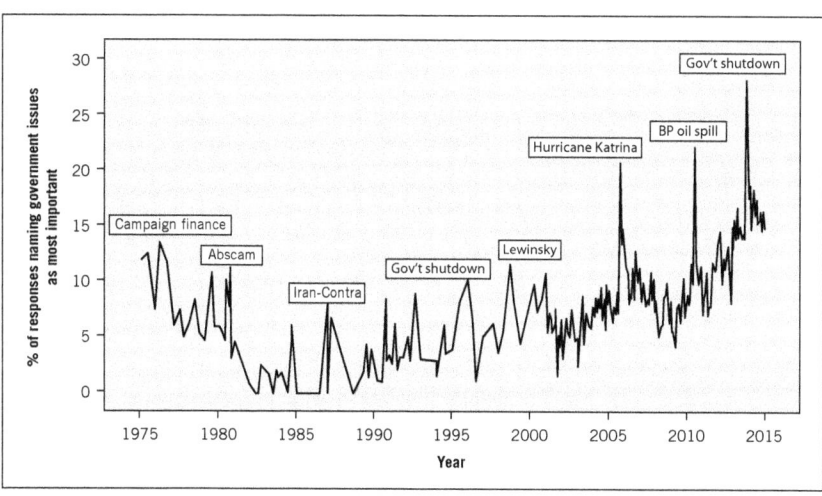

Figure 2.5. Public concern about government and politics, 1975–2014.

were sentenced, having been convicted the month before. As the July 1975 poll began, Watergate prosecutors questioned Nixon, and his legal battles over the release of papers and tapes continued. More than 12 percent of responses mentioned government. The April 1976 poll, in which more than 13 percent of responses named government as the most important problem, coincided with a legal tangle over the structure of the Federal Election Commission (FEC), another legacy of the Watergate crisis. The Supreme Court had ruled the FEC's proposed structure unconstitutional, and, despite the pleas of presidential candidates, the Court refused to release federal campaign matching funds until the issue was resolved. The October poll, in which more than 11 percent of responses named government as the most important problem, began a few days after U.S. Secretary of Agriculture Earl Butz's resignation, prompted by racist comments he made.

Only three of nineteen polls taken during Carter's term in office (1977–1981) registered public concern about government at more than 10 percent of responses. In August 1979, following Carter's televised public address on what he called a national crisis of confidence and a subsequent White House cabinet shakeup, concern about government reached more than 10 percent for the first time in his presidency. In July 1980, concern about government was more than 10 percent, following the indictment of two members of Congress and a mafia don implicated in corruption and bribery by the FBI's Abscam sting operation. It also spiked to more than 11 percent in October, during the first of the Abscam trials. Eventually, seven members of Congress would be convicted, though public concern about government does not remain high throughout this time frame.

There were twelve nonconsecutive months during the Reagan administration (1981–1989) when polls showed no one naming the government as the nation's most important problem. The earliest such poll was in June 1982, while the latest was in September 1988, and polls with this result were split fairly evenly between the two terms. No other president in this series has presided over a public that did not name government as a problem. In the twenty-seven polls taken during Reagan's presidency, concern about government peaked at slightly less than 8 percent of responses in a poll taken in January 1987, during the Iran-Contra affair. Infrequent and irregular polling on the most important problem may have obscured the impact of other Reagan-era scandals. However, Attorney General Edwin Meese's resignation and press secretary Lyn Nofziger's conviction (later overturned) for inappropriate lobbying during the Wedtech scandal and Deputy Chief of Staff Michael Deaver's perjury conviction, for example, were not associated with increased public concern about government.

All polls taken during George H. W. Bush's presidency (1989–1993) include some mentions of government as a most important problem, but none of the twenty taken during his term register levels of concern of more than 10 percent. Concern peaked at about 9 percent of responses in August 1992, perhaps owing to problems with the government's response to Hurricane Andrew, which hit Florida shortly before the poll began. However, during the investigation of the Keating Five—U.S. senators accused of influence peddling during the savings and loan crisis—public concern about government peaked at less than 5 percent of responses. Congressional confirmation hearings in which Supreme Court nominee (and ultimately Justice) Clarence Thomas was accused of sexual harassment by former staffer Anita Hill also provoked no discernable rise in public concern about government.

Although many think of Clinton's presidency as scandal-plagued, there are only two polls out of the twenty-two taken during his terms in office (1993–2001) in which concern about government was recorded at more than 10 percent of responses. The first, at slightly more than 10 percent, appeared in January 1996 and may have been in response to a federal government shutdown lasting from December 16, 1995, until January 6, 1996, a period immediately preceding the poll. The second, slightly more than 11 percent, was recorded the month after Clinton admitted to an improper relationship with Monica Lewinsky. Neither the Whitewater scandal nor the death of White House aide Vince Foster seems to have had much effect on public concern about government. The average level of concern about government during the Clinton years (almost 6 percent) was not much higher than it had been in the George H. W. Bush administration (not quite 4 percent), or even in the Reagan White House (2 percent).

George W. Bush's first term (2001–2005) looked much like those of his predecessors. The only time public concern about government exceeded 10 percent was the month he took office. This may have been due to the remarkable circumstances of his ascension to the presidency, which came in the wake of a virtually tied election that was ultimately decided by the Supreme Court more than a month after Election Day. The average level of public concern about government across the forty polls taken in his first term was 6.4 percent, an incremental increase similar to those seen in previous administrations. It was in Bush's second term (2005–2009) that public concern about government became chronically high. In September 2005, following the botched federal response to Hurricane Katrina, concern about government rose to more than 20 percent of responses for the first time in the series, and it continued at more than 10 percent until

March 2006. In July 2006, following the resignation of U.S. House Majority Leader Tom DeLay, who was implicated in the Abramoff lobbying scandal, it again topped 10 percent of responses. With the fallout and resignations from the scandal, public concern about government remained at more than 10 percent of responses, with one exception, through December. September and November of 2007 also saw public concern exceeding 10 percent of responses, perhaps due to an ongoing Justice Department scandal involving the dismissal of seven U.S. attorneys that was said to be politically motivated. Attorney General Alberto Gonzales, implicated in the scandal, resigned that September.

Overall, public concern about government in Bush's second term averaged slightly more than 9 percent of responses, and fourteen of forty-eight polls saw more than 10 percent of responses naming government as the most important problem. Nevertheless, some major revelations provoked little change in public concern. Disclosure of the National Security Agency's domestic surveillance program in December 2005 did not further elevate levels of concern about government. The Walter Reed Army Medical Center patient neglect scandal and the conviction of former White House Chief of Staff Lewis "Scooter" Libby, in connection with leaks of classified information about CIA operative Valerie Plame, both in the spring of 2007, failed to produce appreciable changes in public concern about government.

In some respects, Obama's first term (2009–2013) was like George W. Bush's first term. The forty-eight polls taken showed public concern about government up a bit from what was typical in Bush's second term, averaging 10 percent of responses. However, levels of public concern exceeding 10 percent were much more common in Obama's first term, occurring in twenty-three of forty-eight months. Concern was first recorded at more than 10 percent in September 2009, as conservatives objected to a back-to-school speech Obama planned to deliver to public schools nationwide via the internet. Eleven percent of responses named government as the most important problem just after Obama signed the Affordable Care Act into law in April 2010. Public concern spiked to more than 22 percent of responses in June 2010 following the BP oil spill in the Gulf of Mexico and remained at more than 10 percent, with one exception, until December. The battle over raising the U.S. debt ceiling that began in late July 2011 preceded another increase in public concern to more than 10 percent, and in some ways, it represented a sea change in the series. In only two succeeding months would public concern about government ever drop to less than 10 percent of responses.

During Obama's second term of office, 2013 through the end of the series, public concern about government never dropped below 13 percent of responses, and the average level of concern across twenty-three polls was above 16 percent, suggesting another important change in public attitudes toward government. Two spikes of more than 20 percent, including the highest recorded, at 28 percent, coincided with a sixteen-day government shutdown that began just before the October 2013 poll. However, other than this spike, the numbers are so chronically high that it is difficult to tie them to specific events or initiatives.

Robert Entman (2012) has written persuasively about the differential news coverage of political scandals and how media coverage impacts whether scandals have meaningful consequences for public opinion and political fortunes. John Zaller (1998) suggests that the consequences of scandal can also depend on the overall performance of an office holder: perceived success at one's job can ameliorate the impact of one's bad behavior on public opinion. Results here reveal that time may play a role as well. Public concern about government has grown over the past forty years, incrementally in some cases but in a huge rush in Bush's and Obama's second terms. As Entman might suspect, public reaction to political scandal is quite scattershot and does not seem meaningfully tied to the seriousness or plausibility of the accusations. However, the four months when public concern surpassed 20 percent of responses coincided not with scandals but with occasions when government failed to do its job: Hurricane Katrina, the Gulf oil spill, and the 2013 government shutdown. Other notably high levels of concern during the Clinton and George H. W. Bush administrations, as well as during the debt ceiling crisis, also suggest public impatience with a government that does not perform well. This indicates an encouraging degree of event-driven public pragmatism rather than a public distracted by elite-driven scandal machines. Chronically high levels of concern about government during Obama's second term, unresponsive as they seem to be to any actual government behavior—scandalous or incompetent—are more troubling.

Conclusion

This forty-year history of issues rising and falling on the public agenda reveals just how unpredictable the content of the public agenda can be. Not only is it impossible to judge the relative importance of events or conditions; some events that seem important in retrospect provoked little public concern at the time they occurred. Indeed, the analysis shows something even more complex is going on: it is not always clear what sort of issue is raised by particular events. School shootings raise public concern about law and order, but they also raise concern about social relations, suggesting different citizens perceive them differently. Federal budget battles raise the level of concern about government spending but also about government itself. During the Great Recession, some poll respondents identified the most important problem as jobs, while others said it was the economy in general. These diverging perceptions of an event almost certainly emerge from the respondents themselves, who gave differing answers to the Gallup "most important problem" question, rather than a product of the way those answers were coded by Gallup. They suggest the presence of aspect, or second-level, agenda setting, in which the same event or issue is perceived differently because different aspects of it are emphasized by public officials and in news coverage, and they hint at the potential for public fragmentation. Reality matters, but representation matters, too.

Not only are there differences between people in the ways that issues are perceived in the moment, the same issues may be perceived differently over time. For example, after the Clinton government shutdown ended in 1996, concern about spending topped 20 percent of responses, while concern about government was 10 percent. During the Obama shutdown in 2013, slightly less than 10 percent of responses named spending while more than 28 percent of responses named government. This fits a larger pattern in the data of rising levels of concern about government and suggests the public blames government for more things today than it once did. In the case of terrorism, both poll respondents and the Gallup coders themselves may have been caught up in an evolving understanding of the issue. Coders in our study treated mentions of Iran during the hostage crisis as references to terrorism, but it may be that either Gallup coders or survey respondents (or both) thought of the hostage crisis as an aspect of Middle East or international relations rather than as terrorism. The apparent lack of public reaction to the Oklahoma City bombing may be a methodological artifact of people naming some aspect of law and order, or of Gallup coders interpreting public responses as an aspect of law and order. Acts of terrorism occurred throughout the time frame under study, but terrorism became a salient category only after September 11. It could be that earlier acts of terrorism were not seen as most important problems, but it is also very possible they were perceived by respondents or by coders as some other kind of public problem so that their impact on the public agenda cannot be traced.

Other new categories introduced by Gallup also indicate changing public perceptions of social issues over time. Public problems must be perceived as public problems before they can emerge on the public agenda. Apparently, before 1982, not enough people mentioned the economy in general for it to merit its own category; presumably, respondents mentioned more specific concerns or were encouraged by interviewers to do so. After 1998, enough people named the media as a most important problem to warrant the creation of its own category. Smith (1985) discovered a similar sort of evolution: in the 1950s, civil rights were not seen as a public problem. It underleverages the data to treat changes in categorization over time as "coder error." Instead, the data document cultural-level changes in our shared understanding of the social world, although these data present further evidence that the content of the public agenda cannot be effectively modeled or predicted. The data also demonstrate that while events are real, communication about those events matters for the way they manifest on the public agenda.

As Lippmann (1922) pointed out long ago, communication processes are another complicating factor in the ebb and flow of public concern. Smith (1980, 1985) found no evidence that political leaders shape the public agenda, perhaps because he was not looking for it. This analysis suggests political communication can and sometimes does influence the distribution of public concern, yet it did not do so in line with expectations about obtrusive and unobtrusive issues or about event-driven and elite-driven news. Foreign affairs might be expected to be especially susceptible to elite-driven communication processes (Bennett 1990; Entman 1991), in part because it is so unobtrusive, but the rise and fall of public concern about these issues in fact tends to be shaped by events to a considerable degree. Political leaders may steer the United States toward or away from international conflict, but when conflict breaks out, the ebb and flow of events affect the ebb and flow of the issue on the public agenda. As the Iraq conflict deteriorated, George W. Bush was unable to distract the public from it or to reshape public perceptions. Similarly, partisan scandal machines—elite-driven representations of unobtrusive issues—may influence the public's perception of government as the most important problem. Yet the biggest spikes in public concern tend to be associated with events, moments when government failed, such as in a government shutdown or in the federal response to Hurricane Katrina.

Conversely, while one might expect economic issues to be obtrusive and largely driven by events, there is evidence Carter's speeches enhanced public concerns about the economy. Public concern about some unobtrusive issues seems entirely shaped by political leadership, such as elite conflicts over government spending and the debt ceiling, but, curiously, public concern about some issues that appear very obtrusive are also driven by elite leadership. Concerns about health, education, and welfare emerge on the public agenda when political leaders work to enact policy to address these issues. There is little evidence that changes in real-world conditions, such as rising health care costs or failing schools, move public concerns. Together with the evidence that recent mass shootings, widely reported in the press, do not always increase public concern, these findings suggest political leadership may be needed to raise the profile of some issues on the public agenda. This presents an important counterpoint to critical scholars' concern about manipulations of the public agenda by political elites. While leaders may steer the public toward unnecessary wars or distract it from pressing social and environmental problems, leadership may also be needed to put some issues on the agenda as "most important problems." Without that support, the inability to afford health insurance or to make ends meet on welfare or Social Security might be seen as personal failings rather than social problems. Both government surveillance and mass shootings could be perceived as the price of freedom.

This detailed look at the public agenda offers insight into how history is understood by those who live it as well as a view into the complexity and unpredictability of the communication processes that influence public concern about particular issues. Clearly, events are not the only influence on the public agenda. As political leaders and media organizations offer representations of civic life to the public that influence the expression of public concern about issues, mediated communication processes interact with, and sometimes generate, events. The importance of these representations suggests that although public concern about any given issue is unpredictable, changes in the media ecology that communicates representations of public affairs have the potential to alter the character of the public agenda.

At this level of detail, the broader outlines of the public agenda are difficult to discern. Patterns of public concern about the economy or foreign affairs are difficult to identify, as are the ways far-reaching changes in the social environment, such as the end of the Cold War or the growth in media choice, have shaped the public agenda. Considering each issue individually makes competition between issues difficult to observe, and looking issue by issue does not reveal the increasing fragmentation of public concerns. Thus, Chapter 3 employs broader categories as well as statistical analysis to document the changing character of the public agenda. Although the content of the public agenda is unpredictable, its character is not, and the content of the agenda and its degree of fragmentation are related to each other.

3

The Character of the Public Agenda, 1975–2014

A detailed look at the public agenda reveals how the public has responded to historical events, news media representations, and political leadership. However, considering the agenda at such a granular level makes larger trends and changes in the public agenda hard to spot. Widening the analytical lens lets us observe relationships between issues as they rise and fall on the public agenda. It is these patterns of relative concern about issues that give the public agenda its character. It is here where we can see evidence of a public agenda that is growing more diverse and, by extension, a public that is growing more fragmented. Throughout this book, we use terms like *fragmented*, *unfocused*, *broad*, and *diverse* more or less interchangeably as descriptors of the public agenda, although when we use the term *diversity*, we are referring to a specific statistical measure. We also use terms like *focused*, *unified*, and *compressed* as descriptors of a public agenda that is less diverse. All these terms refer to the degree of public agreement about the most important issue facing the country. When the public agenda is more focused, there is more agreement on what the most important issue is. When the public agenda is more fragmented, there is more variety in the issues individuals name as most important. Unlike the content of the public agenda, which seems to

---

Portions of this chapter were previously published as Jill A. Edy and Patrick C. Meirick, "The Fragmenting Public Agenda: Capacity, Diversity, and Volatility in Responses to the 'Most Important Problem' Question," *Public Opinion Quarterly*, December 27, 2018, available at https://doi.org/10.1093/poq/nfy043.

fluctuate over time in response to historical events and persuasive campaigns, the character of the public agenda evolves.

In this chapter, we consider theories about the character of the public agenda and how changes in the media environment have undermined some of the foundational assumptions of these theories while, potentially, changing the character of the public agenda. Then we explore how the public agenda as a whole has evolved over time by depicting the interplay in different time frames between the twenty categories whose history we examine in Chapter 2. These figures show changes in the character of the public agenda over the course of the late twentieth and early twenty-first centuries, both as history unfolded and as the media environment changed. We then examine the character of the public agenda using statistical techniques that can give us continuous, more precise measures of the changing character of the public agenda. We use these techniques to document how the characteristics of the public agenda interact with one another in ways that defy the expectations of existing theory. Not only do they reveal a diversifying public agenda; they suggest that existing theories about how fragmented the public agenda can become do not apply.

Limited Capacity and Issue Competition: Assumptions about the Public Agenda

Scholars typically posit that the public agenda has a limited "carrying capacity" so that issues compete with each other for public attention. Max McCombs (2004) describes "intense competition" among issues for a place on the public agenda, observing, "No society and its institutions can attend to more than a few issues at a time" (38). Apocryphally, this number was said to be between five and seven (McCombs and Zhu 1995; Shaw and McCombs 1977; Zhu 1992), but McCombs (2004) suggests the range is really more like two to six. Agenda setting was thus described as a "zero-sum game" (McCombs 2004; Zhu 1992), a place where the power of political leaders, social elites, and news media professionals could be observed. Getting an issue on the limited public agenda (or keeping one off) involved the exercise of both political and media power.

Jian-Hua Zhu (1992) identified a number of constraints limiting the size of the public agenda, including the limited carrying capacity of the news media (such as twenty-two-minute evening news broadcasts and the size of a newspaper's front page), and an individual's limited cognitive capacity. Despite the transformation of the U.S. media system over the past forty years, there are some reasons to think little has changed since Zhu's explication of these constraints. Individual cognitive capacity probably has not changed. Traditional news media are still an important source of news content, no matter where audiences encounter that content (Leccese 2009; McChesney and Nichols 2010; Pew Research Center 2010; Webster 2014). News judgment is highly similar across news organizations (Ryfe 2006), and journalists are reluctant to change their practices (Anderson 2013; Ryfe 2012). The declining economic fortunes of the news media (McChesney and Nichols 2010) might actually produce contraction in the public agenda if traditional news lacks the resources to cover a wide variety of issues. The front page of the *New York Times* contains fewer stories now than it did a decade ago (Boydstun 2013). On a broader level, Russell Neuman (1991) argues essential similarities in audience tastes generate uniformity rather than dissimilarity in media content, and James Webster (2014) points out that media audiences are overlapping.

Yet, in many ways, the assumptions underlying the view of the public agenda's limited capacity are problematic. From the early 1980s to the present, people's media choices have dramatically expanded. Broadcast network news and printed newspapers are now supplemented by cable news, news-oriented websites, and social media, which have profoundly altered the information environment available to American citizens. Online and twenty-four-hour news organizations are not faced with the same space and time limitations of their "old media" counterparts. Moreover, there are many more news outlets today, so, while each outlet's carrying capacity may be limited, together their carrying capacity may be virtually unlimited. Cable news fills many programming hours with punditry (Jurkowitz et al. 2013), profiting from audiences' differences rather than their similarities (see Turow 1997). Bruce Williams and Michael Delli Carpini (2011) argue changes in the media environment have effectively ended the agenda-setting and gatekeeping power of traditional news media, suggesting they no longer filter information or drive public attention and, thus, no longer serve an agenda-setting function. How, then, has the character of the public agenda changed?

Several scholars have examined the impact of the changed media environment on individual citizens and suggest that media and elite agenda setting still occur but operate differently. Their findings suggest two different mechanisms through which the public agenda might be transformed by the media's expansion. First, growing media choice could undermine the ability of news media to build public consensus around a limited range of issues as public attention to news declined. Toshio Takeshita (2005) observes that increased audience choice is a key threat to the media's agenda-setting power. Markus Prior (2007) demonstrates in the "high choice" media environment made possible by cable and internet technologies, a substantial proportion of the television audience opts out of watching news in favor of entertainment programming, resulting in a growing knowledge gap between informed and uninformed citizens. In this scenario, as the audience for news shrinks, the public agenda falls apart, becoming more diverse in the absence of news cues.

A second possibility arises from people's tendency to choose news that suits them. Shanto Iyengar and Kyu Hahn (2009) show that the availability of partisan news sources encourages viewers to select politically congenial media, and Natalie Stroud (2011) demonstrates that individual media choices result in different issue priorities. Lance Bennett and Iyengar (2008) argue that changes in the media environment have resulted in a new era of limited media effects in which individual opinions are reinforced rather that swayed by media exposure. Cass Sunstein's (2009) analysis of the impacts of self-selection suggests worse consequences, for he argues that in environments lacking dissent, people's opinions become more extreme and their decisions riskier. In this scenario, the consensus-building features of news media are not undermined; rather, competing media agendas fragment the public agenda. In other words, the public agenda is driven apart, becoming more diverse as the issue agendas of news organizations become more distinctive.

Underlying these individual-level studies of media effects is an unarticulated insight about the collective quality of the public agenda, for while it is true that any given individual may have limited attention and cognitive capacity, the public as a whole does not have the same degree of constraint. These studies suggest that citizens making individual choices in a diversified media environment may engage in the social equivalent of parallel processing, expanding the carrying capacity of the public agenda beyond the cognitive limits of its individual members, much as issue publics expand the limits of public knowledge and expertise (Page and Shapiro 1992; Popkin 1991). In other words, a parent of young children who watches no news, an older news junkie, and recent college graduate who gets news from social media might each be cognitively capable of worrying about only a short list of public problems. However, if their lists are dissimilar, their combined agenda would be quite diverse. Thus, a media environment with enormous potential carrying capacity is encountered by a public that has substantial carrying capacity as well.

Historical Eras, Media Eras, and the Public Agenda

Chapter 2 reveals that elite leadership, news attention, and historical events move the public agenda and exert different levels of influence on

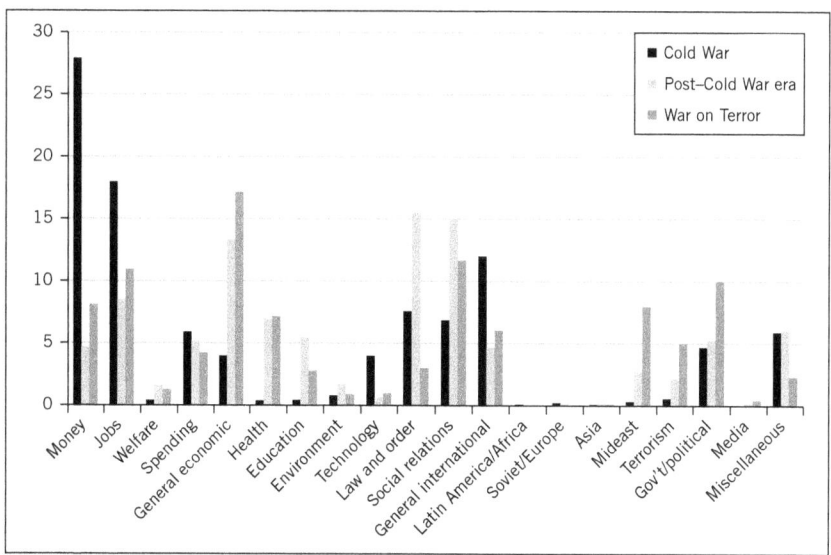

Figure 3.1. Public concern about issues during different historical eras.

different issues. Examining the distribution of public concern within different periods of time instead of looking at the specific histories of each issue illuminates the patterns of influence more clearly. History clearly plays a role in shaping the public agenda. One might think of three distinct historical periods as shaping world events since 1975: the Cold War, the ongoing standoff between the communist Soviet bloc and the capitalist West (1975–1989);[1] the post–Cold War era, the period of U.S. global dominance following the Cold War (1990–2001); and the War on Terror, the period following the September 11 attacks in the United States (2002–2014). Figure 3.1 suggests history's impact on the public agenda. It shows the mean level of public concern (measured as a percent of total responses) for each issue in each era.

During the Cold War and the War on Terror, public concern with international issues was substantially higher than it was in the post–Cold War era. Public concern about the Middle East and about terrorism during the War on Terror is substantially higher than in previous eras. These eras also happen to demarcate economic events that are reflected in the public

---

1. Historians date the end of the Cold War to the collapse of the Soviet Union in 1991, but defining the end of the Cold War as the year the Berlin Wall fell enables us to divide our time frames somewhat more evenly, providing more measures of the public agenda during the post–Cold War era.

agenda. During the Cold War era, the economy experienced "stagflation" and what was known as the "Reagan recession." The War on Terrorism time frame includes both the collapse of the so-called dot-com bubble and the Great Recession. In contrast, the post–Cold War era included years of budget surpluses and general economic good times, fueled in part by the expansion of the economic bubble that would burst and trigger the Great Recession. The public agenda reflects these economic environments. While jobs are a perennial public concern, they were a greater concern during the Cold War and War on Terror eras. Concern about money shows a similar pattern, though concern about general economic issues does not (a point to which we shall return).

One might also consider the objects of public concern during the post–Cold War era. Figure 3.1 shows that while the economy and international affairs dominated the Cold War public agenda, law and order and social relations emerged on the agenda during the post–Cold War era. In some ways, this change does not reflect a public response to "real world" events. Although violent crime peaked in the 1990s, social relations were surely just as problematic during the struggles for the civil rights of women and people of color in the 1970s as during the gay rights and immigration struggles of the 2000s. However, to the extent that the public agenda must, by definition, have some object of concern, it should follow that when items fall off the public agenda, public concern must go somewhere. During times of peace and prosperity, if public attention is responding to social reality, it should surely drift from economic and international concerns and settle somewhere else.

The apparent impact of history on the public agenda demonstrates that changes in its content have many different sources, and it would be a mistake to imagine that changes in the character of the public agenda have a single cause. However, many scholars reason that changes to the media environment may have affected the public agenda by altering the influence of news media and political elites. Key changes include the rise of cable television, of partisan television news, and of social media. Thus, one might parse the forty-year time period in terms of media changes: the broadcast era (1975–1985); the cable era, whose beginning can be defined by the moment when cable was present in half of all U.S. households (1986–1996); the partisan news era, defined by the launch of Fox News and MSNBC (1997–2008); and the social media era, defined as starting after Facebook reached 100 million active accounts worldwide (2009–2014). Figure 3.2 illustrates how these changes in the media environment are reflected in the public agenda, again in the form of the mean level of public concern about each issue in each era.

Explainable patterns of public concern are more difficult to sort out when history is parsed in terms of media expansion rather than historical events. For example, attention to jobs, money, and general international issues do not seem intelligibly linked to changes in the media environment. However, there are a few places where the media era seems to offer better insight than the historical era regarding patterns in the public agenda. Particularly notable is public concern with government. Both Figure 3.1 and Figure 3.2 show that concern about the government (a category that includes concerns about inefficiency and corruption) has risen over the past four decades. In Figure 3.2, parsing by historical era, one finds a fairly steady rise in concern, even though Richard Nixon's resignation would be a fresh memory and the movement for "clean government" inspired by the Watergate scandal was ongoing in 1975, when the timeline begins. Parsing the pattern by media era offers more insight. It reveals the major spike in concern about government emerges during the partisan media era and grows in the social media era. This spike has its "real world" connection because partisan news media came into their own as news sources during the Clinton impeachment hearings in 1998. However, as Williams and Delli Carpini (2011) point out, these scandals were themselves largely driven by media and particularly by partisan media. Further, as analysis in Chapter 2 reveals, concerns about government during Clinton's presidency did not rise nearly as much as they did in George W. Bush's and Barack Obama's second terms.

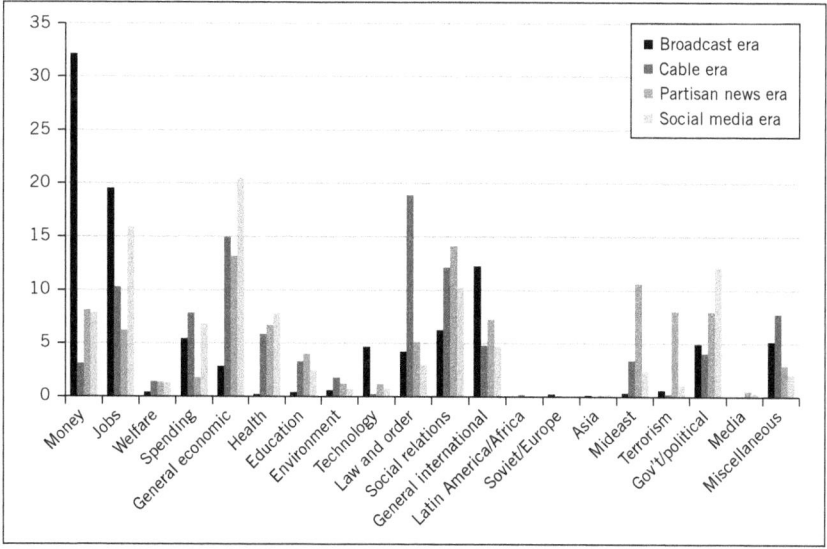

Figure 3.2. Public concern about issues during different media eras.

Although the pattern is less clear than with concerns about government, a similar argument could be made with regard to public concern about general economic issues, which has increased as the media environment has become more diverse. Of course, economic problems have many tangible forms experienced by average people, but this general concern is more susceptible to media and elite influence than concrete economic issues, such as jobs, inflation, or personal debt might be (evidence of which can be seen in Chapter 6). Another pattern that shows evidence of potential elite and media influence but could also be driven by the public's experience of changing social conditions is public concern about health. The analysis in Chapter 2 reveals that public concern about health is largely driven by elite policy initiatives that address health care costs. But these attempts at reform were made in increasingly hostile political environments that were reflected in an increasingly intemperate media environment. Thus, both the changing media environment and the changing social reality may explain rising concerns about health care.

Both Figure 3.1 and Figure 3.2 suggest the public agenda has become more diverse over the past four decades. One way to illustrate this is to consider the number of issues that could be seen as "on" the public agenda during a given time period. McCombs (2004) suggests using 10 percent as the lower limit of public attention an issue must receive to be considered "on" the public agenda. During the Cold War, average levels of public attention reach 10 percent of responses for only three public problems: jobs, money, and general international issues. In the post–Cold War era, although the public issue agenda is transformed, only four public problems—general economic issues, law and order, social relations, and jobs (at 9.9 percent)—earn average attention levels of nearly or more than 10 percent. During the War on Terror, public attention is divided among six public problems: jobs, money, general economic issues, Middle East, government, and social relations. Parsing the time series by media era reveals a similar pattern. In the broadcast era, public attention focuses on three public problems: jobs, money, and general international issues. In the cable era, the public agenda grows to four public problems: jobs, general economic issues, law and order, and social relations. In the partisan media era, it reaches six public problems: money, general economic issues, the Middle East, government, social relations, and terrorism. In the social media era, it encompasses a somewhat different group of six: jobs, money, general economic issues, health, government, and social relations.

Although there are hopeful signs that the public agenda is still governed to a meaningful extent by the social conditions average people experience, there is also evidence that the changing media environment may be fragmenting the public agenda by shaping public concerns about aspects of public life beyond personal experience, in line with the more general principle that public and political life are becoming increasingly mediated. More sophisticated statistical techniques can help detail these trends and substantiate that the patterns observed in the data are probably not due to chance, and it is to those techniques we next turn.

The Changing Character of the Public Agenda

Max McCombs and Jian-Hua Zhu (1995) develop three statistical measures of the public agenda to help illuminate its character and explain its dynamics. Capacity is the number of issues on the agenda at a given point in time. Diversity is the degree of entropy in the public agenda—that is, over how many issues public concern is spread and how evenly concern is spread over the issues. Volatility is how quickly an issue cycles onto and off of the public agenda, which can also be thought of in terms of its likelihood of surviving on the agenda from one point in time to the next. Looking at the public agenda from the 1950s through the mid-1990s, they find evidence of increasing agenda diversity and volatility, which they attribute to increasing levels of education. However, they find no linear relationship between time and carrying capacity. They observe that carrying capacity rises moderately into the mid-1970s and then falls again to 1950s levels by the mid-1990s.

Believing the carrying capacity of the public agenda to be limited to a handful of issues, McCombs and Zhu (1995) hypothesize that limited capacity and rising diversity lead to rising volatility as more issues compete for limited space. They argue, "When a greater number of issues are competing for attention and space on a public agenda that has major constraints on its capacity, volatility is a likely outcome" (497). Thus, they expect diversity and volatility to move together—as one increases, so does the other. However, if the carrying capacity of the public agenda is less limited because greater media choice is met with an audience's carrying capacity rather than an individual's cognitive capacity, issue competition would be less intense. This might produce increasing diversity with little or no change in volatility, a phenomenon more like *agenda stagnation*, in which the individual issue agendas making up the public issue agenda are both idiosyncratic and stable.

To find out how the character of the public agenda and its dynamics have evolved since the Cold War, as the media system expanded exponentially, we adapt McCombs and Zhu's (1995) measures to analyze responses to the "most important problem" question from 1975 through 2014. As

McCombs and Zhu do, we use ordinary least squares (OLS) regression with time and "time squared" as the independent variables. This allows us to see whether the changes over time are statistically significant (probably not due to chance) and whether they are linear (changing at a steady rate) or curvilinear (rising and falling, or vice versa, at a rate that changes).[2] The figures used to illustrate the findings show the individual data points representing how capacious, diverse, or volatile the public agenda was when a particular poll was taken and a regression line depicting the trend over the past forty years. Because the 254 time points when Gallup asked the "most important problem" question are not evenly spaced across the forty-year time frame, in all the figures presented here, data are plotted by the start date of the poll, and the x-axis is scaled in months.

Capacity

McCombs and Zhu (1995) operationalize issue-carrying capacity as the average number of issues named by respondents. Tom Smith (1980) claims that 106 of 125 times Gallup asked the "most important problem" question between 1946 and 1976, multiple responses were permitted, and this practice appears to have continued, for total responses across issue categories typically exceed 100 percent. McCombs and Zhu simply divide this total by 100 to arrive at mean issues named per respondent, a reasonable approach given their hypothesis that an individual's level of education is related to the public agenda's issue-carrying capacity. Applying this approach to the Gallup "most important problem" data from 1975 through 2014 produces Figure 3.3. It shows that while the average number of issues named by respondents in the surveys declines from 1975 until about 1990, it rises afterward and has been consistently greater than 1.3 since 2001, suggesting the issue-carrying capacity of the public agenda has risen since the end of the Cold War. Regression shows time has both a positive linear relationship[3] and a positive quadratic (U-shaped) relationship[4] with number of issues named. This suggests that the number of issues named by respondents has generally grown and may have grown at an increasing rate over time.

The difficulty with using total responses as a gauge of either the capacity of an individual's agenda or that of the public as a whole is that the

---

2. To minimize collinearity between predictors, time (in months) is centered in months over the 480-month span of the data, and then the centered variable is squared.
3. $\beta = .41, p < .001$.
4. $\beta = .16, p < .01$.

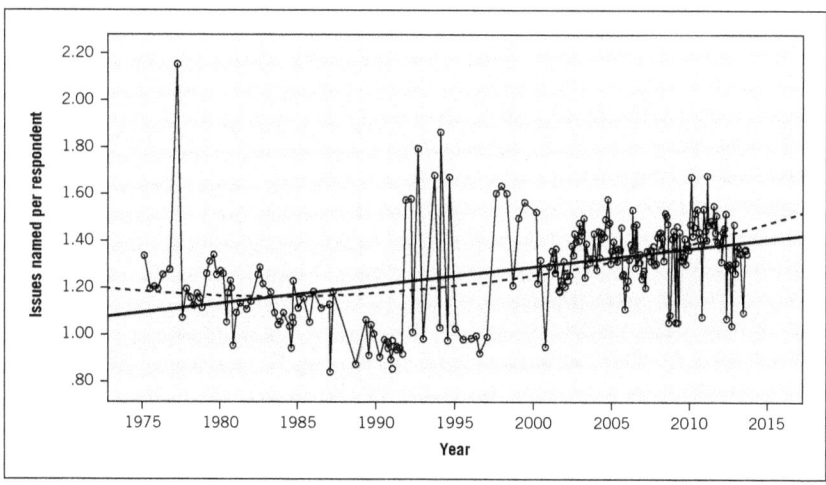

Figure 3.3. Number of issues named as most important per poll respondent, 1975–2014.

measure contains a great deal of potential noise. It weights quite heavily whether the poll permits multiple responses as well as respondents' willingness to defy the question's request to name the *most* important problem (a formulation that implies a single answer is desired). By contrast, when German researchers ask, "In your opinion, what are the most important political problems?" respondents choose an average of about four and one-half issues from a list of sixteen (Brosius and Kepplinger 1992). It is also a very "noisy" measure in the sense that it is susceptible to changes in Gallup's coding practices. A second approach to measuring issue-carrying capacity is to count the number of issues "on" the agenda for each poll. In fact, McCombs and Zhu (1995) employ this sort of approach when they measure issue volatility. To find out how quickly issues cycle on and off the public agenda, they establish an operational definition of what it means to be "on" the public agenda. Like Russell Neuman (1990), they consider an issue to be on the agenda if 10 percent or more of respondents name it as the most important problem. We adapt this measure with a modification: We concur with Smith, who argues for considering "responses rather than respondents as the unit of analysis" within a poll (1980, 165). Therefore, the second operationalization for issue-carrying capacity is the number of issues garnering 10 percent or more of the total responses, an approach that aligns with the issue history in Chapter 2.

This threshold approach to measuring carrying capacity has limitations as well. Although public attention is undoubtedly a scarce resource (Webster 2014), we are uncertain as to the maximum carrying capacity of the public agenda. In politics and public life, how salient an issue must be to have a place "on" the agenda is probably defined normatively and flexibly. Setting a threshold, a percentage of total responses an issue must receive to be considered "on" the agenda, arbitrarily operationalizes salience and creates an artificial maximum. If an issue must garner 10 percent of responses to be "on" the agenda, then the maximum potential capacity of the public agenda is arbitrarily set at ten issues (100 percent divided by 10). A lower threshold for an issue to be on the agenda would increase the maximum potential capacity but would dilute the meaning of being on the agenda by reducing the required degree of salience. A higher threshold would decrease agenda capacity and make the assumption that the public agenda encompasses a maximum of five to seven issues an untestable truism.[5] In addition, given the colloquial meaning of the word, it is important to clarify that our measure of *capacity* pertains to how many issues meet the 10 percent threshold of concern in a given poll, not to how many issues could theoretically fit. To borrow imagery from plumbing, the 10 percent threshold is much like the diameter of a pipe. Just as a ten-inch pipe has a maximum *potential* capacity that is arbitrarily set by the builder, adopting this threshold sets a maximum number of issues that can be said to be on the public agenda. But what's measured is capacity in the sense of how much *actually* flows through the pipe, how many issues are *actually* on the public agenda in a given month.

Another consideration with this measure is that to control for variations in the total number of responses, it assumes a fixed level of total public concern. That is, regardless of how many responses the poll records, it is the percentage of responses falling into a particular category that defines its status as "on" or "off" the agenda. This adjustment has to be made because without it, we could not be sure whether the total number of responses to a poll is really signal (indicative of high public concern) or noise (a product of the way Gallup coded the responses). In general, this approach represents a tougher test of whether the character of the public agenda has changed. Using the number, rather than the proportion, of responses typically makes the trends presented even stronger.

Figure 3.4 shows gently rising capacity in the public agenda. In the first eight years of the data set, capacity rises above three issues only twice; in the last five years, it falls below three issues only three times. These results confirm with greater specificity and rigor evidence of an ex-

---

5. Setting a threshold of 5 percent for an issue to be considered on the agenda strengthens the relationships with time that we observe. Setting a threshold of 20 percent or more results in the nonintuitive conclusion that in nearly one-third of the polls, there are no issues on the public agenda.

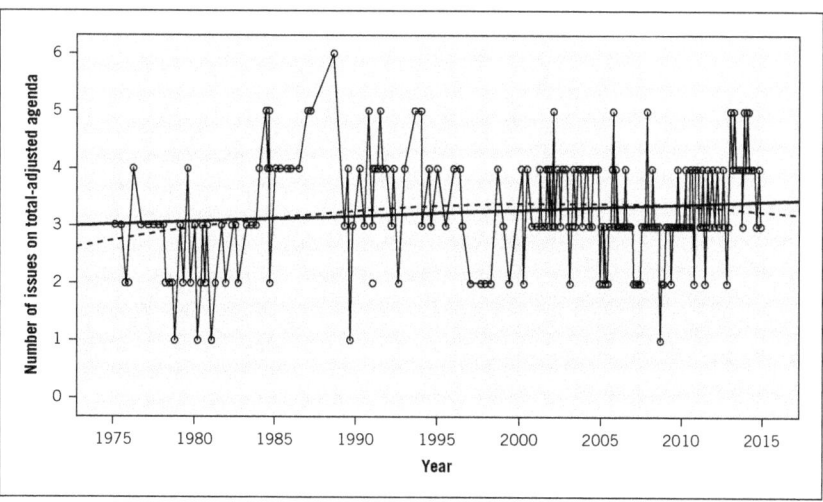

Figure 3.4. Number of issues "on the agenda" (named in 10 percent of Gallup poll responses), 1975–2014.

panding public agenda, revealed when the public agenda is parsed by era, as in Figures 3.1 and 3.2. With this more rigorous statistical approach, time has a positive significant linear relationship with the number of issues on the agenda,[6] meaning that, in general, the capacity of the public agenda increases slightly over time. Time also has a negative quadratic (inverted U-shaped) relationship that approaches significance,[7] suggesting that the rate of change in agenda capacity is inconsistent. Whichever way issue-carrying capacity is measured, its significant and mostly positive relationship with time suggests that the carrying capacity of the public agenda has increased since 1975. The public divides its attention among more issues today than it did when Gerald Ford was president.

Diversity

Another way to think about the character of the public agenda is to consider its diversity. Diversity refers to how evenly public concern is spread across issues. A commonly used measure of diversity is the Shannon index of entropy, also called the H statistic (Shannon and Weaver 1949). Detailed information about how it was computed appears in Appendix B. Essentially, the measure calculates how evenly public concern is spread

---

6. $\beta = .16, p < .05$. For a 5% threshold, $\beta = .51, p < .001$.
7. $\beta = -.11, p < .10$. For a 5% threshold, $\beta = -.15, p < .01$.

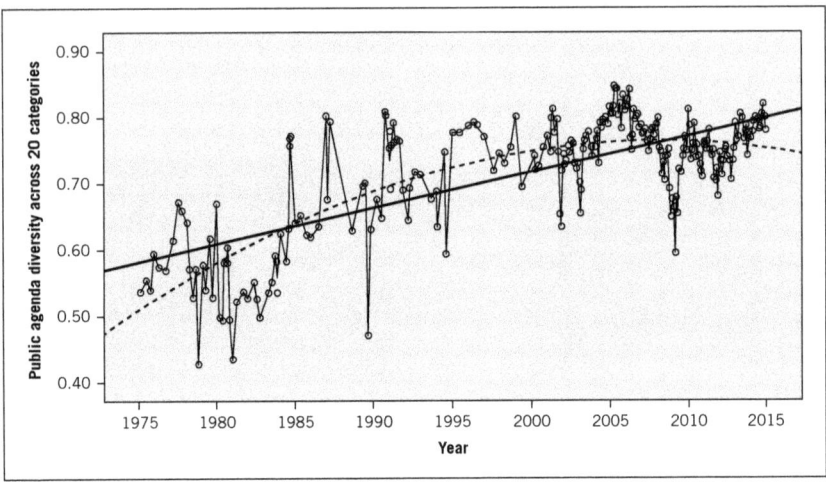

Figure 3.5. Public agenda diversity measured across twenty categories, 1975–2014.

across the issue categories. The maximum and minimum values of the H statistic are affected by the number of categories, so to make it easier to interpret, we have normed the statistic so that it varies from zero, which would mean that all the public's concern was focused on a single issue, to one, which would mean that the public's concern was evenly divided across all issue categories.

Figure 3.5 shows the normed value of the H statistic for the twenty categories of issues that make up the public agenda. It suggests the public agenda generally has been diversifying over the time frame, but not at a steady rate. This is confirmed by the regressions of diversity with time. Time has a positive linear relationship with normed H,[8] which suggests the overall trend has been toward growing diversity in the public agenda. However, time also has a negative quadratic relationship with normed H, indicating an inverted U-shaped curve.[9] This is because diversity rises and falls at different rates across the time frame. Issue entropy increases between 1975 and the early 1990s, rises less steeply in the early 2000s, peaks around 2006, and falls during the Great Recession. In the most recent polls, it is beginning to rise again.

A closer look at the figure shows just how dramatic the changes have been. All ten of the lowest values for H (those polls in which the public agenda was the least diverse) appear before 1990, and only one of the

---

8. $\beta = .81, p < .001$.
9. $\beta = -.31, p < .001$.

twenty-five lowest values for H has been recorded in the new millennium. In contrast, eight of the ten highest values recorded for H (those polls in which the public agenda was the most diverse) appear in 2004 or later, and twenty-two of the twenty-five highest values for H are measured in the last eleven years of the time frame.

It is also apparent that crises no longer focus the public agenda to the same extent that they once did. The economic difficulties of the late 1970s and early 1980s focused the public agenda on jobs or money in eight of the ten moments when the public agenda was least diverse, and economic concerns also accounted for five of the ten lowest values recorded since 2000. The lowest value recorded since the new millennium appeared in February 2009, when the economy in general swamped other public concerns during the depths of the Great Recession. However, inflation in October 1978 drove public agenda diversity down to .43, with 67 percent of responses naming money as the most important problem. The most serious economic crisis since the Great Depression, the Great Recession reduced diversity to only .60, with just 48 percent of responses naming the economy as the most important problem. Even the September 11 terrorist attacks did not serve to focus the public agenda in the same way. The poll in which the public agenda was the most focused subsequent to the attacks was taken in November 2001, and terrorism accounted for only 40 percent of responses to the "most important problem" question. There are more than 50 polls when the public agenda was more focused than it was that month.

Looking more closely reveals how elite leadership can focus public attention and reduce the diversity of the public agenda, but, as is the case with the impact of crises on agenda diversity, elite leadership in the twenty-first century has less impact than elite leadership in the twentieth. One of the ten lowest diversity values was recorded following George H. W. Bush's "crack speech" (see Chapter 2). The lowest level of diversity recorded over the forty years under study occurred after a speech given by Jimmy Carter addressing the rising inflation rate—a poll result that probably indicates a conflation of economic events and elite leadership. Elite leadership also seems to account for some lower diversity moments since 2000. One of the five lowest values recorded in the new millennium appeared in September 2012, as Republicans geared up to defeat Obama's reelection run, focusing public attention on an economy that was only beginning to return to prerecession performance. One of the ten lowest values recorded since 2000 was in October 2013, when the focusing issue was government. Although this coincided with a sixteen-day government shutdown, the budgetary conflict driving it was largely elite-driven rather than "real." Nevertheless, the impact of political leadership on public agenda diversity has declined. Following Bush's speech, agenda diversity was .47, and nearly 63 percent of responses to the "most important problem" question named law and order. Concerted Republican efforts to defeat Obama in 2012, combined with lingering unemployment, produced a level of public agenda diversity at .71, with public concern divided between jobs and the economy, each of which accounted for about 25 percent of responses to the "most important problem" question.

These results are persuasive, but there are some reasons to approach the findings in Figure 3.5 with caution. Although we have recoded the raw data to make the "most important problem" polls comparable across the time frame, changes in the ways Gallup polled people and coded the data might have influenced the results. One concern is the distribution of the polls over the time frame, for the "most important problem" question was asked only sporadically from 1975 through 2003 but has been asked more or less monthly since 2004. Could the greater availability of more recent data lead us to overestimate the rise in agenda diversity? Weighting the polls to adjust for the greater availability of more recent data produces virtually no change in the observed relationships between diversity and time,[10] so the increase in diversity is not just an artifact of more frequent "most important problem" polls since 2004.

A second potential issue is that although the Gallup "most important problem" question is the most consistently coded (McCombs and Zhu 1995), the coding process may vary over time. As Tom Smith (1980) observes, some polls that include the "most important problem" question do not code multiple responses. Moreover, the level of sensitivity in the Gallup coding may vary. That is, while some polls may have very elaborate coding schemes for recording responses, others may have more rudimentary coding categories. This would have an impact on estimations of agenda diversity. More sensitive coding would appear to be greater agenda diversity, so if coding schemes become more elaborate over time, or are more elaborate in some periods and less elaborate in others, the conclusion that the public agenda becomes more diverse over time or that diversity rises and falls would be false. Both recoding the data into twenty categories and normalizing the value of H by dividing it by its theoretical maximum help minimize the potential problem. However, there is some indication in the issue-by-issue exploration of the public agenda in Chap-

---

10. $\beta = .74$ for time weighted vs. .81 unweighted; $\beta = -.31$ for time^2 weighted vs. $-.26$ unweighted; $R^2 = .61$ for both.

ter 2 that the recoding might not eliminate all the inconsistencies in the Gallup coding.

A related but distinct aspect of this problem is distinguishing between the issue agenda and aspects of issues. When people agree on an agenda of public problems, debate over how to address those concerns becomes possible, even if different people consider different aspects of public problems to be the most salient. Thus, a public divided over what the issues are has a different set of challenges than a public that disagrees over how to address them. However, it is not always easy to see whether responses to the "most important problem" question represent issues or aspects of those issues. For example, are jobs and government spending separate issues, or are they aspects of a broader issue—the economy? In the Reagan era, these two categories seem related but distinct. However, during the Great Recession, they appear to distinguish alternative approaches to handling the economic crisis.

One way of addressing these potential analytical problems is to reduce the number of coding categories, which typically increases coding reliability and makes the distinction between issues and aspects even clearer. Smith's (1980, 1985) approach to the problem of changing Gallup coding practices between the 1930s, when scientific polling was in its infancy, and the 1970s is to vastly simplify the coding. Ultimately, he uses just two categories: foreign issues and domestic issues, although he does discuss some subcategories, such as the economy and civil rights, in more detail. We adopt a somewhat less drastic approach to see whether the public agenda still seems to be diversifying when a simpler coding system is used. We recode the twenty categories of most important problems into just five: Economic (jobs, money, welfare, spending, general economic), International (general international, Soviet/Europe, Asia, Mideast, Latin America/Africa), Domestic Policy (law and order, health, environment, education, social relations, technology), Government (government/political), and Other (terrorism, media, miscellaneous). We call the resulting public agenda diversity variable H-5 to distinguish it from the diversity measure generated by all twenty categories (H-20).

Figure 3.6 shows what happens. Again, the public agenda is diversifying over time, but the shape of the distribution is subtly different. With H-5, there is a steeper (and earlier) rise in agenda diversity starting around 2000, a steeper and longer-lasting decline during the Great Recession, and a steeper increase in diversity in the last two years of the data set. Once again, there is a positive linear relationship between time and H-5,[11]

---

11. $\beta = .40, p < .001$.

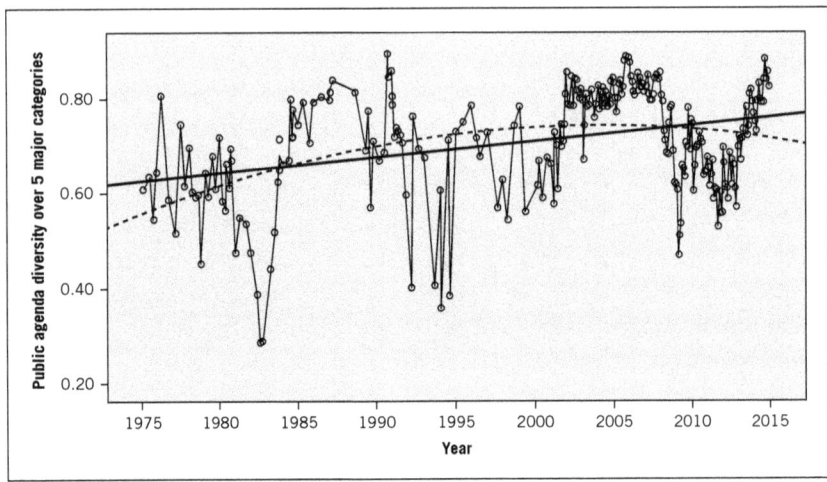

Figure 3.6. Public agenda diversity measured across five broad categories, 1975–2014.

suggesting an overall increase in agenda diversity over time. Time's quadratic relationship with diversity remains negative and significant,[12] indicating the rate of change in agenda diversity has been uneven and that decreases in diversity associated with the Great Recession flatten its overall upward trend.

A clearer understanding of the reasons for the differences between the two figures emerges from a closer examination of the data points themselves. A closer look also helps explain some counterintuitive aspects of both figures, most notably the high level of agenda diversity following the terrorist attacks of September 11. Recall that the value of H rises in response to high levels of public concern across multiple categories. In the early 2000s, one might expect public concern to focus on terrorism and international issues, but, in fact, these issues compete with an economic recession for public attention, and the terrorist attacks have both domestic law and order and international dimensions (see Edy and Meirick 2007). Consequently, in January 2002, for example, public concern is evenly divided between the categories of Economic (named by 39 percent of respondents), Domestic Policy (32 percent), and Other, which includes terrorism (37 percent).[13] This divided public attention continues for several months and helps to explain why the public agenda is actually quite

---

12. $\beta = -.22, p < .001$.

13. Including terrorism under the International category in Figure 3.6 does not substantively alter the shape of the curve.

diverse in the months following the terrorist attacks. The broader range of categories included in Figure 3.5 slightly muffles this trichotomy, but neither Figure 3.5 nor Figure 3.6 suggests that September 11 focuses public attention on a single issue of concern.

A more substantive change in interpretation might be implied by the differences between Figure 3.5 and Figure 3.6 for the years since 2000. Both figures show a peak in diversity around 2005, followed by compression of the public agenda during and immediately following the credit crisis and Great Recession in late 2008. But the magnitude of the peak and, especially, the plunge differ considerably, appearing much greater in Figure 3.6. Keep in mind that the post-September 11 issue trichotomy constitutes three out of the five issue categories for Figure 3.6, making H appear highly diverse in the wake of the terrorist attacks. When the Great Recession hits, economic categories dominate the issue agendas represented in each figure, as expected. However, Figure 3.6 compresses all respondents' expressions of economic concern into a single category. Figure 3.5 spreads them across five categories, and four of those categories split public concern about the recession and how to address it. By August 2011, public attention is split between concern about the economy generally (31 percent of responses), jobs (30 percent), spending (18 percent), and money (14 percent). Thus, the normed H value that month for the 20-category agenda is a robust .71, versus .51 for the five-category H. This split continues in subsequent months, driving up the level of entropy in the public agenda as represented in Figure 3.5.

Which figure paints the more accurate picture might depend on the facet of agenda diversity with which one is concerned. Figure 3.6 suggests that public concern was highly focused on the economy, much as it had been during the recession and stagflation of the late 1970s. Figure 3.5 suggests that while this may be the case, there are important differences between the time periods. In the 1970s and early 1980s, when people were focused on the economy, they defined the problem in relatively the same way, such that their responses consolidated into a single category—usually money. The two figures paint relatively similar pictures of this time period. During the Great Recession, it would seem that different people defined the problem differently, their responses placing them in several categories. Therefore, the difference between Figure 3.6 and Figure 3.5 might be said to reflect the difference between an issue and an aspect, or a first-level agenda and a second-level agenda. The former captures the salience of the larger issue, while the latter captures the aspects of an issue that are most salient for people and, thus, in a way, how they think about the problem (McCombs et al. 1997). Finally, one might note that the steep decline in entropy depicted in Figure 3.6 does appear to end with the 2012 presidential election. Beginning in November 2012, a steady rise in entropy begins again.

Volatility

A third way to examine the character of the public agenda is to consider its volatility, how quickly issues cycle on and off the public agenda. To measure this, we adapted a statistic used to estimate the likelihood of survival—the Kaplan-Meier estimator—and defined an issue as being "on" the agenda if it garnered 10 percent of total responses. Details of how the statistic is computed are presented in Appendix B.

The Kaplan-Meier estimator was designed to examine the survival function: how long a patient survives after diagnosis, for instance. Survival becomes less likely as time intervals grow, so it is important to look at survival over consistent periods of time. If Gallup polls had been taken at regular intervals throughout the decades, we could simply look at survival and mortality from the previous poll, but that is not the case; polls are conducted as infrequently as seventeen months apart in the 1980s, while they increase to monthly in 2004. To even out these differences, we specify the interval for analysis to be four to six months, allowing us to include more than 90 percent of our data set (twenty-seven polls, all from 2001 or earlier, had no poll taken four to six months previously and had to be excluded from the volatility analysis) and allowing us to compare modern, monthly polls to the sporadic polling of earlier eras. To make the statistic easier to interpret as a representation of agenda volatility, we present it not as the likelihood of survival but as the likelihood that an issue will drop off the public agenda within four to six months. The value of the statistic can vary from a minimum of zero, if all the issues from the previous poll are still on the agenda four to six months later, to a maximum of one, if there is complete turnover in the issue agenda four to six months later.

Figure 3.7 shows the results. McCombs and Zhu (1995) would expect that issue volatility might increase as agenda diversity rises because there is more competition for a spot on the public agenda; in fact, there is no significant relationship between time and volatility, despite increasing agenda diversity.[14] Instead, the regression with time squared suggests volatility rises and falls over the time frame.[15] Early in the period, an issue has less than a 20 percent chance of dropping off the agenda within four

---

14. $\beta = .05$, *ns*.
15. $\beta = -.18, p < .01$.

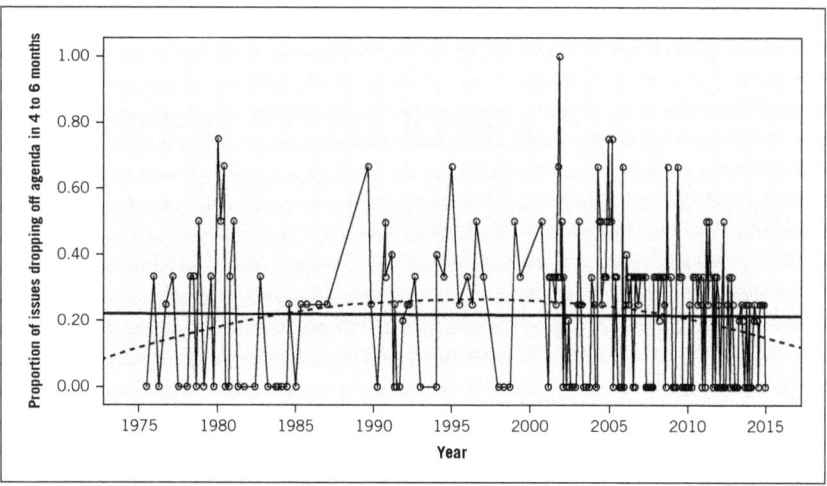

Figure 3.7. Public agenda volatility (the proportion of issues no longer being named in 10 percent of responses after four to six months), 1975–2014.

to six months. The probability of dropping off the agenda rises gradually, a sign of increasing volatility, and in the mid-1990s, an issue is almost twice as likely to drop off the agenda in four to six months as it is in 1975. But in the last decade of the time frame, the probability of an issue falling off the agenda decreases again; that is, volatility declines. By the end of 2014, volatility is roughly where it was in 1975.

Digging into the data points, however, it becomes apparent that the recent low volatility is not your father's low volatility. By way of comparison, let us look at the year of Reagan's first inaugural, 1981, and the year Obama took office, 2009. Economic crises loom both years, but the public's focus is clearer in 1981. At the beginning of 1981, money is the only issue on the public agenda, and it dominates (as high as 65 percent of total responses). Jobs enter the agenda in May and international issues in November. Jobs were off the agenda briefly in January 1981, the only agenda volatility that year. By contrast, 2009 averages three issues on the agenda. The general economy is the main concern at the beginning of the year, at 40 percent; that dwindles to just less than 20 percent by the end of the year but never, in the remainder of the time frame, goes away. The other issues in January are the Mideast (for one month) and money (until May). The issue of jobs joins the agenda in February (and remains until late 2013); health joins in June, for a year. By Obama's second inauguration, in January 2013, there are five issues on the agenda, none of them claiming more than 16 percent of total responses. However, January's agenda does not drop any issues from four months before—and four months later, four of the five issues are still on the agenda. Thus, the public agenda is both diverse and stagnant.

Issue Competition and the Character of the Public Agenda

Capacity, diversity, and volatility do not seem to relate to one another in the way that McCombs and Zhu (1995) and others who theorize a highly competitive public agenda would expect. To explore the relationships between these characteristics of the public agenda, we again use correlation and regression. Zero-order correlations, which relate two variables to each other without introducing statistical controls for any other variables, show that carrying capacity, as measured by number of issues on the agenda, is positively related with both measures of issue diversity[16] and negatively related with agenda volatility.[17] That is, when there are more issues on the public agenda, it is typically more diverse but less volatile. Notably, neither measure of issue diversity is related to agenda volatility,[18] contrary to what McCombs and Zhu (1995) would expect.

To further explore the relationships among all three variables, we ran a regression specifying volatility as the dependent variable, with diversity and capacity as the independent variables. Each independent variable in multiple regression is simultaneously a predictor and a control variable. Statistically controlling for agenda capacity is, in essence, holding it mathematically constant, and, thus, treating it as a constraint on the public agenda, as is traditionally assumed. Under these conditions, the predicted relationships between volatility and diversity emerge. Both measures of diversity are positive and significant predictors of volatility.[19] Therefore, if the public agenda had a very limited carrying capacity, as theories of agenda competition hypothesize, diversity would make it more volatile as they predict. However, if the capacity of the public agenda is less limited, as this analysis reveals, and competition for a place on the public agenda less fierce, the agenda may stagnate as a collection of chronic, low priority problems.

Conclusion

The analysis in this chapter reveals that the character of the public agenda has changed over the past forty years. Although the public agenda still

---

16. $r = .32, p < .001$ with twenty-category H; $r = .29, p < .001$ with five-category H.
17. $r = -.31, p < .001$.
18. $r = .02$, ns with twenty-category H; $r = .04$, ns with five-category H.
19. $\beta = .14, p < .05$. for twenty-category H; $\beta = .15, p < .03$ for five-category H.

responds in apparently sensible ways to the events of history and although political leaders can still generate public concern about issues, the public agenda in the twenty-first century encompasses more issues while at the same time being less focused and, in some ways, less competitive than it was in the twentieth. Earlier theories about the dynamics of the public agenda, which suggest that growing diversity in the public agenda leads to increased volatility because the capacity of the public agenda is limited by both media capacity and an individual's cognitive capacity, do not seem to hold. Perhaps we should not expect them to hold. After all, when diversity is greater, issues take up less space on the public agenda (for example, three issues at 20 percent each instead of one issue at 60 percent), creating greater carrying capacity with no effect on volatility. Nevertheless, the significant linear increases in capacity and diversity reveal that something about the social processes shaping the public agenda has changed, and that change has implications for citizenship, media influence, and democratic governance.

There are a number of potential explanations for the changed character of the public agenda. McCombs and Zhu (1995) suggest rising levels of public education in the United States might increase the carrying capacity of the public agenda, but they find no linear trend to support this, and recent changes in the character of the public agenda seem much too swift for the slow-moving demographics of educational achievement. It seems more likely that individual cognitive capacity never was a significant constraint on the capacity of the public agenda. However, it still seems plausible that the public agenda does have some sort of upper limit because one can still think of public attention as a scarce resource, particularly in light of the enormous growth in media choice over the time frame. As James Webster puts it, "The total supply of human attention available . . . has an upper bound. The widening gap between limitless media and limited attention makes it a challenge for anything to attract an audience" (2014, 4).

Some scholars refer to this phenomenon as an "attention economy." Under these conditions, the capacity of the public agenda is defined not by human physiology but by a social norm about what constitutes "a lot" of public attention in a highly competitive attention economy. This norm is both poorly documented and, probably, subject to change as social actors jockey with one another to put favored issues on the agenda and keep threatening issues off. In contemporary times, agenda competition and, therefore, political power struggles may encompass battles about not just refocusing public attention on a different issue but about how much public attention is required for an issue to "count" as "on" the public agenda.

Of course, the changing media environment is almost certainly not the sole reason for the altered character of the public agenda. The expansion of the public agenda has in some respects coincided with the end of the Cold War, a time in which one might expect the public agenda to broaden. However, recent national crises—such as the September 11 terrorist attacks and the Great Recession—have not recompressed the public agenda to Cold War levels. It seems more likely that the increasing capacity of the media system and the ways both political leaders and American citizens use that system have transformed the public agenda. Chapters 4 and 5 examine how changes in the media system correspond to changes in the public agenda's diversity, looking for the system characteristics that might explain the public agenda's transformation and exploring whether the political functions theorists once ascribed to media still work in the context of the public agenda.

No matter the proximate cause, these changes have implications for theories of agenda setting and political power as well as for democratic functioning. The limited capacity of the public agenda and the dynamics of issue competition have underpinned important theories of political and media power. For example, the power to manage the public agenda is implicated in Peter Bachrach and Morton Baratz's (1962) concept of non–decision making and Samuel Kernell's (2007) theory of going public. Bachrach and Baratz suggest that the power to keep an issue off the public agenda allows decision makers to avoid addressing politically uncongenial issues. Kernell argues that the ability to bring an issue to the public's attention allows a political actor—the president, for Kernell—to mobilize public demand for change, providing leverage for dealing with recalcitrant decision makers by threatening their constituent support. The agenda stagnation documented in this study suggests that political power may work differently in an era of high diversity and low volatility. If it is virtually impossible to get the public to focus intensely on a small number of issues, power may lie in picking and choosing among a large number of low-intensity public concerns.

The dynamics of a stagnating public agenda offer new insights on research findings documenting declining political responsiveness over time (e.g., Jacobs and Shapiro 2000) and the public's general dissatisfaction with government. Lawrence Jacobs and Robert Shapiro (2000) note that growing polarization in Washington makes it less likely political leaders will be responsive to centrist voters, but the trends in the public agenda identified here suggest the central concerns of a fragmented public grow progressively more difficult to identify. Even if we assume political leaders want to respond to citizen concerns rather than shape them, the limited decision-making capacity of governmental institutions makes the diffuse concerns of the contemporary public difficult to satisfy. Where would one start? At the same time, the low levels of volatility, suggesting that the same issues stagnate on the public agenda for long periods of time, offer a substantive reason for public complaints that the government is unresponsive to their concerns.

Changing dynamics in the public agenda signal not only the decline of mass audiences but also a transformation of majoritarian democracy that may require reconceptualizing both media power and political power. Chapters 6 and 7 consider the changing relationship between the public and its political leaders through the lens of agenda dynamics, exploring the power of elite leadership to focus the public agenda and whether the character of the public agenda influences how political leaders respond to it.

4

Broadcast News and the Public Agenda, 1968–2010

For people born after 1980, it may be difficult to even imagine the mass media environment of the 1960s, 1970s, and early 1980s. Most Americans took a daily newspaper that landed on their driveways every morning, missing, one hoped, the sprinklers in summer and the snowdrifts in winter. Many large- and medium-sized cities still supported multiple newspapers. Television, largely in color by the late 1960s, came into American households over the air. "Rabbit ear" antennas on the sets themselves or larger rooftop antennas tuned in the picture. The United States is divided into 210 television markets, from the largest, New York City, to the smallest, Glendive, Montana. Most markets had affiliate stations for each of the three broadcast television networks (ABC, CBS, NBC), although very small markets, even today, have stations that share an affiliation with two networks. Most had a public television station (PBS). Larger markets had independent stations, with no network affiliation, that aired syndicated programs, often reruns of older network programming, but did not usually carry a newscast. Typically, then, people had perhaps half a dozen channels of television to choose from. Commercial radio stations had by this time moved away from the drama and comedy programming of the pretelevision era to a music format. Although national radio news still exists today, led by NPR, it had largely been supplanted by television news by the 1970s. Programming could not be stored for later viewing: one had to watch a program at the time it was broadcast.

If there was "nothing on," there was nothing on: one could not rent or buy programming to subvert the television schedule.

In this media environment, each national broadcast network televised a half-hour nightly news program. In most markets, all three news programs aired simultaneously on weeknights, so nightly news was virtually the only kind of program on the air in that time slot. Professional norms, similar work practices, and institutional relationships meant these programs were very similar to one another and very similar to newspapers in their content (Cook 1998; Ryfe 2006; Sparrow 1999). These programs and the local daily newspaper were the main sources of public affairs information available. In the 1960s, about one in four Americans watched a network newscast on any given day. In 1970, there were about 63 million American households, and about 60 million newspapers were sold each weekday (though, of course, some households took more than one). It was in this media environment that agenda-setting theory was born and ideas about the role of news media in democratic processes were initially tested.

Although evidence of the mass media's behavioral and attitudinal effects on individuals was elusive, the idea that mass media could effectively control the public's information environment showed more promise. As Walter Lippmann (1922) points out, the public is highly dependent on communications media for information about events and trends beyond their personal experience. Distant wars, government scandals, and national election campaigns are beyond the scope of almost everyone's everyday life experience. All we know about them is what the media tell us. In 1948, Paul Lazarsfeld and Robert Merton posited that the mass media had a "status conferral" effect: when the media paid attention to issues, organizations, and people, the public thought them important. In 1972, Max McCombs and Donald Shaw published an empirical test of the mass media's ability to set public priorities, and agenda-setting theory was born. The small number of media outlets and the similarity of their content were an important source of the theory's normative weight: these few organizations represented the wider social world to the public, who in turn were expected to hold democratically elected leaders accountable for their management of it. The quality of the news media's performance was vital to democratic functioning.

Naturally, one of the main concerns was that news media would draw attention to the wrong issues. Since the U.S. news media are profit-driven, they might seek to draw larger audiences by covering celebrities and sporting events at the expense of economics or foreign policy. They might favor sensation and visuality over substance and deliberation. Dependent on public officials for access and information, they might overlook official negligence or misconduct to preserve that access. A white-dominated, male-dominated profession, news might systematically neglect the issues affecting women and racial minorities. Yet implicit in these critiques was a recognition that the news media served as a national public forum. The problem with news media covering the "wrong" issues was that for the public, there was no alternative to this mediated representation of the social world. Citizens were limited to the information mass-mediated news provided them.

But the ability of the news to generate a national public forum had benefits, too. As Markus Prior (2007) observes, in this era, it was very difficult for anyone to completely avoid exposure to public affairs information. Almost everyone knew at least a bit about what was going on in the nation and the world. The public forum could also help generate a shared public agenda, which was important to democratic functioning. As McCombs (1997) puts it, "Achievement of consensus among the members of a public is the focal point of *agenda setting theory*, a social science perspective that attributes significant influence to the news media in the process of achieving community consensus about the most important problems and tasks of the day" (443). The reasoning underlying this line of thought was that the news media had a limited carrying capacity (Zhu 1992). There were only so many stories one could tell in a half-hour broadcast or place on the front page of a newspaper. Thus, the news media engaged in gatekeeping, limiting the issues and problems presented in the news. Since different news organizations made highly similar decisions about news content, the agendas of news outlets were very similar. When the public consumed news, its priorities were influenced by media agenda setting, and a shared public agenda emerged as the public agenda came to resemble the news agenda. This shared public agenda might be manipulated by political elites, but it could also potentially give direction to legislators. Clear signals from the public about which problems were seen as most important could enable them to effectively marshal their own limited agenda capacities to focus on key issues. Moreover, the shared agenda and focused public attention were important for accountability processes. Where official misdeeds came to light, widespread public agreement on their seriousness (Ettema and Glasser 1998; Zaller 1998) or officials' fear of public condemnation (Protess et al. 1987) was an essential component to holding the wrongdoers responsible and provoking change.

When the media environment began to change in the 1980s and 1990s, scholars expressed concern over the impact of the changes on the public forum media generated and for the public agenda. In the 1980s, videocassette recorders allowed television audiences to shift network programming schedules and watch what they wanted when they wanted. Cable television began to offer other programming options in the early evening time slot once dominated by national and local news programs. Now, one could watch entertainment programming instead of news. Cable television not only offered far more entertainment options, it also offered more news. News junkies could watch television twenty-four hours a day on cable networks devoted to news coverage, and by the mid-1990s, each could choose the cable news station that most closely matched his or her political point of view. The internet offered even more options, both for avoiding information about public affairs and for accessing more such information than ever before. Now, news junkies could acquire information from news organizations around the world. Users could tailor the news content they received to their personal tastes and interests. If they wanted only football scores or local crime news, such things were possible. If they chose to avoid public affairs information altogether, this, too, could be done. By the early 2000s, the internet was connecting people with one another as never before, through social media. Now, people could acquire (or not acquire) public affairs information from one another. Of course, gossip over back fences is as old as back fences, but now one's garden fence could overlook the world. Public affairs information need no longer come from news organizations or political leaders; it might come from friends and neighbors who shared information on social media platforms like Twitter and Facebook. They might stand up to an oppressive regime, but they might also spread false or unsubstantiated rumors. If people now had so many opportunities to customize their media to suit their tastes, what might happen to the public forum that had existed in the mass media era? Was it still possible for traditional news media to shape an agenda of common concerns for the public?

Much of the accumulating empirical evidence suggested the public forum generated by broadcast news was in decline. The audience for broadcast television news had dwindled from 55 million in the 1960s to about 24 million by 2009 (Uscinski 2014). In real terms, the decline was even starker: about one in thirteen Americans watched national broadcast news on any given day. Elihu Katz (1996) argued that if the news media did not command national attention—if viewing the same program was not a shared experience—then the national forum provided by television news would no longer exist. There was evidence of both fragmentation, in the form of smaller audiences for any given channel or program, and polarization, in the form of audiences choosing news sources with which they agreed (Iyengar and Hahn 2009; Prior 2007; Stroud 2011). All of this suggested that the public forum the news once generated might be vanishing with no social process to replace it. Donald Shaw and Bradley Hamm (1997) envisioned the advent of fragmented, competing public agendas and the dissolution of national consensus into mutually hostile interest groups. Steve Chaffee and Miriam Metzger suggested that this could mean "the kind of widespread collective action seen in the past may not be possible in the future" (2001, 375).

Not all the predictions about the decline of the national forum created by broadcast news were negative. Scholars who worried about the potential for tyranny and demagoguery inherent in a national forum largely managed by political elites applauded advances in communications technology that undermined their control. Minority and oppressed groups whose voices had been largely silenced in the mass media era could find an outlet in the emerging user-driven communication environment where audience size was not the driving principle (Chaffee and Metzger 2001). The airless, objective news forms that stifled public debate (Carey 1987) but appealed to a generic mass audience might give way to partisan news that generated meaningful public discussion between citizens (Chaffee and Metzger 2001). Still, the underlying assumption of both the scholars who worried and those who hoped was that the national forum generated by broadcast news was in decline and that the public agenda would grow more diverse.

Yet other forms of evidence did not indicate a public forum in decline. Traditional news media still strongly influenced the content of newer news outlets (Leccese 2009; Pew Research Center 2010). Audience tastes were not all that different, so content might not vary that much across venues (Neuman 1991), and while people did not seek out information that contradicted their views, they did not seem to avoid it, either (Garrett 2009). Newer media might seek niche audiences (Turow 1997), but the media audience still clustered around a small number of media outlets (Webster 2014). Moreover, there was no reason to imagine the fundamental processes underpinning the agenda-setting phenomenon had changed. Agenda setting should still involve the transfer of salience from media to audience (or if Uscinski [2014] was right, from audience to media), making some issues more accessible than others both socially and cognitively.

Despite declining public attention to traditional news sources, evidence of change in the size of the traditional media's agenda-setting effect on the public is mixed at best. Yue Tan and David Weaver's analysis of quarterly agenda-setting data for the *New York Times* and Gallup "most important problem" polls find "no discernable trend" (2013, 779) over time. Jae Kook Lee and Renita Coleman (2014) look at the relationship between public concern and *New York Times* coverage for nine years between 1968 and 2004. Agenda-setting effects fell short of significance in 2000 and 1996, but also in 1968 and 1980. Generational studies assume that if agenda-setting effects are fading, they should be more pronounced in older generations and less pronounced in younger ones. Here, too, results are mixed. Coleman and Max McCombs (2007) see some evidence in two studies of newspaper agenda setting that the effects were weaker (but still substantial) for those ages 18 to 34 than for older cohorts. But Lee and Coleman (2014) find that agenda-setting effects of the *New York Times* are similar for the civic generation (born between 1926 and 1945), baby boomers (born between 1946 and 1964), and Generation X (born after 1965). If anything, the boomers are the odd generation out. Although Coleman and McCombs (2007) find evidence that heavy internet use undermines the agenda-setting effects of newspapers, other studies also find differences in agenda-setting effects across media (Lopez-Escobar et. al. 1998; McCombs 2004). In principle, of course, agenda-setting effects could further fragment the public if newer media and traditional media pursued distinctive agendas and have agenda-setting effects (a possibility Chapter 5 explores). However, with decades of research supporting an agenda-setting effect and no clear evidence that the size of the agenda-setting effect is significantly smaller in more recent years or among younger generations, McCombs concludes, "The agenda-setting role of the media endures" (2014, 18).

Altogether, the evidence points in conflicting directions. While the agenda-setting effects of traditional media endure, the public agenda is becoming more diverse. How could both these things be true?

News Media Influence on the Public Agenda

One possible explanation for a diverse public agenda despite continued agenda setting by traditional news media is that the consensus-building process does not work the way scholars had assumed. In fact, relatively little is known about exactly how the news media contribute to establishing a shared public agenda. In the broadcast era, news content was so limited that the role of the news media as consensus builders probably seemed unproblematically obvious. An argument could be made that agenda-setting effects themselves amount to building consensus around a shared public agenda. A geographically, racially, and economically diverse population would surely be concerned about a panoply of public issues. The influence of a common news source that had a carrying capacity of perhaps seven or eight issues per day (the size of a front page or the length of a half-hour newscast) on their individual agendas would surely reduce the diversity of their issue agendas, creating a shared understanding of common concerns. Thus, agenda-setting effects should be consensus-building effects.

Perhaps because this logic seems so sound, few studies of news media consensus building have been undertaken. The typical test is whether demographic groups whose issues agendas are assumed to be different have more similar agendas when they are heavier users of news. For example, Donald Shaw and Shannon Martin (1992) found men and women who were heavier news users had more similar agendas than men and women who were less exposed to news. Studies were undertaken in particular cities, such as Chapel Hill, North Carolina, in the case of Shaw and Martin, and Pamplona, Spain, in research conducted by Lopez-Escobar, Llamas, and McCombs (1998), which may have understated agenda diversity among demographic groups. Although some tests produced mixed results (Chiang 1995; Lopez-Escobar, Llamas, and McCombs 1998), the preponderance of evidence suggested news exposure reduced differences between groups.

This approach to the public agenda assumed that news produced overlapping personal agendas among citizens, leading to a less diverse and more focused public agenda. This seemed likely because the size of the public agenda was seen as limited by the cognitive capacity of an individual, who could worry about only a few problems at a time (Zhu 1992) and because the size of the media agenda was limited to the few issues that would fit into a newscast or onto the front page (Zhu 1992; McCombs and Zhu 1995). Yet if the news media work in the way Lippmann (1922) imagines, it is just as likely if not more likely that the news media make people aware of problems beyond their immediate experience and so make their personal agendas more diverse, not less. Agenda setting by news media might serve to make people aware of each other's problems, broadening their narrow personal agendas by showing them what else is going on in the world. For example, in the 1960s, news media coverage of African Americans attacked by police as they attempted to march from Selma to Montgomery, Alabama, demanding voting rights, brought the brutality of the Jim Crow South into American living rooms (Garrow 1978).

Consequently, news media agenda setting might contribute to a public agenda that was widely shared but also one that included a more diverse collection of issues than the public might otherwise have been concerned about. Instead of one issue taking priority over another in a blending of agendas, issues could be added to a relatively short list, creating a more diverse agenda. Men, initially concerned about defense and taxes, could add health and crime to their lists as a result of news exposure. Women, concerned about health and the environment, could add defense and taxes. Their agendas would be more similar to each other as a result of news exposure, but also more diverse. In other words, the public agenda could be more diverse, not less, than the agendas of individual groups as a result of news exposure, and media consensus building via agenda setting would be compatible with a diversifying public agenda. This kind of consensus building has very different implications for how public life works, for it does not suggest that attention to news encourages the public to home in on key problems but rather that it expands the list of public concerns.

History and the Public Agenda

History is a second complicating factor in understanding how fragmenting audiences and declining attention to traditional news could be reconciled with strong agenda-setting effects, for as the media environment transformed, history continued to unfold. Broadcast news became a household staple following John F. Kennedy's assassination in 1963 (Zelizer 1992). Over the course of the late twentieth century, dozens of events and issues occupied the news agenda, including Vietnam, Watergate, the Cold War, the Iran-Contra scandal, the fall of the Berlin Wall, the Los Angeles riots, the O. J. Simpson trial, the Gulf War, Clinton's impeachment, the September 11 terrorist attacks, wars in Afghanistan and Iraq, Hurricane Katrina, and the Great Recession. Longer term trends—such as the struggles for African American rights, women's rights, and the rights of LGBTQ people; rising income inequality; police violence against people of color; climate change; and waves of immigration—were also in the news.

In studying how changes in the media environment have affected the public agenda, it is tempting to treat history as a constant—to assume the issues in the news at a particular point in time are more or less random in relation to the changes in the media environment. Wars and recessions come and go as the media environment continues to evolve. This would allow researchers to use time as a proxy for change in the media environment and ask, "Has this proliferation of new channels diminished the agenda-setting impact of the legacy media?" (McCombs 2004, 18). If change over time were observed, it could be chalked up to change in the media environment. However, it is likely that something much more complex is going on: research has shown that news has different levels of agenda-setting influence under different historical circumstances.

Psychological variables, such as the need for orientation, affect the size of the agenda-setting effect (McCombs and Weaver 1985), which would suggest that in moments when public participation is expected, like elections, or in moments of national crisis, agenda-setting effects would be larger. These kinds of wobbles would not necessarily result in longer term trends, but they encourage us to pay attention to the time frames being studied. If a study concluded that the agenda-setting effects of broadcast news were roughly the same in 2002 as they were in the 1970s, it might be because the national crisis provoked by the 2001 terrorist attacks produced an unusually high need for orientation and, thus, an unusually large agenda-setting effect during the time frame under study.

History can also affect trends over time because research has shown that the issues themselves have an impact on the agenda-setting effect. Unobtrusive issues, those for which people are dependent on media for information, are said to exhibit larger agenda-setting effects than obtrusive issues, those where people have more direct experience of the issue (Neuman 1990; Zucker 1978). If this were the case, one might expect larger agenda-setting effects in time frames dominated by wars abroad or national politics and smaller agenda-setting effects in time frames when unemployment or inflation dominated the public agenda. Wayne Wanta and Yu-Wei Hu (1993) found that the way international issues were presented to the public influenced the size of the agenda-setting effect. Stories suggesting that the world system was working well or that world problems were irrelevant to Americans actually had negative agenda-setting effects: more news coverage was associated with less public concern. These findings suggest the content of news matters for agenda setting, and they might help explain the lack of trend in studies looking for changes in traditional media's agenda-setting effects over time (Tan and Weaver 2013) and across generations (Lee and Coleman 2014). If the news agenda has evolved over time, paying more attention to some issues once neglected and less attention to others once prominent, then it is not only the number of channels or the diversity of information sources that is changing.

There are at least two dimensions on which the news agenda might have changed over time. One possibility is that the world has become more complicated in the past four decades. If news media spread their attention more evenly over more issues in the face of that complexity, news cues about issue importance are less clear to the public, and the public agenda might consequently become more diverse. A second possibility is that the news agenda has substantively changed over time. For example, international news coverage has declined over the past half century as news organizations closed foreign bureaus and pooled coverage to help their bottom line. Yet the news agenda is a zero-sum game (Zhu 1992), so the news attention once given to international affairs had to go somewhere. The issues to which attention was diverted might have larger or smaller agenda-setting effects, which would mean that the size of the news media's agenda-setting effect would change with the news agenda rather than moving with audience size. Those agenda-setting effects might generate a focused public agenda or a diverse one, depending on which issues received news attention and the size of the agenda-setting effects associated with them.

The analysis that follows considers how the broadcast news agenda has changed from 1968 through 2010 and how those changes are related to both news media agenda setting and the diversity of the public's issue agenda.

Agenda-Setting Effects and History Effects

To examine how the news agenda and the public agenda have interacted with each other over the past forty years or so of historical change, we use a different data set than we did to analyze the public agenda in Chapters 2 and 3. These data, collected for the U.S. Policy Agendas Project (https://www.comparativeagendas.net/us), were designed to examine how the public policy agenda of the federal government is related to the public agenda.[1] They enable us to compare the public agenda to the agenda of broadcast news, which was coded by Joseph Uscinski (2012) using the project's standardized categories.

The Policy Agendas Project uses the same raw Gallup data from the "most important problem" question, which are the basis of the analysis of the public agenda in Chapters 2 and 3, but it uses a different kind of coding scheme to reclassify people's responses into categories. Because the project's goal is to link the public agenda to the policy agenda, its coding uses categories that align well with congressional policy-making structures, like committees and subcommittees. This makes it possible to use the same codes to document both the policy agenda and the public agenda, and to look for connections between them (a task we undertake in Chapter 7). However, to achieve this, it loses some detail that the McCombs and

---

1. The public opinion data used here were originally collected by Frank R. Baumgartner and Bryan D. Jones, with the support of National Science Foundation (NSF) grant numbers SBR 9320922 and 0111611, and were distributed through the Department of Government at the University of Texas, Austin. Neither the NSF nor the original collectors of the data bear any responsibility for the analysis reported here.

Zhu (1995) categories give the "most important problem" data. For example, in the Policy Agendas data, all the public's economic concerns are folded into the single category of macroeconomics because economic policy-making structures drive the categories rather than public concerns (which include unemployment, inflation, and taxes). The coding also includes categories of policy making, such as public lands and water management, that the public never mentions as most important problems, again, because these are significant policy-making categories. Generally, then, the Policy Agendas Project's "most important problem" data is structured by the way legislators think about public affairs more than it is by the way the public thinks about them. Its public agenda data is also parsed into longer periods of time. Rather than considering each poll individually, as we did, it groups polls together into quarterly averages and interpolates for those quarters when no Gallup data exist. These longer time frames, again, lose some detail but are a very sensible approach, given the relatively slow pace at which government institutions generate public policy. It is lasting rather than momentary public opinion to which these institutions can respond.

Despite the differences in time frames and coding categories, the Policy Agendas Project data on the public agenda shows the same pattern of change in the diversity of the public agenda as is documented in Chapter 3. Figure 4.1 presents changes in public agenda diversity across twenty coding categories over time from Chapter 3 in black and changes in public agenda diversity across the nineteen categories of the Policy Agendas Project over the same time frame in gray. The figure demonstrates that the two measures of public agenda diversity generally move together and are strongly correlated with each other.[2]

Uscinski (2014) used the coding categories of the Policy Agendas Project to code the news abstracts of the Vanderbilt Television Archives, which provide a summary of the content of each evening's newscast for the three major broadcast networks, beginning in August 1968. His coding, along with the Policy Agendas Project's public agenda data, allows us to look at the agenda-setting effects of broadcast news over time. Uscinski coded the first two stories of each broadcast on each night for which they were available (sports broadcasts preempted news programming in some markets on some weekend evenings, making the Vanderbilt Archives incomplete [Althaus, Edy, and Phalen 2002]). He compiled the coding by quarter so that the news agenda data line up with the public agenda data, and his coding covers 167 quarters, from 1968 through the first quarter of 2010.

---

2. $r = .78, p < .001$.

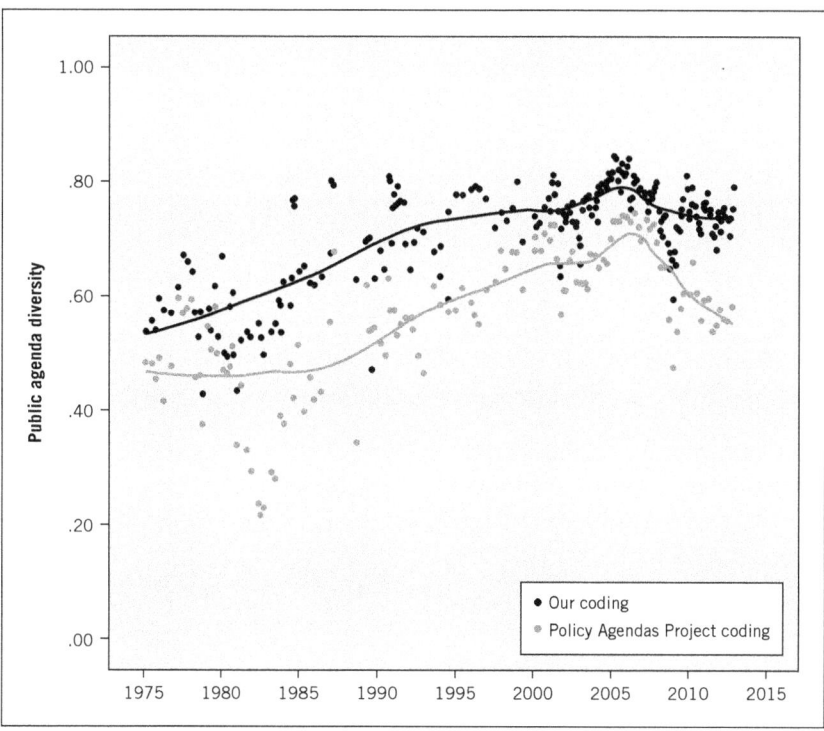

Figure 4.1. Public agenda diversity over time as measured by the authors' twenty-category H and nineteen-category coding of the same data from the Policy Agendas Project.

Although Uscinski's (2014) coding categories are designed to overlap with those of the Policy Agendas Project, the match is not quite perfect; therefore, we have made a few adjustments so that the data sets align. In some cases, Uscinski broke a public agenda category down for his broadcast news agenda coding, such as having separate categories for abortion and civil rights. In those cases, we recombine those news categories to ensure a match with the public agenda data. The resulting nineteen issue categories are: macroeconomics, civil rights (including abortion), health, agriculture, labor (including immigration), education, environment, energy, transportation, law/crime (including family issues), social welfare, community development/housing, banking/finance and domestic commerce, defense (including domestic terrorism and homeland security), space/science/technology/communication, foreign trade, international affairs, government operations (including state and local government administration), and public land/water management. We exclude Uscinski's other categories because they have no parallel in the Policy Agendas

Project public agenda data. We also exclude the other/miscellaneous category from both the public agenda data and the broadcast news agenda data because there is no way to figure out whether the "other" things named match across the data sets, and it is very likely they do not.

Using these data, we explore the agenda-setting effects of traditional broadcast news and its impact on the diversity of the public agenda over a time period in which the media environment evolves from dominance by the three broadcast networks to the hundreds of media options available by the early twenty-first century.

Agenda-Setting Effects and Agenda Diversity

The classic test for agenda-setting effects is to compare news coverage to public concern and see how well they match. The effect can be measured at both the issue level and the agenda level. At the issue level, correlation is used to measure how changes in the amount of news coverage about a particular issue are related to the amount of public concern about that issue. Does increasing news attention to the Iraq War produce more public concern about the Middle East? At the agenda level, correlation is used to measure how closely the overall news agenda and the overall public agenda resemble each other at a given point in time. The analysis that follows uses both kinds of measures, and we begin by documenting how the relationship between the news agenda and the public agenda evolves over time.

The Public Agenda and the Broadcast News Agenda

To get a broad sense of how the relationship between the broadcast news agenda and the public agenda has evolved, we consider how closely those agendas have resembled each other in each of our 167 quarters of data on the broadcast news agenda. For each quarter, we have a TV news agenda of coverage of nineteen issues and a public agenda of concern about the same nineteen issues. The more similar the patterns of coverage and concern are across those nineteen issues, the stronger the agenda-setting effect is for that quarter. We compute this relationship using a Pearson's correlation coefficient.[3]

Of course, there are other decisions to make about how to compare news agendas and public agendas. First, one would expect a certain amount of delay between changes in the news agenda and changes in the

---

3. An alternative approach to measuring agenda setting uses Spearman's rank correlation coefficient, or rho. Appendix C discusses the differences between these measures and why Pearson's correlation is the preferred approach here.

public agenda. Previous research has shown that agenda-setting effects are typically at their strongest at between one and eight weeks and that the lag in agenda-setting effects for television is especially short (Wanta and Hu 1994). Since the time frames in the data we are using are relatively long, with each data point representing three months, we compare the news agenda to the public agenda in the same quarter. A second issue that arises is the question of which direction the causal effects go. Does the news influence the public agenda by highlighting particular issues or problems? Or is it the case that audiences influence the agenda of the profit-driven broadcast news, which seeks to present news the public will find interesting and engaging? From our perspective, the key question at this point is not which way the causal effects go but, rather, whether the relationship between the news agenda and the public agenda has changed over time. One might expect that since the public's media choices have grown exponentially and audiences for broadcast news have declined dramatically between 1968 and 2010, the relationship between the broadcast news agenda and the public agenda has faded. However, Figure 4.2 shows something very different is going on.

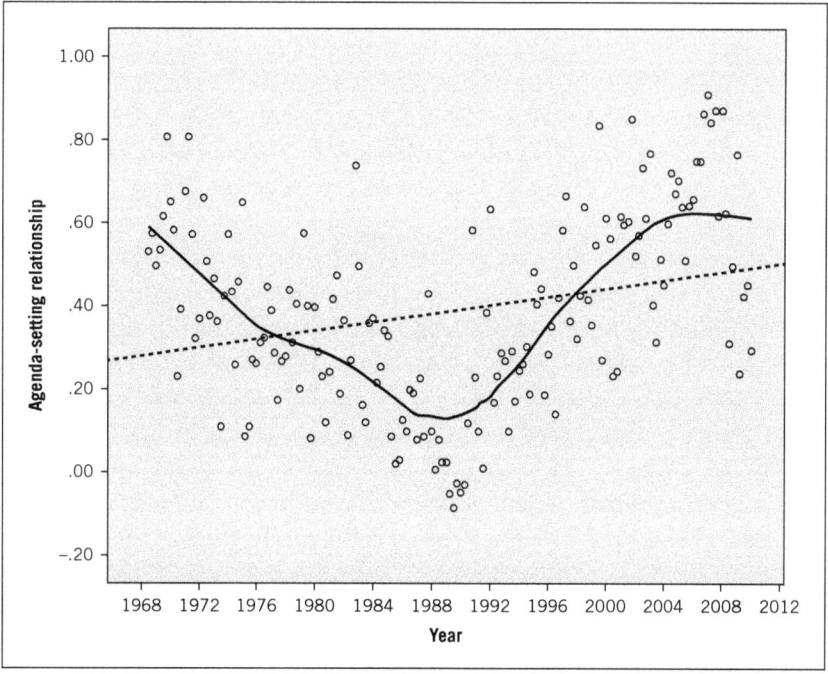

Figure 4.2. Agenda-setting relationship (Pearson's *r*) between broadcast news and public agendas, 1968–2010.

Figure 4.2 examines the relationship between the broadcast news agenda and the public agenda. Essentially, it depicts the extent to which the issue priorities of news (as measured by the number of stories about each issue) match the issue priorities of the public (as measured by number of responses naming that issue). The individual points on the graph show the strength of the agenda-setting relationship in each quarter. The straight line depicts the trend over time in the strength of the agenda-setting relationship using ordinary least squares (OLS) regression. It shows that the relationship between the news agenda and the public agenda has actually gotten stronger over time.[4] It is also clear that this has not been a steady increase. The curved line on the graph uses a technique called locally estimated scatterplot smoothing (or LOESS) to show trends over shorter periods of time. This approach captures the ups and downs a bit more smoothly than individual data points do. It reveals that the strength of the relationship between the news agenda and the public agenda declined until the early 1990s, then rebounded by 2010 to become even stronger than it had been during the broadcast era.

Issue-Level Agenda Setting

When we look at the agenda-setting relationship between the news and the public at the level of individual issues, we get a similar sort of unexpected result. Table 4.1 shows how the agenda-setting effect varies for sixteen of the nineteen issues these data sets explore. Here, the correlations depict the strength of the relationship between news coverage of a particular issue and the proportion of responses to the "most important problem" question naming that issue. For example, is more coverage of the environment associated with greater public concern about the environment? Three issues could not be tested because there was never any public concern about them. Agenda-setting effects are measured overall and in three time frames: (1) the broadcast era, defined as the time before twenty-four-hour cable news existed; (2) the CNN era, defined as the time frame when CNN and broadcast news coexisted; and (3) the partisan news era, defined as the period since Fox News and MSNBC began transmitting. The z scores in the last column of the table measure the change in the size of the agenda-setting effect between the broadcast era and the partisan news era.[5] Most commonly, there is no appreciable change in the agenda-setting effect for broadcast news from the earliest to the latest time pe-

---

4. $r = .26, p < .001$.

5. In three cases, this comparison is not possible, so comparisons are made between two adjoining eras.

Table 4.1. Issue-specific agenda-setting relationships between news coverage and public concern across the entire time span and three time periods

Issue	1968–2010	1968–1979	1980–1996	1997–2010	z
Macroeconomics	.52***	.57***	.64***	.46***	.73
Banking and commerce	.29***	—	-.03	.20	-1.24
Social welfare	.08	.27	.12	-.12	1.93†
Civil rights	.17*	.38**	.06	-.22	3.04**
Health	.30***	.30*	.13	.44**	-.79
Agriculture	.18*	.37*	.02	—	1.90†
Labor	.17*	.58***	-.13	.10	2.74**
Education	.20**	.20	.31**	.27*	-.36
Environment	.16*	.02	.21	.35**	-1.68†
Energy	.77***	.77***	.83***	.62***	1.44
Transportation	—	—	—	—	
Law and crime	.56***	.24	.63***	.54***	-1.75†
Space and science	-.13†	.13	—	-.30	2.14*
Community development	.02	.06	—	—	
Defense	.69***	.83***	.33**	.74***	1.16
Foreign trade	.30***	—	.21	.40**	-1.12
International affairs	-.03	.05	.07	.13	-.39
Government operations	.49***	.70***	.19	.31**	2.66**
Public land management	—	—	—	—	
Mean r		.36 (.28)	.24 (.27)	.26 (.30)	
N	167	46	68	53	

Note: Coefficients are Pearson's correlations. The last column shows a z test for the difference between earliest and latest available correlations, with a positive sign indicating a decline over time. Cells with missing values indicate that a correlation could not be computed because public concern was a constant (0). *p < .05; **p < .01; ***p < .001; †approaches significance at p < .10.

riod. This is the case for eight issues: Macroeconomics, health, education, energy, banking and commerce, defense, foreign trade, and international affairs. For two more issues, the environment and law and crime, agenda-setting effects get marginally stronger over time. Thus, for the majority of issues, the agenda-setting effect stays the same or gets stronger. Only six issues show the effects one might expect: over time, the agenda-setting effect for civil rights, agriculture, labor, social welfare, space and science, and government operations weakens.

One other element of this table is important to note: the size of the agenda-setting effect varies by issue. In other words, for some issues, public concern closely follows news attention, but not all issues generate agenda-setting effects.

How Issue Coverage Affects Agenda Setting and Public Agenda Diversity

None of this evidence supports the conventional wisdom that broadcast news has become largely irrelevant in the information age, but the question remains: If, as theorists have supposed, the news media build consensus on a public agenda, and the news media's agenda-setting relationship with the public is stronger than ever, why is the public agenda growing more diverse? The answer may lie in the confluence of media competition and history, for while the diversity of the news agenda does not directly affect the diversity of the public agenda,[6] its content does, and that content has changed over time. The next series of models reveals how changes in the issues covered in the news have shaped the relationship between the news agenda and the public agenda, preserving agenda-setting effects while fragmenting the public agenda.

Table 4.2 depicts the impact of news coverage of particular issues on the relationship between the overall news agenda and the overall public agenda. In other words, does coverage of particular issues influence how closely the news agenda and the public agenda match each other? It also shows the impact that coverage of particular issues has on public agenda diversity and how the news agenda has changed over time. The first two columns of Table 4.2 break down the news agenda by issue, showing which issues tend to receive the greatest amount of news attention (column 1) and whether the amount of attention being paid to that issue has tended to increase or decrease over time (column 2). Positive numbers in the second column of the table show news attention to the issue has increased from 1968 through 2010. Negative numbers show attention has decreased. The asterisks indicate that the change in the amount of coverage is statistically significant (unlikely to be due to chance). The table shows that five issues have tended to dominate news coverage. Macroeconomics, law and crime, defense (which includes homeland security and domestic terrorism), international affairs, and government operations together have accounted for about two-thirds of the news agenda over the forty-two-year span. The third column in the table shows how these changes in news attention over time have affected the diversity of the news agenda. For most issues, the more attention those issues receive, the more diverse the news agenda is, but the reverse is true for international affairs and defense, the two issues that received the most news attention. The less attention those issues receive, the more diverse the news agenda becomes, suggesting that wars, acts of terrorism, and international incidents produce focused news

---

6. $r = .03$, *ns*.

Table 4.2. Correlations between news coverage of issues and time, agenda setting, news agenda diversity, and public agenda diversity

Issue	% of News	Time	News agenda diversity	Agenda setting	Public agenda diversity
Macroeconomics	7.45	−.14†	.29***	.15†	−.31***
Banking and commerce	2.15	.39***	.20*	.08	.00
Social welfare	1.36	.26***	.42***	−.02	.09
Civil rights	2.00	−.05	.24**	.03	.09
Health	2.37	.49***	.45***	.08	.21**
Agriculture	.46	−.16*	.17*	−.06	−.07
Labor	1.74	−.23*	.28***	.14†	.10
Education	.26	.08	.27***	−.13†	−.06
Environment	.60	−.04	.35***	−.15*	−.08
Energy	2.17	−.15*	.06	.08	−.01
Transportation	2.53	.32***	.28***	−.03	.12
Law and crime	8.55	.28***	.38***	.22**	.27***
Space and science	1.53	−.19*	.12	.09	−.14†
Community development	.19	.02	.14†	.02	.01
Defense	14.92	.18*	−.19*	.42***	.32***
Foreign trade	.98	.00	.29***	−.19*	−.08
International affairs	24.18	−.46***	−.22**	−.60***	−.44***
Government operations	11.04	−.14†	−.02	−.10	−.08
Public land management	.05	−.14†	.10	−.05	−.07

Note: Coefficients are Pearson's correlations. $N = 167$ quarters. Other news topics totaled 15.47 percent of coverage. Agenda setting is the correlation between the overall news and public agendas for a given quarter, so positive signs in that column indicate more coverage makes overall agenda setting stronger. *$p < .05$; **$p < .01$; ***$p < .001$; †approaches significance at $p < .10$.

agendas. As we see in later models, the diversity of the news agenda has implications for the diversity of the public agenda, although diversity in the news agenda in and of itself does not fragment the public agenda.

The fourth column of Table 4.2 shows how coverage about each issue influenced the overall agenda-setting effect. Notably, international affairs coverage tends to produce a weaker correlation between the news and public agendas as a whole. The more attention broadcast news pays to international affairs, the less the public agenda resembles the news agenda. That might seem contradictory, but it actually makes sense in light of what the news would have been. As Christopher Wlezien (2005) points out, something can be salient without being perceived as a problem, and many international issues have these kinds of characteristics. For example, the end of the Cold War or the end of South African apartheid (both international issues) generated considerable news attention but not much public concern; if anything, they were causes for celebration. Other issues might have been considered problems but not necessarily ones "facing the nation" if national interests were not clearly at stake, such as the Ethiopian famine of the mid-1980s. In contrast, coverage of both defense and law and crime tend to strengthen the overall agenda-setting effect: more coverage of these issues improves the match between news and public agendas. Macroeconomics has a marginal effect on agenda setting, and government operations has a statistically insignificant negative relationship with agenda setting.

Column 5 shows the relationship between news coverage of an issue and the diversity of the public agenda. Macroeconomic coverage tends to reduce the diversity of the public agenda: when news pays a lot of attention to the economy, public concern tends to be more focused. International affairs coverage also tends to reduce the diversity of the public agenda, although not because it encourages the public to focus concern on international affairs. In contrast, more news coverage of law and crime and of defense is associated with a more diverse public agenda. Although it represents a very small proportion of news coverage over the time frame examined, news coverage of health-related issues also has a substantial positive effect on the public agenda's diversity.

Now, consider columns 2 and 5 in relation to each other. International affairs coverage, which is associated with lower public agenda diversity, has declined sharply over time. From the beginning of our time frame, 1968, until the fall of the Berlin Wall, 1989, international affairs coverage accounted for almost one-third of television news; afterward, it amounted to 17 percent. Coverage of macroeconomics, which also seems to focus the public agenda, has declined marginally over time. In contrast, news coverage of law and crime, defense, and health, all of which are associated with greater diversity in the public agenda, have increased significantly over the forty-two-year span. Using the same Cold War (1968–1989) versus post–Cold War (1990–2010) comparison, defense coverage rose from not quite 13 percent to more than 17 percent of the television news agenda; crime coverage more than doubled, from less than 6 percent to almost 12 percent; and health coverage tripled, from just more than 1 percent to almost 4 percent.

With the information from Table 4.2, Figure 4.2 begins to make better sense. The decline in agenda-setting effects occurs in an era when the economy and international affairs dominated the news agenda. Inflation, stagflation, government spending, and the Cold War are leading issues in the 1970s and 1980s. However, rising media attention to international affairs weakens the agenda-setting relationship between news and public concern, so as the Cold War reached its climax and the Berlin Wall fell, the public's list of most important problems was very far out of step with the news agenda. Following the Cold War, as the War on Drugs (a law and crime issue) and the War on Terrorism (a defense issue) joined repeated government attempts to reform the health care system on the news agenda, the resemblance between the public agenda and the news agenda became stronger. These issues both had stronger issue-level agenda-setting effects and increased the similarity between the public agenda and the news agenda.

Statistical modeling is useful in understanding the factors that may have driven change in public agenda diversity over time. Table 4.3 depicts a model that essentially asks which factors make stronger contributions to agenda-setting effects (the relationship between the news agenda and the public agenda—column 1) and contribute to diversity in the public agenda (column 2). The model disentangles the effects of the different predictors by statistically controlling for them. Essentially, it shows us the effects of each predictor as if all the other predictors were held constant. Because the size of the contribution of each predictor is standardized to vary between –1 and 1, we can directly compare how much each one contributes to changes in agenda-setting effects and public agenda diversity. A value close to 0 means the predictor has little influence, while bigger values, whether positive or negative, indicate stronger influence. Positive values mean that when the value of the predictor gets larger, the value of

Table 4.3. Linear regression predicting agenda-setting relationship and public agenda diversity from time, news agenda diversity, and news coverage of issues

	Agenda setting	Public agenda diversity
Prior agenda setting	.35***	
Prior public agenda diversity		.62***
Time	−.04	.11†
Macroeconomics	.43***	−.25***
Health	.03	.02
Law and crime	.22***	−.03
Defense	.37***	−.11†
International affairs	−.37***	.06
News agenda diversity	−.18**	.06
Agenda setting		.30***
Adjusted R^2	.68***	.69***

Note: Coefficients are standardized regression betas. "Prior" indicates the dependent variable in the previous quarter. Agenda setting is the correlation between the overall news and public agendas for a given quarter, so positive signs in that column indicate more coverage makes overall agenda setting stronger. $N = 167$ quarters. *$p < .05$; **$p < .01$; ***$p < .001$; †approaches significance at $p < .10$.

what is predicted does, too. Negative values mean that when the value of the predictor gets bigger, the value of what is predicted gets smaller. For example, the more attention the news media pay to macroeconomics, the more the public agenda resembles the news agenda but the less diverse the public agenda.

The model includes five kinds of predictors. First, agenda setting and agenda diversity from the previous quarter control for the existing levels of agenda setting and agenda diversity and let us focus on how the other variables change the size of the agenda-setting effect and the amount of public agenda diversity. Since agenda setting and agenda diversity typically do not change very much from quarter to quarter, controlling for them also makes for a tougher test of the other predictors because prior levels of the dependent variables explain a great deal of variance. Second, controlling for time confirms what other researchers have found: agenda-setting effects do not weaken over time. Time matters a bit more for public agenda diversity, but several other predictors matter even more.[7]

Third, we test the impacts of the five issues that are most strongly connected with both agenda-setting effects and with the diversity of the public agenda. With other variables controlled for, some of the relationships in Table 4.2 change. News about defense now focuses the public agenda, and international affairs news does not. Macroeconomics coverage still focuses the public agenda, but coverage of health and of law and crime, which appear to promote public agenda diversity in Table 4.2, are statistically insignificant in Table 4.3. These changes are likely due to the very large impact of the previous quarter's agenda-setting effects and public agenda diversity. While these predictors need to be taken into consideration, the next two are more important to understanding how changes in the news agenda have affected the diversity of the public agenda.

Fourth, the diversity of the news agenda influences its ability to set the public agenda. When the broadcast news agenda is more diverse, the agenda-setting relationship between the broadcast news media and the public is weaker. In other words, when news coverage offers the public less clear cues about which issues are most important, the public agenda does not match the media agenda as closely. However, news-agenda diversity does not have a direct relationship with public-agenda diversity. Last, aside from the diversity of the public agenda in the previous quarter, the biggest predictor of increasing public agenda diversity in the current quarter is the overall agenda-setting effect. The model suggests, then, that

---

7. See Appendix C for diagnostic statistics and alternate analyses, including ARIMAX modeling, which attempt to control for prior levels of the dependent variable and time trends. The results remain very similar.

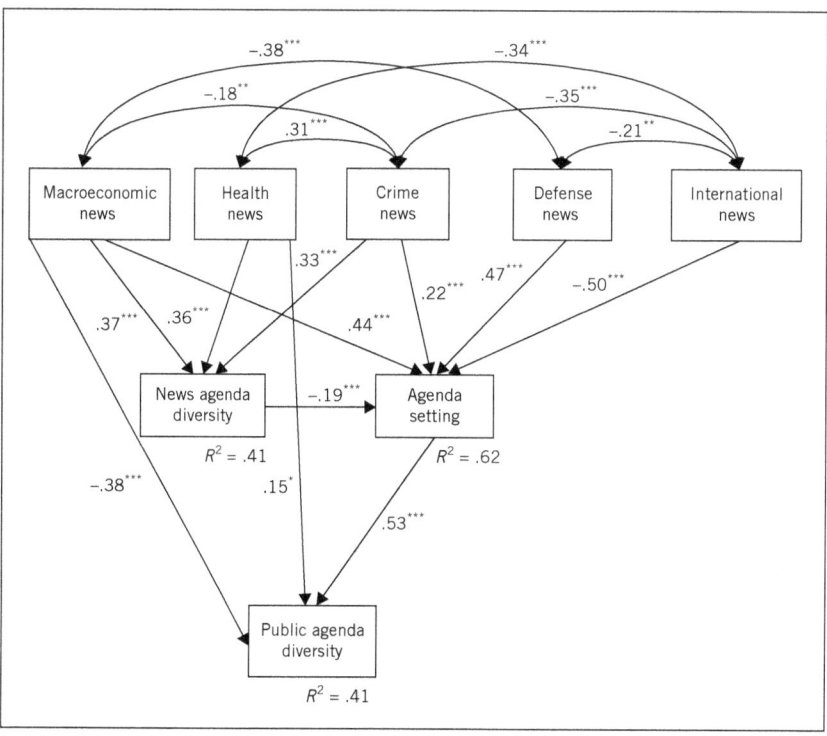

Figure 4.3. Path analysis model for issue coverage, news agenda diversity, agenda setting, and public agenda diversity, 1968–2010. *Note:* Standardized coefficients. Curved lines show covariances. *p < .05; **p < .01; ***p < .001.

news media agenda setting contributes substantially to the growing diversity of the public agenda.

A more sophisticated form of statistical modeling, structural equation modeling, lets us put all the variables into one model to see how they interact with one another. Figure 4.3 displays a structural equation model that depicts the news agenda in terms of the five issues that have been the strongest predictors of public agenda diversity in the analysis so far—macroeconomics, health, law and crime, defense, and international affairs. The figure presents these issues as they relate to news agenda diversity, overall agenda-setting effects, and public agenda diversity.[8] The

---

8. The model shown in Figure 4.3 is a path analysis model using AMOS 21. This is like a multiple regression model that allows variables to be predicted and predict others simultaneously, which permits analysis of direct and indirect effects. Unlike typical structural equation models, it uses only observed variables and no latent variables, a strategy recommended for sample sizes of less than two hundred; 167 quarters of data are represented here. The model has a good fit as indicated by a

model confirms the conventional wisdom about the limited size of the news agenda (Zhu 1992). The relationships between issues in the news agenda are mostly negative, meaning that more coverage of one issue is associated with less coverage of another issue. This is what one might expect given the limited time available in a nightly newscast. The only exception is the positive relationship between crime news and health news. These two issues have both received increased news attention across the forty-two years the model covers, with the growth in health coverage being the greatest of any of the nineteen issues.

When we consider the news agenda's relationship with the other variables in the model, the dynamics of public agenda diversity emerge. The model depicts the strength and direction (positive or negative) of relationships between the variables, and the R^2 values tell us how much of the change in value of one variable (for example, news agenda diversity) is explained by the variables that link to it. This model explains 42 percent of the variance in public agenda diversity. To keep the model tidier and easier to read, only the statistically significant links between variables are included here. Looking more closely at the model, only macroeconomic news and health news are directly connected with public agenda diversity. The more macroeconomic news there is, the less diverse the public agenda; the more health news, the more diverse the public agenda, though this effect is not as strong.

All the other elements in the news agenda are related to diversity in the public agenda through the mechanisms of news agenda diversity and/or agenda setting. News agenda diversity tends to undermine the agenda-setting effect of news, which one would expect if a diverse news agenda offered less clear cues about issue importance. Macroeconomic, health, and crime coverage all tend to make the news agenda more diverse. However, the effects of news diversity are much smaller than the effects of news' issue content on agenda setting, and this agenda-setting effect tends to promote a more diverse public agenda. Economic, defense, and crime coverage all are associated with stronger agenda-setting effects, meaning that the more attention news pays to these issues, the more closely the public agenda and the news agenda resemble each other. On the other hand, international affairs coverage has a strong negative relationship with agenda setting, meaning the more international affairs coverage, the less the public agenda follows the news agenda; thus, it has a negative indirect effect on public agenda diversity.

---

nonsignificant chi-square (χ^2 = 7.15, df = 11, p = .79) and other fit indexes (CFI = 1.00, RMSEA = .000).

In general, the model shows the forces that have been at work in shaping the public agenda over the last half century and helps explain why that agenda has become more diverse. The issues for which there is a strong positive effect on agenda setting are issues that have tended to receive more broadcast news attention over the time frame, while the issue with the largest negative effect, international affairs, has seen a steep decline in coverage. Although the attention once paid to international affairs may be distributed across more issues now, contributing to news agenda diversity and thus weakening the relationship between the news agenda and the public agenda, this impact is offset by the strong agenda-setting effects of each issue. Increasing news coverage of crime, defense, and health has increased the similarity between the news agenda and the public agenda, scattering public attention across more issues. Intriguingly, even economic news tends to have a positive effect on public agenda diversity when it influences the public agenda through the mechanisms of news agenda diversity and agenda setting, even though its overall effect on public agenda diversity is negative.[9]

Is It News, or Is It History?

So has the news agenda changed because the world has changed or because the news business has changed? Both explanations are plausible. One grounded in history might go like this. As broadcast television came of age, so did the Cold War, which divided the world into opposing ideologies of communist and capitalist and offered a prism for making international affairs relevant for Americans following World War II even if its agenda-setting effects seem to have been negligible. What were at the time the worst economic problems since the Great Depression together with Cold War concerns dominated the news in the 1970s and 1980s. When the Cold War ended with the fall of the Berlin Wall in late 1989 and the dissolution of the Soviet Union in 1991, good economic times together with a relatively peaceful world meant public and news attention moved to domestic issues like crime and health care. Historical events that tended to focus the public agenda reached their conclusion and issues that tended to diversify the public agenda came to the fore. Although a massive recession in the 2000s refocused the public agenda temporarily, the

---

9. $\beta = .20, p < .001$. AMOS estimates indirect and total effects on public agenda diversity using bootstrapping. Health news has similarly contradictory effects by path, a negative indirect effect ($\beta = -.04, p < .01$) that, despite its positive direct effect, has a nonsignificant total effect on public agenda diversity ($\beta = .11, p = .14$, ns).

multipolar and globalized international threats of the new century did not recreate the ideologically orderly world of the Cold War.

Yet it is also the case that the news industry was changing dramatically over this time frame, and this, too, offers a plausible explanation for the transformation of the news agenda. During the 1980s, news organizations consolidated, becoming part of larger corporate entities (Bagdikian 2004). These corporate entities expected all units of the organization to be profitable, including news (McChesney and Nichols 2010). One way to make news more profitable was to reduce production costs, and one way to reduce production costs was to reduce the amount of international affairs news, which was very expensive and (as the data here reveal) unlikely to matter much to news consumers. Crime news, in particular, represented a relatively inexpensive means of attracting and maintaining audiences, giving rise to the local news mantra, "If it bleeds, it leads." Initially, these changes to the structure of news organizations, and thus to the news agenda, were instituted to improve profitability. However, as the news environment became more competitive, with entertainment programming and cable news competing for audiences and the internet competing for both audiences and advertising niches once unique to local news outlets, the changes became economically necessary for survival. This story suggests that the commercial news media's search for profit is a key part of the explanation for why the public agenda has become more diverse. It also suggests that the changing media environment has affected the public agenda not (or not only) by altering the means by which the public can acquire or avoid public affairs information but by altering the news agenda through restructuring the competition for audiences.

Since the observed changes are what actually happened rather than an experiment conducted under laboratory conditions, it is impossible to know for sure which explanation is right or exactly how much each explanation contributes to our understanding of what happened. However, we can use the concept of volatility, which we explore in Chapter 3, along with measures of news agenda diversity and some statistical tests suggestive of causal directionality, to give us clues about whether the commercial values of the industry have affected the public agenda.

Amber Boydstun (2013) demonstrates that news agendas tend to shift suddenly rather than gradually, lurching from one issue to another. In some cases, news attention to an event is fleeting, but, in others, the attention persists and results in a broader look at the issue, producing a lasting wave of attention to the issue until the next distraction comes along to move news attention to the next event. She refers to this as the alarm-patrol hybrid model of news. Joseph Uscinski (2014) argues that longer lasting news attention to an issue (Boydstun's patrol mode) is commonly affected by the public's concern about the issue. If the news media have become more aggressive over time in their search for audiences, we might expect that the volatility of the news agenda has increased over time. That is, searching for audiences, the news media lurch more quickly from one issue to the next than they once did, making the news agenda more volatile now than it used to be. If the news agenda is more volatile, not only would it suggest more commercial competition among news outlets, but it might also contribute independently to the diversity of the public agenda. As the news cycles move more and more rapidly from one issue to the next, we might expect the public agenda to grow increasingly diverse. To calculate television news volatility in the quarterly Vanderbilt data, we identify the proportion of issues that "fall off the agenda"—that account for at least 10 percent of stories in the previous quarter but fall short of the threshold in the next quarter.[10] Broadcast television news agendas do not grow steadily more volatile over time,[11] although they are more volatile in the partisan cable news era of 1997–2010[12] than they are in the CNN era of 1980–1996, which is a low ebb for news volatility.[13] This suggests that, in general, growing competition among news media has not sped up the alarm/patrol cycles of broadcast news. Moreover, it turns out that agenda volatility in broadcast news is not related to public agenda diversity.[14] This evidence does not support a history-driven explanation for changes in the news agenda, but it does not support one grounded in increased media competition, either.

A second way in which growing competition among news outlets might have left its mark on the broadcast news agenda is by making that agenda more responsive to public concerns. To keep an audience, the news media might engage in "patrol mode" for those events and issues that audiences seem to care about, whether or not those issues are objectively "important." Over time, the public's influence on the news agenda might grow relative to the news agenda's influence on the public, and this altered relationship between news and its audience could explain the growth in agenda-setting effects despite the decline in audience size. To help identify whose agenda led whose, we test how well the news agenda in one quarter predicts the public agenda in the following quarter (which would

---

10. For a discussion of how agenda volatility is calculated, see Chapter 3 and its appendixes.
11. $r = .11$, ns.
12. $M = .30$, $SD = .33$, $t(86.96) = 1.94$, $p < .10$.
13. $M = .19$, $SD = .23$.
14. $r = .07$, ns.

suggest the news leads the public) and how well the public agenda in one quarter predicts the news agenda in the quarter that follows (which would suggest the news responds to the public). Overall, there is no significant difference between the size of the news-led and the public-led agenda-setting effects.[15] Thus, we cannot say which is stronger: the effect of news on the public agenda or the effect of the public on the news agenda. However, the news-led correlation increases somewhat more than the public-led correlation over time,[16] and while the public-led effect is slightly stronger at the beginning of the time frame, by 2010 the news-led effect is stronger. This suggests that television news is increasingly leading rather than following the public agenda.[17]

In general, then, there is no strong evidence that growing competition for audiences among profit-driven news organizations has changed the content of news or the pace at which issues cycle through the news. Of course, the quarterly measures cannot capture the ebb and flow of the twenty-four-hour news cycle in which news stories are updated every few hours, if not every few minutes, and one must keep in mind Wlezien's (2005) caution that the "most important problem" question does not measure salience per se. However, as Uscinski (2014) points out, focusing on this kind of event-centered coverage tends to overestimate the agenda-setting effects of news relative to that of the public, and, as Webster (2014) argues, internet uproars are often generated by the noisy few and unrepresentative of the public as a whole. From a democratic perspective, the fact that short-lived media sensations do not seem to register in the public agenda is a hopeful sign that people can distinguish hoopla from concerns. Nevertheless, it remains very possible that news organizations seek to improve profitability by reducing organizational costs and that this alters the news agenda. Stories that require fewer resources and less expertise to cover may be more appealing to news media with more limited production budgets, themselves the product of smaller audiences that produce less revenue. Both market competition and history thus remain viable explanations for the changes in the news agenda that are associated with greater public agenda diversity in the post–Cold War years of growing media choice.

---

15. News-led mean $r = .383$, $SD = .24$; public-led mean $r = .367$, $SD = .23$, $t(167) = 1.46$, ns.

16. News-led $r = .32$, $p < .001$; public-led $r = .23$, $p < .001$.

17. One final nail in this argument: There is no relationship between news agenda volatility and the agenda-setting effects of either the public on news ($r = -.04$, ns) or news on the public ($r = -.03$, ns), suggesting that if news agenda volatility represents a search for viewer interest, it does not work.

Conclusion

The relationship between broadcast news and the public agenda supports a "driven apart" explanation for the growing fragmentation of the public agenda, but the mechanism is very different from what existing theories of media expansion and audience fragmentation might predict. Many expected the agenda-setting relationship between broadcast news and audiences to fade as media choice expanded, causing the public agenda to "fall apart"; instead, it grew stronger as the broadcast news agenda evolved. Issues that generate large issue-level and overall agenda-setting effects, such as crime and defense (which includes terrorism), began to occupy more space on the news agenda. At the same time, an issue that had once been prominent but failed to cue public attention, international affairs, faded. This changing news agenda sustains the agenda-setting relationship between the broadcast news media and the public even as it contributes to a more diverse public agenda. News attention to international affairs has tended to reduce the diversity of the public agenda, but attention to crime and defense tends to fragment it. Essentially, coverage of international affairs may not give the public anything new to worry about, but attention to crime and terrorism does. On a smaller scale, more coverage of health care does as well. As the coverage pattern shifted, the public agenda became more diverse.

These results also raise questions about whether the public forum of broadcast news media generates public consensus on an issue agenda as studies from the 1990s suggest (Lopez-Escobar et al. 1998; Shaw and Martin 1992). If by consensus one means similarity between the news agenda and the public agenda, the results of the present analysis are generally supportive. The agenda-setting effects demonstrate a match between the public agenda and the news agenda, and that match could reduce intergroup differences. However, these results also demonstrate that consensus and diversity are not conceptual opposites: it is possible for the public agenda to resemble the news agenda but also be diverse. Indeed, the analysis shows that the content of broadcast news reduced public consensus about the most important problem; that is, it contributed to public agenda diversity. This is not a function of the diversity of the broadcast news agenda, which is typically very diverse. Rather, it is a product of the issues to which broadcast news pays attention. Studies from the 1990s may equate consensus with a lack of diversity in part because the news paid more attention to issues that either focused the public agenda (like the economy) or that had small issue-level agenda-setting effects (like international affairs). However, this analysis demonstrates that a public forum may not necessarily generate a focused public agenda.

Though the enormous expansion of the media environment did not reduce the agenda-setting relationship between broadcast news and the public as many had expected, it may have played an indirect role in changing the broadcast news agenda in ways that fragmented the public agenda. U.S. news media are profit-driven commercial entities, and their emphasis on profit became more pronounced in the late twentieth and early twenty-first centuries, as media companies went public, accumulated debt, and were acquired by business conglomerates expecting profit from every unit in the company. Those pressures increased as media choice expanded and television news alternatives emerged, and, by the early twenty-first century, traditional news organizations struggled to stay afloat. Two ways to increase profits (or, in later years, keep the doors open) were to reduce production costs and attract audiences. Coverage of international affairs was expensive and, as the analysis above shows, failed to move audiences. Crime and terrorism were cheaper to cover and more likely to provoke public reaction and, potentially, draw audiences. This explanation for the changing news agenda is at least as plausible as one grounded in late twentieth century history, which marked the end of the Cold War and the emergence of the United States as the only remaining superpower. In all likelihood, both growing media competition and the events of the late twentieth and early twenty-first centuries had a hand in shaping a broadcast news agenda that contributed to public agenda diversity.

This chapter's evidence offers support for a driven-apart explanation of public agenda diversity rather than the falling-apart-" argument typically ascribed to the decline of broadcast news. However, the falling-apart argument may still have merit if we consider the structure of public attention to television news rather than the content of the news agenda. Moreover, we have yet to examine the more traditional form of the driven-apart argument, that competing cable news channels may promote differing issue agendas. Chapter 5 looks at these more traditional explanations of the impact of expanding media choice on the public.

5

Media Choice, News Agendas, and the Public Agenda

During the late twentieth and early twenty-first centuries, the media system grew immensely, offering the potential for the public's attention to disperse across a wide variety of media content. Many have argued that the growth in media choice and content diversity have undermined the media's ability to set the public agenda. However, Chapter 4 reveals that changes in the broadcast news agenda, possibly due to increased competition from alternative sources of news, played a significant role in fragmenting the public agenda by *strengthening* broadcast news' agenda-setting effect. These results suggest the public agenda has been "driven apart" by a changed news agenda rather than "fallen apart" because the agenda-setting influence of the news media has declined. Nevertheless, it is still possible that the public agenda has fallen apart, to some degree, as public attention to news media has declined. It is also possible that cable news networks further contribute to driving the public agenda apart by pursuing their own distinctive issue agendas.

In this chapter, we consider both possibilities: that audiences' choices about media consumption affect the public agenda (that the public agenda has fallen apart) and that different news media sources promote different issue agendas (that the public agenda is driven apart). In some ways, these two dimensions of change represent a kind of chicken-and-egg problem. If, despite being spoiled for choice, public attention remains focused on a few outlets, we would expect little change in the public agenda. If public attention spreads across a large number of media sources but all those sources present roughly the same issue agenda, again, we would expect little change. Conversely, either change in the patterns of public attention or differences in the issue agendas of news organizations could be associated with a diversifying public agenda. It is also possible that these two influences interact with each other.

Falling versus Driven Apart: Expanding Media Choice and the Fragmenting Public Agenda

The concept of selective exposure, that people choose which media content to consume and which to avoid, dates back to the 1940s. Early studies produce mixed results (Freedman and Sears 1965; Frey and Wicklund 1978), which is perhaps unsurprising, given how few media choices were available. Three networks dominated television, and their goal was to maximize the size of their audiences, so their programming was very similar (Webster 2014). However, since the 1980s, growth in media choice has been exponential. As of 2013, more than 90 percent of U.S. households had either cable or satellite television (Television Bureau of Advertising, n.d.), the average U.S. cable household received 189 television channels (Nielsen 2014), and 70 percent of American households had broadband internet service (Zickuhr and Smith 2013). Given this extraordinary growth, selective exposure is virtually inevitable. Indeed, Nielsen points out that of the 189 channels available to them, most people watch about seventeen. The idea that people pick and choose among media, and that this might have substantive effects on the public agenda, seems highly plausible.

Two key theories about the effects of selective exposure on individuals offer some insight into the likely effects of media choices on the public agenda, although the different mechanisms of influence they postulate have somewhat different implications for the public agenda. Markus Prior (2007) argues that the expansion of media choice has allowed the politically disinterested majority to turn away from broadcast news in favor of entertainment programming, while those interested in politics can consume more news than ever before. Evidence for his conditional political learning model documents a widening political knowledge gap between heavy news consumers and those who prefer entertainment. This knowledge gap could contribute to growing public agenda diversity if those who consume a great deal of news are particularly influenced by news agendas, while those who prefer entertainment either give uncued, top-of-the-head responses (Zaller 1992) or refer to obtrusive issues in their own lives (Neuman 1990; Popkin 1991) when asked to name issues of concern. The shift in public attention from news to entertainment programming would increase public agenda diversity as the public agenda fell apart in the absence of news cues.

Prior notes that polarized news could further exacerbate the effects of the knowledge gap, but some scholars believe the ability of audiences to choose the news that suits them ideologically is the main driver of political divides that, in turn, might explain a fragmenting public agenda. These scholars focus not on the growth of media choice in general but rather on the development of partisan television news—in other words, Fox News and MSNBC, both of which debuted in 1996. Shanto Iyengar and Kyu Hahn (2009) find in an experimental setting that people prefer news they associate with their own ideology. Matthew Levendusky's (2013) experiments show that when people consume partisan media, it has a polarizing effect. Talia Stroud (2011) finds evidence in survey data that those who attend to conservative news sources have different issue priorities than those who attend to liberal news sources, an effect that holds across party lines. Consumers of conservative and liberal news also differ from those who attend to other media sources. However, Stroud does not find evidence that media choice is governed by issue priorities. Rather, agenda influence seems to flow from media to audiences, much as it did in the broadcast era, supporting Max McCombs's observation: it was possible audiences in a fragmented media environment would be exposed to "vastly different media agendas" (2004, 147). If a substantial portion of the public selects ideologically congenial news sources, and those sources promote distinctive issue agendas, the public agenda would be driven apart by the agenda-setting effects of partisan media.

Both these visions of selective exposure have been questioned by other scholars. James Webster (2014) argues people are not as able to filter out unwanted content as those who decry "filter bubbles" (Pariser 2011) and "opinion enclaves" (Sunstein 2007) claim. This is because the tendency of both user tools (like search engines) and marketing tools (like ad servers) to cater to someone's personal taste are countered by the tendency of these tools to point up what is widely popular. Webster also makes the case that among the plethora of media choices now available, a very large segment of audience attention is dominated by a very small number of channels and websites. Matthew Baum (2002) argues that "soft news" programs make audiences who avoid traditional news aware of public affairs, although Prior (2003) argues that users of these programs do not acquire much information. These analyses suggest the size of the "knowledge gap" may be bounded: a person can be only so politically uninformed; therefore, a public agenda might be similarly bounded in terms of its diversity, despite lower levels of public attention and knowledge. Kelly Garrett's (2009) survey experiment shows that while people prefer ideologically congenial information, they do not actively avoid alternative points of view. Webster's data reveal that partisan media viewers typically sample content from the "other" channel. Kevin Arceneaux and Martin Johnson (2013) suggest that partisan media tend to preach to the choir, while those who are most likely to be influenced by them are the most likely to avoid them. These findings suggest that polarization may have limits, too.

The shift in public attention to media could also mean that the public agenda is influenced by sources other than the traditional news media, and this change could contribute to a more diverse public agenda. Many critical scholars who have decried the news media's choices about where to direct public concern (e.g., Bennett 1990; Bennett, Lawrence, and Livingston 2007; Entman 1989; Hallin 1986) might be pleased that the public now has greater power to determine its own agenda, using social media to connect and focus on problems or issues the news has neglected. Several scholars have pointed out that the internet gives individuals the potential to address audiences big enough to be politically meaningful (e.g., Quandt 2012; Williams and Delli Carpini 2011). This might occur through at least two processes. First, people might generate content through citizen journalism or sharing personal narratives about issues and problems they face. These might be shared and popularized by social media like Facebook or blogging sites, regardless of whether the traditional news media ever picked up on them, although Bruce Williams and Michael Delli Carpini point out that popular stories from such sources commonly do migrate into the news. Second, content from the traditional news media might be picked up and passed around through social media, a tendency that is better documented (Leccese 2009; Pew Research Center 2010). Although this content might originate in traditional news, there is no reason to imagine the agenda of traditional news would be preserved. In other words, the problems and issues journalists believe are most important would not necessarily be the ones most shared via social media. For example, Webster (2014) notes that media content creators have a poor track record of predicting which content will become popular, and Pablo Boczkowski, Eugenia Mitchelstein, and Martin Walter (2012) observe that the top stories on a news website are not typically the most read. Thus, the public agenda might diversify in part because social media compete with traditional news to influence the list of public concerns, driving apart the public agenda.

To explore these possibilities, we use archival data about how the media environment has changed from 1975 through 2014 and our poll-by-poll coding of the Gallup "most important problem" data presented in Chapters 2 and 3. Our analyses consider the impact of media evolution in ways that are distinct from previous research on two key dimensions. First, many studies of the contemporary media environment explore its impact on individuals. They consider how a person's opinions might change or be reinforced by exposure to news or what governs a person's choice about which media to use. They then extrapolate the social consequences of these individual attitudes and behaviors by aggregating them—essentially saying, "What if everyone did this?" Here, we unpack the problem from the other direction, considering the measured behaviors of the public—of audiences. These data reveal patterns in *public attention* rather than individual behaviors. Second, where many studies rely on experimental results obtained by bringing subjects into the lab, the data here are historical. They represent what actually happened as the media environment transformed over the course of forty years. This approach has its pros and cons. It does not provide airtight causal explanations for the changes observed, as well-designed laboratory research can do. However, it captures a much wider sweep of issues and a much greater span of time than typical experimental research. In some cases, not enough data are available to draw conclusions, and because social reality is what is being measured, no more data are forthcoming until more time has passed. Sometimes, too, history happens and confounds simple explanations grounded in changing patterns of attention. Nevertheless, the data represent what really happened and so have the potential to confirm or disconfirm the social changes about which other scholars have speculated. First, we examine key changes in the media environment and in patterns of public attention to news. Then, we put the variables representing these changes into a model that helps us understand the relative influence of each factor on the public agenda's diversity.

The Evolution of the Media System: 1975–2014

Media choice. People's media choices grew substantially in the years from 1975 through 2014 on many dimensions. Cable technology was available as early as the 1960s, used primarily to retransmit broadcast signals where terrain features put certain homes in a broadcast area out of the broadcast transmitter's line of sight. By the 1970s, however, cable technology was being used to transmit, for a fee, unique content into people's homes that was unavailable through over-the-air television. HBO was created in 1972, and ESPN was launched in 1979. In 1977, not quite 17 percent of households with television had cable (TV History, n.d.). Satellite television was also available in the 1960s, and, like cable, home satellite dishes were initially used to receive broadcast signals from distant transmitters. Direct broadcast satellite and other alternative ways of delivering television content that viewers would have to pay to receive emerged in the 1990s to compete with cable. By 2013, only 10 percent of television households still got their television over the air. The rest had cable or some other form of subscription service (Television Bureau of Advertising, n.d.). The growth in homes receiving television via cable and similar delivery services was matched by growth in the number of channels those systems offered. In 1975, a typical household received an average of about seven and a half channels (Compaine and Gomery 2000). By 2013, it had ballooned to 189 (Nielsen 2014).

Along with the growing diversity of television programming, the internet offers the public enormous choice in content consumption, and technical advances have only expanded the content possibilities of the medium. The World Bank (2015) estimates that in 1990, fewer than one in one hundred Americans used the internet from any location at any time. By 2000, more than one-third of U.S. households had dial-up internet access, and a few early adopters already had broadband service, which enabled them to access content much more quickly and to easily stream video and audio content. By 2013, 73 percent of U.S. households had internet access, 70 percent of them via broadband (Zickuhr and Smith 2013).

To explore the relationship between expanding media choice and the public agenda, we gathered historical data on the proportion of television households with cable or other alternatives to broadcast, the number of channels available, and the proportion of households with internet access over the course of our forty-year time frame. Details on the data sources, how we resolved discrepancies between the data sources, and how we coped when data were missing can be found in Appendix D. It turns out these three factors are very strongly related to one another. That is, they have grown together and their patterns of growth have been very similar, which makes sense given their interdependence. For example, more unique content makes cable more desirable for households and larger audiences make content creation more profitable for programmers, so the number of cable subscribers and the number of channels grow together. This means we can create a single, indexed variable that combines all three measures into one variable that represents the concept "media choice" (again, see Appendix D for details about this computation).

Broadcast news. Broadcast television news was the first documented source of media agenda-setting effects (McCombs and Shaw 1972), and when the theory was formulated in the late 1960s and early 1970s, the news media might have been expected to perform a kind of consensus-building function for the public (McCombs 1997). With relatively few news outlets focused on relatively similar issues and events owing to professional news norms (Cook 1998; Sparrow 1999; Tuchman 1973), the public might have been expected to focus on the few issues that were widely reported in the news. Empirical research bore this out (Lopez-Escobar, Llamas, and McCombs 1998; Shaw and Martin 1992). However, when media choice expands, public attention to news tends to decline (Prior 2007). Those who have never been much interested in public affairs take the opportunity to watch something else. If the public pays less attention to broadcast television news, what happens to the public agenda?

To find out, we used annual ratings data for evening broadcast newscasts from 1975 through 2014 (again, see Appendix D for details about how we gathered this information). Using ratings rather than number of viewers is helpful given the long time frame. Rating points represent viewership for a program as a proportion of the total television audience, so the growth in the U.S. population over the forty years does not affect it. Moreover, ratings data measured through set-top meters represent the actual behavior of audiences rather than what they say they do, which is notoriously inaccurate (Webster 2014). Since there is no theoretical reason to separate the networks, the variable is the combined rating for all three broadcast networks—ABC, NBC, and CBS.

Cable news. The first twenty-four-hour news network, CNN, launched in 1980. Though conservatives sometimes label it as the liberal alternative, its editorial stance is not overtly partisan. For example, arch-conservative Glenn Beck had a program on CNN before moving over to Fox (and eventually to the internet). Previous scholarship and the analysis in Chapter 4 offer ambiguous guidance about how nonpartisan cable news might affect the public agenda. If one thinks of the emergence of CNN as an aspect of growing media choice, higher ratings for the channel could be associated with greater agenda diversity because they would contribute to the knowledge gap generated by varying levels of attention to the news. The public agenda would fall apart as public attention varied from those who got news cues all day long from CNN to those who got no news cues because they watched entertainment programming, instead. However, if the public agenda were driven apart by public attention to partisan news that offered distinctive news agendas, attention to CNN could have a consensus-building effect similar to that of attention to traditional broadcast news. As we learn in Chapter 4, news media consensus-building is not incompatible with public agenda diversity, but this mechanism is distinct from the possibility that partisan news channels promote idiosyncratic issue agendas.

To find out how public attention to the network has affected the public agenda, we, again, used ratings data (see Appendix D). When CNN began transmission, not quite one-quarter of U.S. television households had cable (TV History, n.d.), and the new network's ratings were so low that ratings services like Nielsen did not track them. Quarterly ratings data are available starting in 1988, and monthly ratings data from 1997 through 2013 were obtained. The ratings data are quarterly for 2014. Thus, it is important to keep in mind that our measures of ratings are more sensitive in some time periods than others.

Overtly partisan cable news emerged in 1996, when both MSNBC and Fox News began transmitting. Many scholars have traced growing political polarization in the United States to the advent of such ideologically congenial news sources (e.g., Iyengar and Hahn 2009; Stroud 2011). They suggest users split themselves into opposing camps, ignoring opinions and even information with which they do not agree. The networks themselves, courting loyal niche audiences, may promote such polarization (Stroud 2011; Turow 1997; Webster 2014). A divided public might have a more diverse public agenda than one exposed to mainstream, centrist news, which would suggest that the public agenda has been driven apart by the issue agendas of partisan news. Again, we used ratings data to find out. Our analysis uses monthly ratings from 1997 through 2013, and quarterly ratings for 2014.

Social media. In 2005, only 7 percent of Americans engaged in online social networking; by 2014, more than 60 percent of all Americans and three-quarters of American internet users used social media (Perrin 2015). Some have suggested that the advent of social media like Twitter and Facebook has enabled the public to take its agenda into its own hands. Even if the content they share among themselves via such platforms originated in news outlets, they can easily disrupt the agenda presented in the news in the choices they make about what to share. For instance, the top news story of the day may be about a war in the Middle East, but the most shared public affairs content on the web might be a news story about health care. This suggests the public agenda might become increasingly divorced from the news agenda, but whether this would diversify or focus the public agenda is unclear. Studies of internet news use have reached complex conclusions. Scott Althaus and David Tewksbury (2002) find that people using online news are less likely to conform to the news agenda. Boczkowski and colleagues (2012) present similar results, but they find the match between the public agenda and the news agenda improves as an election nears. Reflecting on the online environment more generally, Webster (2014) points out that some of its features have a tendency to personalize content, tailoring it to match individual tastes and preferences, which would suggest that growth in social media use diversifies the public agenda as opinion enclaves of similar preferences emerge. However, Webster also notes that other features of the online environment tend to popularize content, making the attention-rich even richer, as the web's most popular content is pointed out to users. This would suggest that growth in social media could result in a more focused public agenda.

We explore the impact of social media on the public agenda by focusing on the number of active Facebook accounts. Facebook is enormously popular—almost 70 percent of Americans report using Facebook (Pew Research Center 2018). Moreover, Facebook has the advantage of being one of the oldest forms of social media to survive to the present, giving us a longer time frame to explore its potential effects on the public agenda. Quarterly measures of the number of active Facebook accounts exist from 2004 through 2014 (see Appendix D).

The Media System and the Public Agenda

A first look. When we look at the relationships between the variables representing changes in the media system and public agenda diversity, measured across all twenty issue categories and across the five larger issue categories defined in Chapter 3, we see some evidence of a public agenda that is falling apart as public attention to news declines. Table 5.1 depicts zero-order correlations between our measures of media expansion (choice), public attention, and public agenda diversity. Each of our 254 polls is a case, and for each case, we consider the relationship between the agenda diversity measured in that poll, the state of the media ecosystem, and how public attention is distributed. The patterns revealed in the table represent the relationship between each pair of variables without considering any competing factors. As Prior (2007) might have predicted, more media choice almost exactly mirrors falling ratings for broadcast news, and both are strongly correlated with a more diverse public agenda. This suggests that as news cues weaken, the public agenda falls apart. This impact is so powerful that if we think of this as a causal relationship, more than half of the increase in public agenda diversity across the twenty issue categories can be attributed to declining attention to broadcast news.

Table 5.1. Zero-order correlations between public agenda diversity measures and their predictors

Variable	N	H-20	H-5	Prior H-20	Prior H-5	Time	Media choice	Broadcast news ratings	CNN ratings	Fox News ratings	MSNBC ratings
H-20	254										
H-5	254	.67***									
Prior H-20	253	.83***	.54***								
Prior H-5	253	.54***	.72***	.67***							
Time	254	.72***	.33***	.72***	.33***						
Media choice	254	.71***	.35***	.71***	.34***	.995***					
Broadcast news ratings	254	-.73***	-.35***	-.73***	-.35***	-.985***	-.980***				
CNN ratings	203	-.26***	.04	-.21**	.07	-.53***	-.53***	.50***			
Fox News ratings	171	-.14†	-.04	-.16*	-.04	.56***	.55***	-.65***	.34***		
MSNBC ratings	171	-.46***	-.41***	-.41***	-.40***	.55***	.50***	-.59***	.40***	.76***	
Facebook adoption	122	-.07	-.26**	-.08	-.28**	.966***	.982***	-.50***	-.48***	.10	.29**

Note: H-20 = twenty-category public agenda diversity. H-5 = five-category public agenda diversity. "Prior" indicates the dependent variable in the previous poll. *p < .05; **p < .01; ***p < .001; †approaches significance at p < .10.

Perhaps more intriguingly, it tends to fall apart when the public pays less attention to any sort of news, even partisan news. Attention to MSNBC in particular is associated with a more focused public agenda, while attention to Fox News is associated with a more focused agenda at the twenty-category level and has no significant relationship at the five-category level. The results for CNN are quite similar: more attention is related to a more focused twenty-category public agenda but has no significant relationship with the five-category measure. Nowhere in the zero-order correlations do we see support for the driven apart thesis. The growth in Facebook accounts, like everything else, is associated with a more focused public agenda, where we see any relationship at all.

The contrast between these results and those supporting a "driven apart" model in Chapter 4 suggest something more complicated is going on. However, the results of the zero-order correlations also indicate we face some challenges in modeling the relationships between these variables. The trouble is that they are all so strongly related to each other that the conventional statistical technique, OLS regression, cannot be used. Further complicating matters is that all these variables are strongly related to time. For example, the more time passes, the lower the ratings for broadcast news. Our model needs to take into account whether it really is changes in news attention or just the passage of time that is related to public agenda diversity. Finally, we need to take into account existing levels of agenda diversity (as we do in Chapter 4) to get at how attention to various media sources is related to *change* in public agenda diversity.

A closer look. In the model that follows, we use a special statistical technique called ridge regression (explained in more detail in Appendix D) to help tease out the unique contributions of each of our measures of public attention to media. Once again, each poll is a case, but in this model, we consider both the effects of competing variables and the passage of time. We include the previous poll's public agenda diversity as a control variable so that we can focus on how public attention to media is associated with changes in public agenda diversity.[1] Since public agenda diversity does not change very much from poll to poll, its level in the previous poll tends to be a very strong predictor in the current poll, and this makes for a rigorous test of whether anything else might contribute to it. It should lead us to underestimate rather than overestimate the impact of news attention on public agenda diversity. We also include time as a control

---

1. This is similar to creating a difference score in a time series model, which is one way researchers attempt to achieve stationarity.

variable, which means that where we see relationships between public attention to news and public agenda diversity, they are not due to the passage of time. The model does not, however, contain media choice. The relationship between choice and attention to broadcast news is so strong, even ridge regression struggles to untangle their unique influences. In this situation, attention to broadcast news is the conceptually preferable measure because the results from Chapter 4 suggest that news content affects the public agenda. The media choice variable implies merely greater choice, while the broadcast news ratings variable captures the idea of more or less attention to news content.

Although these techniques can manage statistical complexities in our data, it is important to remember that not only is time elapsing; history is unfolding as well. Since the data here are not from laboratory experiments but rather document what has happened to the media environment over the course of the past forty years, history is always there in the background. Of course, history and media are not the only possible sources of changes in the character of the public agenda, but even as changes in the media environment are sometimes linked, history and the media environment can interact. For example, the period in which CNN was the only twenty-four-hour news channel and its ratings were measured (1988–1996) coincides with the end of the Cold War and a period of economic prosperity, making history as plausible an explanation as media for a diversifying public agenda during that time frame. Although there is no statistical solution for this, as a general rule of thumb, the longer the time period over which a relationship between media and the public agenda holds, the less likely that a specific historical event gave rise to it. As war gives way to peace or economic expansion is countered by economic recession, the effects of history on the observed relationships wash out. The exception would be longer historical trends, such as the expansion of civil rights over the course of the late twentieth and early twenty-first centuries. To reduce the chances of history affecting the relationships revealed, the time frames used in the model consider the period "since" the advent of a particular change. This lets us use all the data points available for each change in the media environment, which both reduces the effects of history and increases the chances of finding statistically significant relationships.

The model is divided into four time frames: (1) the entire time frame, 1975–2014; (2) the period since twenty-four-hour cable news, 1988–2014;[2] (3) the period since partisan cable news, 1997–2014; and (4) the

---

2. Recall that although CNN was launched in 1980, ratings data for the network are not available until 1988.

period since social media, 2004–2014.[3] The explanatory variables are broadcast news ratings, cable news ratings, and social media use. The dependent variables are diversity in the public agenda, measured across twenty categories and measured across five categories. The control variables are prior levels of public agenda diversity (a consistent positive predictor, as we would expect) and time (which remains significant only for five-category diversity, and then only for the last two time frames). The coefficients are standardized, so the larger the number, the bigger the impact that variable has on the public agenda. A negative coefficient means attention to that aspect of the media environment tends to reduce the diversity of the public agenda, while positive coefficients suggest that attention to the news source tends to expand public agenda diversity.

The results, presented in Table 5.2, paint a more complex picture and suggest different effects in different time frames. Over the course of the forty-year time frame, public attention to broadcast news tends to focus the twenty-category public agenda, as decades of agenda-setting research might expect, though the relationship falls short of significance for five-category diversity. Yet the relationship is not consistent across the whole time frame. It is large and negative overall, small and not statistically significant when we measure the relative influences of public attention to broadcast and cable news, and significant and positive for both measures of diversity from 2004 to the end of the time frame.[4] Both history and changes in the news agenda may help explain why the relationship between broadcast news and public agenda diversity evolves over time. Chapter 4 shows that after 1988, the broadcast news agenda changed, which may have resulted in a transition from a public agenda that was falling apart as the public paid less attention to broadcast news to one that was driven apart by the news agenda. Although this interpretation is supported by the data, we should acknowledge that the effect may be enhanced by a historical anomaly. The Great Recession produced a decline in public agenda diversity just as public attention to broadcast news bottomed out. As public agenda diversity began to rise again once the recession eased, attention to broadcast news leveled out and even rose slightly.

---

3. Note that these time frames do not exactly match the time frames used in Chapter 3. Here, the beginning of an era is marked by the moment that data on audience use of or attention to a media source become available.

4. Looking only at zero-order correlation in specific time frames, the changed relationship between broadcast news ratings and public agenda diversity is starker. For 1975 through 1987 ($n = 51$), $r = -.55$, $p < .001$ for H-20 and $r = -.34$, $p < .05$ for H-5. For 2004 through 2014 ($n = 131$), $r = .55$, $p < .001$ for H-20 and $r = .65$, $p < .001$ for H-5. These differences between the time frames' correlations are significant: ($z = 7.31$), $p < .001$ for H-20; ($z = 6.67$), $p < .001$ for H-5.

Table 5.2. Ridge regression models for news attention predicting public agenda diversity

	1975–2014		1988–2014		1997–2014		2004–2014	
	H-20	H-5	H-20	H-5	H-20	H-5	H-20	H-5
Controls								
Prior H	.620***	.666***	.318***	.562***	.286***	.538***	.244***	.564***
	(.048)	(.045)	(.030)	(.044)	(.025)	(.042)	(.026)	(.044)
Time	−.076	−.022	.015	−.024	.066	.241**	−.001	.128*
	(.137)	(.091)	(.038)	(.067)	(.044)	(.084)	(.018)	(.051)
Predictors								
Broadcast news	−.345*	−.135	−.042	−.077	.036	.064	.103***	.124*
	(.139)	(.092)	(.037)	(.067)	(.043)	(.080)	(.029)	(.053)
CNN			−.056†	.025	−.037	.199**	−.047†	.075
			(.033)	(.050)	(.035)	(.067)	(.028)	(.051)
Fox News					.109**	.125*	.012	−.013
					(.037)	(.064)	(.028)	(.049)
MSNBC					−.183***	−.386***	−.108***	−.203**
					(.040)	(.079)	(.031)	(.064)
Facebook							.042*	−.021
							(.020)	(.049)
Constant	.007	.003	.226	.050	.294	.045	.471	.177
	(15.95)	(15.95)	(16.63)	(15.41)	(14.54)	(13.25)	(14.76)	(13.60)
Adjusted R^2	.709	.505	.356	.398	.583	.698	.630	.780
Ridge K	1.6	5.6	18.7	13.0	6.4	1.7	13.4	4.1
N	254	254	203	203	171	171	122	122

Note: H-20 = twenty-category public agenda diversity. H-5 = five-category public agenda diversity. "Prior H" is the previous poll's public agenda diversity. Scaled ridge regression coefficients with standardized data; standard errors are in parentheses. Time periods reflect when data exist for sets of predictors. *p < .05; **p < .01; ***p < .001; †approaches significance at p < .10.

In other words, attention to broadcast news and agenda diversity declined together and then rose together in the last few years of our time frame in a pattern that could suggest a historical coincidence.

Many scholars have expressed concerns about the polarizing effects of partisan cable news. When we consider the impact of public attention to partisan news on fragmentation of the public's issue agenda, the evidence is mixed. Public attention to Fox News is associated with a more diverse public agenda over the course of its history as a network, but not for the most recent decade, again perhaps because of the anomalous dip in public agenda diversity during the Great Recession. However, attention to MSNBC is always strongly associated with a more focused public agenda. This suggests that Fox News may indeed have a distinctive news agenda that contributes to driving apart the public agenda, a possibility we explore in more detail later in this chapter.

Public attention to CNN has a complex relationship with the public agenda. It is consistently (but not always significantly) related with a somewhat more focused public agenda when the agenda is measured at the twenty-category level, a relationship that approaches significance in two of the three time frames in which CNN appears. But attention to CNN is associated with a significantly more diverse five-category public agenda from 1997 through 2014. A look inside the data suggests this may in part be a product of the way the content of CNN's news and public attention to CNN interact. Unlike either broadcast television news, with its stable ratings, or partisan cable news, with its steadily growing ratings (both of which suggest more habitual viewing), fluctuations in public attention to CNN seem to be relatively event-driven. This notion that viewership is not steady but expands and contracts in response to events may help explain other oddities in the results as well, and we explore it in more detail both later in this chapter and in Chapter 6.

The number of Facebook accounts is associated with a more diverse twenty-category public agenda, but it has no relationship with the diversity of the five-category agenda. The former result is consistent with the expectation that social media's degree of personalization of news and the homogeneity of social networks would contribute to diversity in the public agenda. Taken with other evidence, it suggests that Facebook users' unique social networks may generate distinctive issue agendas that scatter public concern across more and more issues, driving apart the public agenda. The latter could well have resulted from how much the five-category measure of public agenda diversity contracted during the Great Recession, more so than the twenty-category measure. As the number of Facebook accounts continued to grow, agenda diversity expanded and then contracted. From a statistical perspective, this would make it appear that there was no relationship between the spread of social media and the five-category measure of diversity in the public agenda. Here we may have a case where the time frame is too short to temper the effects of a major historical event.

Some Preliminary Conclusions

Changing patterns of public attention to television news are clearly related to changes in the public agenda from 1975 through 2014. Generally, it appears that both expanding media choice and declining attention to broadcast news help explain why the public agenda has fragmented over the past forty years. Particularly, in earlier years of our time frame, these results support the inference that the public agenda began to fall apart as the public received fewer news media cues about which issues were important. However, the results for broadcast and cable news in more specific time frames are less straightforward and suggest that to truly understand the relationship between the media environment and the public agenda, we must know something about the news agenda. Attention to cable news, even partisan cable news, does not always make the public agenda more diverse; more often than not, the opposite is the case. Consequently, it seems likely that while the amount of public attention paid to a news source influences the size of its effect on the public agenda, whether a news source expands or focuses the public agenda may also depend on its degree of correspondence with the issue agenda of other news providers. Moreover, any given news network may not consistently converge with or diverge from the overall television news agenda, and, as Chapter 4 indicates, the content of the news agenda can affect the diversity of the public agenda, even if it is widely shared across news networks. Therefore, it is to news agendas that we next turn our attention.

Polarized or Parallel? Partisan News, Cable News, and Broadcast News Agendas

Whether the public agenda is driven apart by news content depends to some degree on whether and to what extent news agendas vary across news sources. This is the case no matter what the individual attention patterns happen to be. If particular citizens are dedicated consumers of a single source of public affairs information with a distinctive agenda, the pooled agenda of the public as a whole presumably would become more diverse. If citizens graze across a number of news sources that all have different agendas, the public agenda would also become more diverse.

Leaving aside for the moment the different degrees of news media agenda-setting effects for different issues, which Chapter 4 reveals, there are at least two ways to think about how diversity in the issue agenda of news might be related to diversity in the public agenda. First, if the issue agenda across news outlets becomes more diverse, the public agenda might become more diverse. If Fox News devotes more attention to a government scandal, whereas MSNBC focuses more on economic inequality and CBS News concentrates on national security, the differences in agendas across news sources could result in a more diverse public agenda as the public divides its attention among them. A second way to think about news agenda diversity is the diversity within a particular network. A network evening newscast has only twenty-two minutes of news, so the number of topics it can cover is quite limited. A short list of topics could have the effect of focusing the public agenda. A twenty-four-hour cable news network has vast quantities of time to fill, so it could present a much more diverse news agenda, and the degree of agenda diversity within a single news source could also influence the diversity of the public agenda. However, if news agendas are very similar across news outlets, then public agenda diversity would not be a function of which outlet got more or less public attention.

The differing levels of agenda-setting effects across issues suggest measures of overall news agenda diversity need to be tempered by examination of where those differences lie. This is particularly important because, at least for broadcast news, news agenda diversity does not directly affect public agenda diversity. Chapter 4's analysis shows that a less diverse broadcast news agenda can have larger agenda-setting effects that can diversify the public agenda, depending on which issues are the objects of focus. If cable news networks focus on a short list of issues that tend to diversify the public agenda, their news agendas might not be very diverse but might nevertheless contribute to public agenda diversity. This would be true regardless of whether there was a great deal of overlap between cable and broadcast agendas.

Conventional Wisdom: Cable News and News Agenda Diversity

Pundits, scholars, and public intellectuals have suggested that partisan news channels, particularly Fox News, present dissimilar visions of the social world. There are several theoretical reasons to expect the issue agendas of cable news networks have generated additional diversity in the overall news agenda. During the broadcast era, journalistic norms defining news and practices for producing it were widely shared across news organizations. Commonly shared norms of news selection, what journalists call "news judgment," and objectivity meant traditional broadcast newscasts looked very similar to one another (Cook 1998; Sparrow 1999). However, a number of scholars have argued that the traditional news media have lost their ability to restrict news content to those aspects of public life journalistic norms define as newsworthy (Baym 2009; Uscinski 2014; Williams and Delli Carpini 2011). Thus, cable news content may be less constrained by journalistic norms governing news selection. Furthermore, partisan news may be less influenced by norms of objectivity, which could also contribute to diversity in its agenda.

Media economics offer a second reason for expecting news agendas to become more diverse as the media environment offers more consumer choice. In the mass media era, the closer to the political center a newscast could manage to be, the larger its potential audience and the more potential advertising revenue from that newscast (Webster 2014). When consumer choice expands, as it has in the cable era, competition for audiences encourages media producers to divide audiences, developing small, well-defined niche audiences rather than appealing to broad masses (Mullainathan and Shleifer 2005; Stroud 2011; Turow 1997). In the realm of cable, this has meant partisan audiences, with Fox News appealing to a conservative audience and MSNBC to a liberal one. Catering to those audiences might mean different issue agendas because liberals and conservatives sometimes hold different issue priorities. For instance, a 2014 Gallup poll found 61 percent of Democrats rated climate change extremely or very important compared to 19 percent of Republicans (Newport 2014). Moreover, although network news is expected to cover its expenses and generate profit for shareholders, traditional broadcast networks' profit potential is spread across a wide variety of programming types including entertainment and sports as well as news. Cable news networks' commercial viability depends entirely on their news coverage. Consequently, cable news networks may be driven to distinguish themselves not only from broadcast networks but also from one another. Networks appealing to opposing partisans might be expected to be the most distinctive.

Studies of audience self-selection have suggested dissimilar content across cable news outlets (e.g., Coe et al. 2005; DellaVigna and Kaplan 2007; Iyengar and Hahn 2009), and Talia Stroud (2011) finds evidence of differences between issue agendas of Fox and CNN. However, studies exploring related questions, such as media bias (Aday 2010; Aday, Livingston, and Hebert 2005; Groeling 2008; Groseclose and Milyo 2005) and intermedia agenda setting (Boyle 2001; Heim 2013; Lee 2007; Lim 2006; Lopez-Escobar et al. 1998; Meraz 2011; Vliegenthart and Walgrave 2008) have reached conflicting conclusions about differences between news agendas. Many of these studies focus on one or a few issues and cover a short time frame, such as an election or a particular news event. Broad-based comparisons of the issue agendas of U.S. television news have not been undertaken, perhaps owing to the scale of the task. The contemporary television news environment includes the three broadcast networks (ABC, NBC, CBS) each carrying multiple news programs, and three cable networks (CNN, MSNBC, Fox) devoted to news programming for most, if not all, of the day.

Testing Expectations

An extraordinary data set allows us to test for similarities and differences in news agendas across a five-year time span for issues covering a broad spectrum of American public life. From January 2007 through May 2012, the Pew Excellence in Journalism News Coverage Index content-analyzed tens of thousands of individual news stories. Coders categorized stories from all three broadcast networks and all three twenty-four-hour cable news networks. They included news from morning and evening broadcast programs and samples of coverage from throughout the weekday on cable news. Twenty-six categories were used to document the issues covered: government agencies/legislatures, campaigns/elections/politics, defense/military (domestic), court/legal system, crime, domestic terrorism, business, economy/economics, environment, development/sprawl, transportation, education, religion, health/medicine, science and technology, race/gender/gay issues, immigration, additional domestic affairs, disasters/accidents, celebrity/entertainment, lifestyle, sports, media, U.S. miscellaneous, U.S. foreign affairs, and foreign (non-U.S.). More information about the data set can be found online from the Pew Research Center (2011), but we include a more detailed discussion of the portions of the data set we used in Appendix E.

Comparing the totality of the news networks' agendas across the whole time frame is not really appropriate. First, it seems likely to underestimate the distinctiveness of news media agendas. For example, liberal news outlets might heavily cover scandals involving Republican politicians, while conservative outlets might devote a lot of attention to scandals involving Democrats. Aggregating over the whole time frame, however, might suggest both conservative and liberal news sources cover government scandals about equally. Second, the agenda-setting effects of news do not work that way. News influences the public agenda by making some issues more salient, or cognitively accessible, than others (Scheufele 2000). Recent news coverage of a terrorist incident, for instance, should make terrorism a more salient issue for the public. The effects are relatively short term, lasting for a few weeks, and as the news agenda changes, the public agenda should change as well. As we note in Chapter 4, past studies have shown the optimal agenda-setting effect of the news agenda on the public agenda is found between one and eight weeks (Wanta and Hu 1994). Our own qualitative examination of the public agenda in Chapter 2 reveals the public responding to mediated events such as school shootings or presidential addresses quite quickly, typically within a few days. Social trends such as rising unemployment sometimes take longer to register. Here, we split the difference, examining the news agenda within the context of a month, taking forty months one at a time.

In this analysis, we are looking at the number of news stories aired about each of the twenty-six issues in a particular month. The total number of broadcast and cable news stories included in the Pew data set for each month ranged from about eight hundred to about eleven hundred. For each month, we tested the diversity of the news agenda in two ways. First, we compared the agendas of news networks to one another. If each network selects the same issues to cover and devotes about the same amount of coverage to each issue as every other network, then the larger number of networks does not contribute to the diversity of the overall news agenda. If different networks select different issues, place a different amount of emphasis on each issue, or both, then the proliferation of news networks contributes to the diversity of the overall news agenda and may contribute indirectly to the diversity of the public agenda as well. Second, we considered the diversity of the news agenda within a particular network and among networks using the H statistic to see over how many issues attention is spread and how evenly it is spread across issues. A bigger value for H means a network or group of networks is covering a broader range of issues, devoting relatively equal amounts of coverage to a number of issues, or both. That is, higher values indicate more diversity. To draw conclusions about the diversity of the news agenda both across and within news networks, we consider both in how many months a particular outcome occurred and the average of the values of our statistical measures across all forty months. More details about the statistical measures are presented in Appendix E.

There are two statistical approaches for looking at the differences between the agendas of different news networks. Correlating the agendas of news networks tells us how similar they are. One way to think about this is that correlation tells us how accurately we can predict the agenda of one news network by knowing the agenda of another news network. If we know the agenda of ABC News, how accurately can we predict CNN's? The higher the correlation coefficient, the closer the match is. The second approach, a chi-square test, tells us whether it makes a difference which network you get your news from. If the test reveals no significant difference between the agendas of two networks, then it should not matter how public attention is divided between them.

News Agenda Diversity

Exploring news agendas with correlation reveals substantial similarity in news agendas, but it reveals some differences as well. Since correlation coefficients are not always intuitive, we begin by comparing the agendas of all six news networks in the month when they were most strongly correlated with one another to the networks' agenda in the month when the overall correlation was the lowest.

Table 5.3 depicts the top five issues for each network and the proportion of stories devoted to each of them in September 2008, the month when the news agendas were most similar to one another and also least diverse as measured by the H statistic.[5] This eventful month saw the 2008 presidential election in full swing, the landfall of Hurricane Ike, and the financial crisis coming to a head with the bailout of the world's largest insurer, the largest bank failure in U.S. history, and the biggest single-day point drop in the Dow Jones average. The TV news outlets agreed on what the most important topic was and on what the top three topics were; five of the six agreed on the order of the top three as well. Combined, the six outlets had seven issues in their top five. Also notable is how concentrated news attention is to the top issues when news agenda diversity is low. The topic receiving the most attention from each network—campaigns—received more than a quarter of news attention from every outlet and more than half of MSNBC's attention. The fifth topic in each outlet's agenda received as little as 2 percent of news attention.

Table 5.4 shows the top five issues for each network and the proportion of stories devoted to each of them for May 2009, the month when news agendas were least similar and most diverse.[6] This month lacked huge news, and accordingly, all six TV news outlets chose a different top story. In all, the outlets had thirteen different topics in their combined top five. The high diversity of the news agendas can be seen in the relative equality of attention to different topics. The number one topic on each outlet received between 10 percent and 16 percent of stories about it, while the number five topic got between 6 and 8 percent of news attention.

Now that we have some idea of what high and low levels of news agenda correlation and diversity look like, Table 5.5 depicts the average correlations over forty months between news agendas for each of the six outlets, and for broadcast and cable news overall. The correlations are all positive, meaning that when one network pays more attention to an issue, the others do, too. The large values for the correlation coefficients mean that the overlap between news agendas is considerable, but broadcast news agendas are the most similar. Not only do their mean correlations show a great deal of similarity, but tests show that in any given month, each broadcast network is more like the other broadcast networks

---

5. Average correlation among news outlet agendas is .95, and overall news agenda H is .62.

6. Average correlation among news outlet agendas is .62, and overall news agenda H is .92.

Table 5.3. Top five topics by news attention in September 2008, a low agenda diversity month

ABC	NBC	CBS	CNN	Fox News	MSNBC
Campaigns: 26.5%	Campaigns: 25.5%	Campaigns: 32.0%	Campaigns: 43.8%	Campaigns: 46.0%	Campaigns: 53.6%
Economy: 19.5%	Disasters: 15.7%	Economy: 19.9%	Economy: 24.0%	Economy: 21.8%	Economy: 20.8%
Disasters: 14.8%	Economy: 13.8%	Disasters: 11.9%	Disasters: 11.3%	Disasters: 11.6%	Disasters: 11.7%
Foreign: 6.6%	U.S. foreign: 8.6%	Foreign: 6.8%	Business: 4.7%	U.S. foreign: 6.6%	Government: 3.1%
U.S. foreign: 5.6%	Foreign: 8.4%	U.S. misc.: 6.5%	U.S. foreign: 2.6%	Business: 2.2%	(Tie) U.S. misc.: 2.0%
					(Tie) U.S. foreign: 2.0%

Table 5.4. Top five topics by news attention in May 2009, a high agenda diversity month

ABC	NBC	CBS	CNN	Fox News	MSNBC
Health: 10%	Foreign: 10.0%	Business: 10.8%	U.S. foreign: 13.3%	Government: 16.3%	Terror: 16.0%
Economy: 8.1%	U.S. misc.: 9.4%	Health: 10.6%	Crime: 9.5%	Economy: 12.0%	Government: 12.3%
(Tie) Business: 7.2%	Health: 8.6%	U.S. misc.: 8.7%	Economy: 9.3%	U.S. foreign: 8.5%	(Tie) Courts: 9.5%
(Tie) U.S. foreign: 7.2%	U.S. foreign: 8.0%	U.S. foreign: 7.5%	Government: 8.0%	Terror: 8.3%	(Tie) Campaigns: 9.5%
(Tie) U.S. misc.: 7.0%	Government: 7.1%	Economy: 6.4%	Terror: 8.0%	Crime: 7.6%	Crime: 6.8%
(Tie) Foreign: 7.0%					

Table 5.5. Mean correlations between issue agendas of news outlets

	ABC	NBC	CBS	Broadcast	CNN	MSNBC	Fox News	Cable
ABC								
NBC	.94 (.04)							
CBS	.92 (.08)	.92 (.05)						
Broadcast	.97 (.03)	.98 (.02)	.97 (.03)					
CNN	.81 (.10)	.81 (.09)	.84 (.08)	.84 (.08)				
MSNBC	.64 (.17)	.63 (.16)	.68 (.14)	.67 (.15)	.82 (.12)			
Fox News	.73 (.12)	.74 (.11)	.78 (.11)	.77 (.10)	.89 (.08)	.88 (.07)		
Cable	.76 (.12)	.77 (.10)	.81 (.09)	.80 (.09)	.95 (.03)	.93 (.05)	.97 (.03)	
Total	.88 (.08)	.89 (.05)	.92 (.04)	.92 (.04)	.96 (.02)	.88 (.07)	.94 (.04)	.97 (.02)

Note: Coefficients are mean Pearson's correlations between news agendas of outlets as measured by counts of stories in twenty-six issue categories across forty months. Figures in parentheses are standard deviations. "Broadcast" indicates the composite agenda of ABC, NBC, and CBS. "Cable" indicates the composite agenda of CNN, MSNBC, and Fox News. "Total" indicates composite news agenda across broadcast and cable outlets. All coefficients are significant at $p < .001$.

than it is like cable.[7] On average, each broadcast news channel shares over 94 percent of its variance with the broadcast news agenda overall. The somewhat smaller coefficients for cable news reveal that cable news outlets are different from one another and from broadcast news. However, the nature of the differences is a bit unexpected. MSNBC is the most distinctive network—its agenda shares the least amount of variance with other news channels, between 40 percent and 77 percent. Yet the network with the most similar news agenda to MSNBC is Fox News.[8]

---

7. After computing means and standard deviations of the forty correlations (reported in Table 5.5), we ran paired-samples t-tests, comparing the correlations among the broadcast outlets to the correlations between each broadcast outlet and each cable outlet. ABC's correlations with its fellow broadcast news outlets are significantly greater than its correlations with cable outlets (all t's > 8.74, all p's $< .001$), as were NBC's (all t's > 8.60, all p's $< .001$) and CBS's (all t's > 3.98, all p's $< .001$).

8. Shared variance figures come from squaring the correlations in Table 5.5. The mean correlation of MSNBC's agenda with that of Fox News is .88, which is greater than MSNBC's correlations with the agendas of ABC, NBC, and CBS (all t's > 9.77, all p's $< .001$) and with CNN ($t(39) = 3.30, p < .01$).

Likewise, Fox News's agenda is more akin to MSNBC's and CNN's than it is to any other network's.[9] CNN, for its part, has an agenda more similar to that of broadcast news than its fellow cable outlets do. It shares about 70 percent of its variance with the broadcast news agenda compared to about 60 percent for Fox News and about 45 percent for MSNBC. But CNN is more similar to the other cable news channels than it is to broadcast, sharing about 90 percent of the variance of the overall cable news agenda. These results reveal what many have long suspected: the agenda of broadcast news is different from the agenda of cable news. However, the results do not suggest a liberal news agenda and a conservative news agenda.

Chi-square tests reveal that it does not matter which broadcast network the public gets its news from, since there are virtually no significant differences between their news agendas. The test was significant in only fourteen of forty months;[10] in the other twenty-six months, the broadcast outlets' agendas were practically indistinguishable.[11] However, cable news networks are different, both from one another and from broadcast news. Adding any one of the cable outlets to all three of the broadcast outlets was enough to make the test of independence significant in every one of one hundred twenty (three cable networks times forty months) cases,[12] suggesting that each cable outlet's agenda differs from those of the broadcast outlets. Moreover, the cable networks differ from one another.[13] The overall agenda of cable news is also different from the overall broadcast news agenda.[14] Thus, it matters whether you get your news from broadcast or cable and which cable network you get your news from.

Although the agendas of cable news networks are distinct from the agenda of broadcast news, they are not more diverse in themselves. Figure 5.1 depicts the average value of the H statistic for each network across all forty months. Higher values indicate more diversity, with zero meaning all stories were about one issue and one meaning an equal number of stories about all twenty-six issues. Each broadcast news network has an agenda

---

9. All t's $>$ 5.63, all p's $<$ .001. Fox's correlation with CNN's agenda does not differ significantly from the MSNBC/Fox News correlation: t (39) $=$ –1.06, ns.

10. V's $=$ .155 to .255, all p's $<$ .05. We report Cramer's V, a strength of association measure that can be used with any chi-square test of independence, regardless of the number of cells.

11. V's $=$ .0999 to .185, all p's $>$ .06.

12. V's $=$ .141 to .357, all p's $<$ .01.

13. V's $=$ .155 to .323, all p's $<$ .001.

14. V's $=$ .223 to .439, all p's $<$ .001.

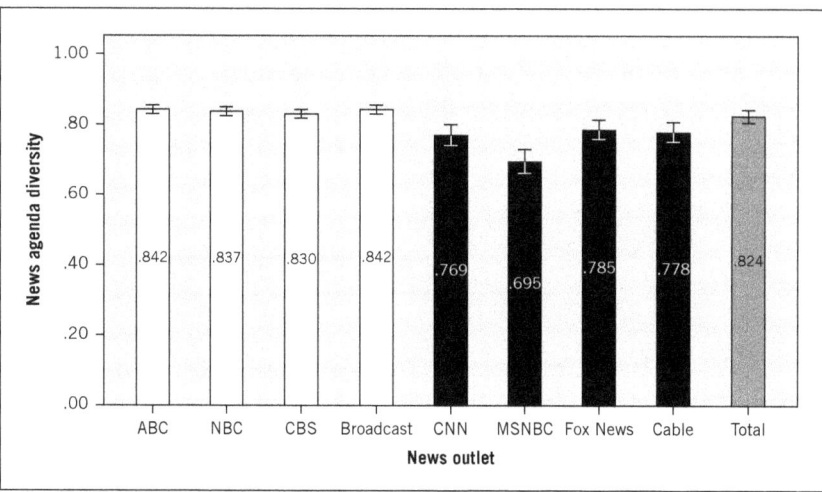

Figure 5.1. News agenda diversity by outlet, 2007–2012. *Note:* Error bars are 95 percent confidence intervals. "Broadcast" indicates broadcast news as a whole. "Cable" indicates cable news as a whole. "Total" indicates all outlets combined.

that is more diverse than any of its cable counterparts.[15] In other words, broadcast networks spread their attention more evenly across more issues despite their relatively brief windows for news. Although they have much more time to present public affairs information, the agendas of cable channels are less diverse. This is true not only when individual networks are compared to one another but also when the cable news agenda as a whole is compared to the broadcast news agenda as a whole.[16] Moreover, cable news has not diversified the news agenda. The diversity of the overall television news agenda (the agendas of all six networks combined) is actually less than the diversity of the broadcast news agenda alone.[17]

Differences in Issue Coverage

Taken together, these results suggest there is not a great deal of difference between the issue agenda of broadcast news and the issue agendas of the

---

15. All three broadcast outlets have greater agenda diversity than MSNBC (all t's > 8.66, all p's $< .001$), Fox News (all t's > 5.87, all p's $< .001$), and CNN (all t's > 6.37, all p's $< .001$).
16. Broadcast news as a whole has greater agenda diversity than individual cable news networks: CNN, $t(39) = 7.42, p < .001$; Fox News, $t(39) = 7.02, p < .01$; and MSNBC, $t(39) = 9.17, p < .001$. The overall broadcast agenda is also more diverse than the overall cable agenda, $t(39) = 7.17, p < .001$.
17. $t(39) = 3.91, p < .001$.

cable news outlets. However, since the evidence from the broadcast context has shown that some issues have larger agenda-setting effects and, through them, greater impact on the diversity of the public agenda, we need to consider where those differences lie. Since we are interested in the general trends of issue coverage on each network rather than similarities and differences in coverage of a specific time period, we can use the entire Pew News Coverage Index to document which networks pay more or less attention to which issues. Chapter 4's analysis offers some guidance about which issues tend to fragment the public agenda and which issues tend to focus it when they receive more coverage from broadcast news. Using this as a guide, we combined news topics into four categories: those that tend to focus the public agenda (macroeconomics and international affairs, except for defense news about U.S. involvement in the Iraq and Afghan wars), those that tend to fragment it (health, crime, defense, and terrorism), those that are neutral in effect, and those that do not correspond well to issue categories in the "most important problem" question.

Broadcast news paid more attention to historically agenda-focusing issues than did cable news. These issues made up almost 30 percent of broadcast news stories, compared with not quite 20 percent for MSNBC and 23 percent for Fox News; CNN's proportion, just more than 29 percent, was most comparable with (and not significantly different from) that of broadcast news. The reverse was true for issues that have diversified the agenda in the past. Fox News led the way with more than 23 percent of its coverage about these issues, followed by CNN and MSNBC, each at almost 22 percent, all significantly more than the not quite 20 percent of broadcast stories on these issues. The most notable difference was on crime, which accounted for nearly 11 percent of Fox News stories and nearly 9 percent of CNN stories, compared to less than 7 percent for broadcast. All three cable news outlets had more coverage of domestic terrorism than did broadcast news.

These patterns are intuitively appealing because they confirm the conventional wisdom about the potential of cable news to offer dissimilar and perhaps diversifying agendas: partisan cable news had less coverage of focusing issues and more of diversifying issues than broadcast. However, the differences in coverage of issues that tend to fragment the public agenda are not very big. Many differences are probably statistically significant only because the Pew News Coverage Index contains tens of thousands of news stories. Moreover, the coverage patterns do not account for the observed relationships in Table 5.2 between public attention to cable news and the diversity of the public agenda. They do not explain why attention to MSNBC, which pays the least amount of attention to focusing issues and is similar to Fox in its attention to issues that diversify, is related to a more focused public agenda. Nor do they explain why the similar news agendas of the partisan networks have opposing relationships with public agenda diversity. Looking instead at where the largest difference lies provides better clues about how the cable news agenda relates to the public agenda.

The biggest difference between broadcast and cable news is the amount of coverage they devote to campaigns. The category of campaigns, elections, and politics occupied less than 10 percent of the broadcast news agenda. In contrast, MSNBC devoted more than 28 percent of its coverage to this category, far more than any other outlet. Fox News was next at almost 19 percent, followed by CNN at more than 17 percent. This explains why MSNBC, which brands itself as "The Place for Politics," has the most distinctive agenda. It also goes a long way toward explaining why MSNBC, Fox News, and CNN have less diverse agendas than broadcast news does. Moreover, this may help explain why attention to partisan cable news has not contributed to a more diverse public agenda in recent years and why attention to MSNBC is associated with a more focused public agenda. Over three-quarters of the campaign category consisted of election coverage, most of which was not coded to allow us to identify it as coverage of a specific issue. Previous content analyses have found the most common type of election coverage, well ahead of policy coverage, is of the horse race: who is ahead, who is gaining or losing ground, and why (Benoit, Stein, and Hansen 2005; Farnsworth and Lichter 2010; Patterson 1993). Consequently, horse race coverage is unlikely to have agenda-setting effects that add diversity to the public agenda. There is, in fact, some statistical support for this interpretation. The public agenda has tended to be more focused in election years than nonelection years, a tendency not in evidence before the advent of partisan cable news.[18]

Harder to explain, given the overall similarities of news agendas and the focusing effects of election coverage, is the tendency of Fox News to fragment the public agenda. It airs less campaign coverage than MSNBC,

---

18. MSNBC and Fox News both launched in late 1996. From 1997 through 2014, the public agenda is more focused in election years, both for twenty-category H (Election $M = .749$, $SD = .037$ versus nonelection $M = .762$, $SD = .044$), t (169) $= 1.797$, $p < .05$, one-tailed, and for five-category H (Election $M = .716$, $SD = .083$ versus nonelection $M = .747$, $SD = .096$), t (169) $= 1.873$, $p < .05$, one-tailed. Before 1997, there is no such difference. If anything, the public agenda broadens slightly in election years, both for twenty-category H (Election $M = .646$, $SD = .097$ versus nonelection $M = .637$, $SD = .101$), t (81) $= -.361$, ns, and for five-category H (Election $M = .685$, $SD = .095$ versus nonelection $M = .642$, $SD = .144$), t (81) $= -1.579$, ns.

leaving more room in its news agenda to cover issues that could potentially fragment the public agenda. It pays the most attention to issues that are known to diversify the public agenda, but its difference from other networks in this regard is small. It is worth pointing out that our documentation of cable news agendas spans 2007–2012, and in that era, attention to Fox News is not associated with a more diverse public agenda. We cannot know what the Fox News agenda was like in the network's early years, and it is only over the entirety of its history that we observe a relationship to rising public agenda diversity. Some pundits have suggested that in its early years, Fox News was "all terrorism, all the time," and evidence from Chapter 4 suggests that news attention to terrorism is associated with greater public agenda diversity. Williams and Delli Carpini (2011) argue that partisan cable news first drew high levels of public attention during the Clinton-Lewinsky government scandal, and increasing public concern about government is associated with a more diverse public agenda.[19] The history of the public agenda documented in Chapter 2 reveals that public concern about government has risen dramatically in the early twenty-first century, but in recent years, Fox News's agenda has not been terribly distinctive from other news networks in the amount of attention it pays to government scandals. Thus, the distinctive relationship between Fox News and a more diverse public agenda may not have continued as other networks began covering major news events such as Hurricane Katrina and the BP oil disaster as instances of government failure and malfeasance.

Part of what makes election coverage such a likely suspect in explaining the counterintuitive finding that MSNBC has in recent years focused the public agenda and Fox News has failed to diversify it is that high levels of coverage coincided with higher ratings. Ratings rose significantly during election years for Fox News and MSNBC but not CNN or broadcast news.[20] If what makes an outlet's agenda distinctive also attracts viewers, it makes an issue-content explanation for the relationship between outlet ratings and public agenda diversity more plausible. However, distinctiveness is not always associated with greater public agenda diversity, as the campaign news on cable reveals. Moreover, events spectacular enough to generate high levels of audience attention are likely to be significant

---

19. In our 254-poll Gallup "most important problem" data set, $r = .44, p < .001$.

20. For Fox News, election $M = 1.56$, $SD = .60$ versus nonelection $M = 1.39$, $SD = .49$, $t(169) = 1.814$, $p < .05$, one-tailed. For MSNBC, election $M = .60$, $SD = .30$ versus nonelection $M = .48$, $SD = .19$, $t(169) = 2.309$, $p < .05$. For CNN, election $M = .83$, $SD = .31$ versus nonelection $M = .85$, $SD = .61$, $t(201) = -.168$, ns. For broadcast, election $M = 24.61$, $SD = 9.67$ versus nonelection $M = 23.59$, $SD = 8.57$, $t(252) = .791$, ns.

enough to produce great similarity among news agendas, which could help explain why rising levels of public attention to cable news do not consistently diversify the public agenda. It also speaks to the ways in which people use news and how events, if they are significant enough, can drive attention to the news, which may then help focus the public agenda, a point that Chapter 6 further discusses.

Public Attention, News Agendas, and the Public Agenda

The evidence presented so far suggests that both the amount of public attention to news and the content of news agendas can contribute to public agenda diversity, which raises questions about the relative impacts of public attention to news and of news agendas on the public agenda. Even if news agendas are highly diverse, they are unlikely to fragment the public agenda if the public is not paying attention to news. Conversely, even if the public is paying attention to news, a focused public agenda may not emerge if numerous issues with sizable agenda-setting effects are on the news agenda. So which is the more substantial contributor to public agenda diversity?

First, let us consider the relative effects of broadcast news agenda setting as it is measured in the Policy Agendas Project data (from Chapter 4) and of public attention to news, in the form of ratings, on the diversity of the public agenda.[21] Since our analysis shows news agendas across news networks are very similar, for this analysis we look at public attention to television news by summing the ratings for all the broadcast networks. Using multiple regression, we can see the independent effects of agenda setting (the similarity between the overall news agenda and the public agenda) and of public attention to news across a time frame from 1975 (the earliest ratings data) through 2010 (the most recent agenda-setting data). When we look only at broadcast news agenda-setting effects, we find that they are strongly and positively related with agenda diversity.[22] The bigger broadcast news' agenda-setting effect, the more diverse the public agenda is. Yet when we add public attention to news as a competing predictor, its strong negative effect[23] on public agenda diversity swamps the agenda-setting effect, which becomes an insignificant contributor to explaining public agenda

---

21. We insert quarterly agenda-setting effects from the Policy Agendas data into our own Gallup coding and ratings data set ($N = 198$) by the quarter in which the poll was taken.
22. $\beta = .42, p < .001$.
23. Broadcast news attention $\beta = -.77, p < .001$; final beta for agenda setting, $\beta = -.05, ns$.

diversity. This suggests that over the whole time frame, it is the declining public attention to television news rather than news media agenda setting that has contributed the most to increasing public agenda diversity.

However, we get a different picture when we take into account what Table 5.2 tells us about the changing consequences of attention to news for public agenda diversity during different time frames. From 1975 to 1987, the more attention television news received and the more its agenda was reflected in public concern, the more focused the public agenda was, although attention had a bigger impact and the agenda-setting impact was only marginally significant.[24] Beginning in 1988, the model changed in two important ways. Not only did the focusing effect of public attention to television news weaken, but the agenda-setting effect of broadcast television news now served to diversify the public agenda.[25] In the period from 2004 to 2010, both attention to news and the agenda-setting effect of broadcast news are associated with a more diverse public agenda, although the effect of attention is relatively stronger and the effect of agenda setting is not statistically significant.[26] These findings suggest that whereas a falling-apart explanation may account for rising public agenda diversity while broadcast television dominated, a driven-apart explanation helps account for more recent growth in public agenda diversity.

The fact that both public attention and news agenda setting are associated with a more diverse public agenda in the last time period helps explain the finding in Table 5.2 that attention to broadcast news tended to diversify the public agenda in the 2004–2014 period. Although the economy was the dominant issue on the public agenda during this time frame, broadcast news tends to be a headline service offering a broad overview of the events of the day. Its attention to issues other than the economy, provided those issues generated positive agenda-setting effects, could expand a contracting public agenda by making people aware of other issues and events beyond their narrow focus.

It is also possible that the content of news agendas could influence the amount of public attention to news, and this, too, would have consequences for public agenda diversity. At particular moments in history, the public may pay more attention to television news. A phenomenon like September 11, 2001, when entertainment programming virtually ceased as

---

24. For broadcast news attention, $\beta = -.51$, $p < .001$; for agenda setting, $\beta = -.21$, $p < .10$.

25. For broadcast news attention, $\beta = -.18$, $p < .10$; for agenda setting, $\beta = .24$, $p < .05$.

26. For broadcast news attention, $\beta = .56$, $p < .001$; for agenda setting, $\beta = .12$, ns.

networks went dark or carried news feeds from other channels, would produce a great deal of attention to news with a highly focused agenda, regardless of the network. Similarly, the onset of the 2008 economic crisis both encouraged Fox News and MSNBC to hew more closely to the overall news agenda, as Table 5.3 shows, and increased public attention to news. This confluence of forces may have helped neutralize the tendency of Fox News to fragment the public agenda and contribute to MSNBC's tendency to focus the public agenda in the most recent time frame. Notably, over the period covered by the Pew data set, the higher the news ratings, the greater the correlations between the news agendas of different networks.[27]

In contrast, if a network were offering a distinctive news agenda during a period of public crisis, it might diversify the public issue agenda, and it could produce different effects at the twenty-category level than at the five-category level. CNN's coverage of the U.S. wars in the Middle East offer a tempting example but not enough content data to draw a conclusion. The events that produced the highest levels of public attention to the network were the 1990 Gulf War and the 2003 Iraq War. As we see in Chapter 3, in the context of the Great Recession, when categories are essentialized, effect sizes can get bigger, and, as we see in Chapter 4, coverage of U.S. military activity produces substantial agenda-setting effects. Here, when the agenda is measured at the twenty-category level, CNN's extensive coverage of the "hot" wars may counterbalance the broad "headline service" coverage of broadcast news and bring increased focus to the public agenda. At the five-category level, however, CNN's extensive coverage may counterbalance the domestic emphasis of network news and make the public agenda more diverse.

In drawing these conclusions, we should nevertheless acknowledge an important limitation of the Pew News Coverage Index. It documents the news environment in remarkable depth, but only for a relatively short period of time. Although the time frame spanned a bit more than a presidential election cycle, which was crucial for understanding the agendas of partisan news, it also coincided with an important historical event: the Great Recession of 2007–2009. Data from the Gallup "most important problem" question shows that this period is marked by an unusual narrowing of the public agenda, and a similar phenomenon may have emerged in the news agenda. Testing for this possibility within the data set is difficult because the election cycle and news about the recession would overlap—at just about the time the effects of the recession began to abate,

---

27. CNN ($r = .60, p < .001$), MSNBC ($r = .32, p < .05$), Fox News ($r = .29, p < .05$, one-tailed), broadcast news ($r = .30, p < .05$, one-tailed), cable news ($r = .44, p < .01$), and all news ratings combined ($r = .59, p < .001$).

which might result in a more expansive news agenda, the 2012 presidential election heated up, which could have contracted the news agenda, particularly on cable. The enormity of the economic difficulties might also have muted the differences in partisan cable news and between the cable news agenda and the broadcast news agenda, although the partisan media's abiding focus on elections and politics suggests their similarities during the 2007–2012 time period are probably characteristic.

Conclusion

In the 1970s and 1980s, declining attention to broadcast news explains far more of the increase in public agenda diversity than does news content, suggesting that, in this era, the public agenda was falling apart. However, by the late 1980s, it is the content of the broadcast news agenda rather than the amount of public attention to news that does more to explain rising public agenda diversity, indicating that the public agenda was driven apart. Nevertheless, the evidence in this chapter does not support a driven-apart model of public agenda diversity that features partisan cable news as the sole driver. In fact, the issue agendas of news sources across the spectrum are quite similar, and the issue agendas of partisan cable news are more similar to one another than they are to other news sources. Cable news is less, not more, diverse in its issue agenda than broadcast news. Although Fox News shows signs of fragmenting the public agenda over the course of the network's history and CNN is associated with a more diverse public agenda at the five-category level during the partisan news era, these effects do not appear consistently in all time frames. Indeed, CNN has had modest focusing effects for most of its history, and MSNBC has had a very strong relationship with a more focused public agenda, regardless of the time frame or of the agenda diversity measure. In contrast, it is attention to broadcast news that is associated with public agenda fragmentation in the most recent decade. Since the available data show that in recent years, news agendas have been highly similar across networks, it seems likely that changes in the overall news agenda, rather than differences between news agendas, drive public agenda fragmentation.

The relationship between news agenda diversity and public attention to news helps explain why attention to news, when considered on its own, is associated with a more focused public agenda. Not only are the cable news agendas highly similar to the broadcast news agenda, but the public tends to pay the most attention to news at moments when the news agenda is most consistent. Contrastingly, when news agendas are the most distinctive, the public is not paying much attention, so news agenda differences between networks are less likely to fragment the public agenda. In other words, cable news agendas per se may not contribute all that much to public agenda diversity.

In Chapter 4, we see some evidence that during a time when audience attention was fading, the broadcast news agenda began to pay more attention to issues with larger agenda-setting effects, which in turn began to drive apart the public agenda. This leads to the counterintuitive conclusion that the more attention the public pays to news, the more diverse the public agenda becomes. The idea of news as an engine for focusing the public agenda does not appear to hold. This is not because the public fails to attend to news but because the news agenda does not necessarily generate consensus on the most important issue.

The complex relationship between when the public attends to news and what the news agenda is like in those moments raises the question of whether the news media can exert a focusing effect on the public agenda under the right set of circumstances. It is to this question that we next turn.

6

Building Consensus on Public Priorities

Can the Public Agenda Be Focused?

By the early 1990s, both declining public attention to television news and the television news agenda itself were associated with a diversifying public agenda. As the news paid less attention to international affairs and the public paid less attention to news, public concern spread more evenly over more issues. Elihu Katz (1996) and Max McCombs (1997), as well as Donald Shaw and Bradley Hamm (1997), feared that the news media no longer built public consensus around a short list of public problems. Although this was true, it was not simply a product of expanding media choice or of shrinking news audiences. The public problems that now received more news attention were problems about which it was easier to raise public concern. As a result, the agenda-setting power of broadcast news seemed to fragment the public agenda rather than focus it. However, from these scholars' perspective, a different question now arises: Is it still possible to focus public concern? For example, if a national crisis arose, such as a war, an economic depression or an epidemic, would the public agenda narrow its focus?

From the perspective of critical scholars who raise normative concerns about the media's leadership of public opinion comes an important related question: Which social actors might have the ability to focus public attention in the wake of these changes to the media system? These scholars raised concerns that the news media ignored public opinion (e.g., Bennett 1990), shaped public perspectives in ways that supported those in power (e.g., Entman 1991), or drew attention to issues inconsistently, making it impossible for the public to evaluate them fairly (e.g., Entman 2012). More broadly, they suggested that political power and commercial incentives shaped the news rather than the importance of underlying issues (e.g., Herman and Chomsky 1988; Uscinski 2014). Following this reasoning, the growing diversity of the public agenda had certain advantages. To borrow from Abraham Lincoln, it appeared that it was no longer possible to "fool all of the people all of the time." However, it was also possible that the changes in the media system made things worse: that the news media, with their growing attention to issues that had greater agenda-setting effects, still distracted the public from important issues, and that public concern failed to consolidate around pressing public problems.

Looking at the evidence presented to this point, narrowing the public agenda to focus on a few important issues seems like a tall order. Not only would focusing the public agenda buck the overall trend of the later twentieth and early twenty-first centuries; times of national crisis since 2000 have not necessarily focused the public agenda. When we look at the public agenda in the 1970s and 1980s, we see moments where it narrows very nearly to a single issue. In October 1978, two-thirds of responses to the most important problem question named money. In other words, almost nothing else mattered. In January 1981, public concern was similarly focused on money. This level of concern emerged in light of a national economy that was, at that time, the worst since the Great Depression of the 1930s and of elite leadership by Presidents Jimmy Carter and Ronald Reagan. In 1989, critical scholars may have been unnerved when President George H. W. Bush's "crack speech" generated intense public concern about crime. Following the speech, more than 60 percent of responses named law and order as the most important problem. However, this is the last moment of extraordinary public focus. National crises like the terrorist attacks of September 11, 2001, the war in Iraq, and the Great Recession did not generate nearly as focused a public agenda. In October 2001, fewer than 40 percent of responses named terrorism as the nation's most important problem. The February 2007 troop surge aimed at ending the protracted war in Iraq produced the greatest level of public concern about the war as measured with the "most important problem" question. In the poll taken that month, less than one-third of responses named the Middle East as the most important problem. The Great Recession was the most serious financial crisis since the Great Depression, and it is notable that during the Recession, the public agenda, which had tended to expand for the previous three decades, became more focused. However, public focus was never as great as it had been during the high inflation and high unemployment of the late 1970s and early 1980s. In November 2008, about 55 percent of responses named the economy as the most important problem. Thus, even substantial national crises seem not to produce the level of focused public concern witnessed during the Cold War era, before the media revolution.

In this chapter, we look more closely at whether and how the public agenda might become more focused, given the modern media environment, and at the social institutions that might be capable of focusing it. In so doing, we articulate the ways in which public attention to news and the news agenda itself interact to influence public agenda diversity.

Refocusing Public Attention: Sounding a Burglar Alarm

The transformed media environment seemed to be restructuring public opinion as people watched less news, and broadcast news, in turn, increased its coverage of issues more likely to provoke public concern. However, concerns that the public might not pay much attention to public affairs are not new, and the models of democratic citizenship they gave rise to offer some insight into how the interaction of public attention and news content might serve to focus the public agenda at critical moments.

Long before the modern, multichannel, multimedia environment emerged, there was clear evidence that many, even most, citizens lacked basic knowledge of public affairs. Anthony Downs's economic theory of democracy, published in 1957, argues that the return on an investment in public affairs information for an individual citizen is so low that it makes no rational sense to gather it. A single vote is very unlikely to change the outcome of an election, so there is not much point in casting a vote, let alone casting an informed one. Philip Converse (1964) demonstrated that most citizens did not think about politics in terms of ideology, as political scientists and politicians did, and that when confronted with public opinion surveys, they commonly offered what he called "non-opinions." In the mid-1990s, Michael Delli Carpini and Scott Keeter's (1996) hugely influential study *What Americans Know about Politics and Why It Matters* confirmed that few Americans knew much about politics and that there were large gaps between informed and uninformed people (see also Tichenor, Donohue, and Olien 1970). Extending this line of research into the evolving media environment, Markus Prior (2007) found that the gaps between informed and uninformed people had expanded as media choice grew.

These consistent empirical findings gave rise to new models of democratic citizenship. The observed low levels of public knowledge were problematic for normative democratic theory that envisioned citizens as informed about public affairs, holding elected leaders accountable and making informed voting choices. The newer models sought to accommodate low levels of citizen knowledge. These models varied in how they envisioned the relationship between the public and the government and in the role they assigned to the news media. Samuel Popkin's "reasoning voter" model portrays citizens as voters who can pick up on partisan cues and other heuristics to get by on "low-information rationality," casting ballots in line with their interests (1991, 7). News media play a minor role as voters gather information on public problems from daily life and interpersonal discussion. Benjamin Page and Robert Shapiro's (1992) rational public model suggests that Americans can be more than mere voters, providing meaningful guidance on policy preferences to public officials by being subject experts rather than generalists. People with an interest and a stake in a particular issue (such as education or the environment) could collect information on that issue and offer informed guidance to public officials making policy in that area. These citizens would need very informative news media to keep them abreast of developments in their area of specialization. Both models resolve the problem of uninformed citizens by assuming that the errors they make will cancel each other out (see also Converse 1990), but both founder on the problem of information inequalities between citizens. Larry Bartels (1996) demonstrates that the actual electorate behaves quite differently from a fully informed electorate, displaying, among other things, a bias in favor of incumbents. Scott Althaus (2003) shows a fully informed public would have quite different public policy preferences than the actual public.

Michael Schudson's (1998) concept of the monitorial citizen differs from models developed in political science, in that it focuses on attention rather than information. He argues that normative democratic theories that envisage highly informed citizens are the product of a historically specific moment, progressivism, and that at other points in history, democracy had functioned with low levels of citizen knowledge. Since the progressive model of a highly informed citizen is clearly a pipe dream and has negative effects on political participation, Schudson (2007) maintains that a better, more realistic model might be a citizen who monitors the situation and acts when necessary, whether by voting or in some other way. Schudson paints the monitorial citizen in this way:

> Picture parents watching small children at the community pool. They are not gathering information; they are keeping an eye on the scene. They look inactive, but they are poised for action if action is required. The monitorial citizen is not an absentee citizen but watchful, even while he or she is doing something else. (1998, 311)

The key to effective low-information democracy in this model is to attract citizens' attention to emerging public problems so they can act. Monitorial citizens need a news media that fulfills Harold Lasswell's (1948) surveillance function of communication, keeping an eye on the political and social environment and alerting the public to problems. Although in more recent work Schudson (2015) emphasizes individual and interest group action in response to public problems, his initial formulation of this model resembles the vision of scholars like Katz (1996) and McCombs (1997), who see news functioning to build consensus about public priorities.

John Zaller (2003) dubs the expectations implied in Schudson's (1998) model the "burglar alarm" model of news and contrasts it to the "full news standard," required by the progressives and by Page and Shapiro's (1992) rational public model. Responding to concerns about the growth of "soft" news, Zaller argues in favor of "intensely focused, dramatic, and entertaining" news coverage that "breaks through the fog of disjointed news and engages the attention of the Monitorial Citizen" (121–122). Ideally, "news would penetrate every corner of public space so few could miss it" (122). The intense coverage would "focus public attention on issues of importance" rather than leading citizens on "wide-ranging patrols of political terrain" (121). For Zaller, the shared public priorities generated by the burglar alarm would be converted into democratic action via mass political behavior: voting.

Lance Bennett (2003) critiques Zaller's initial formulation of the burglar alarm model on three key dimensions. First, he says that Zaller defines the realm of citizen action too narrowly because many social problems occur outside the context of an imminent election. His subsequent work (Bennett, Lawrence, and Livingston 2007) on news media coverage of events such as Hurricane Katrina and prisoner torture at Abu Ghraib offers examples of the kinds of events that might be worthy of public alarm but did not emerge in an election context. In this, Bennett recognizes that public accountability requires mass political behavior in the form of focused public attention, whether the accountability mechanism is an election or takes some other form.

Second, Bennett (2003) rejects Zaller's contention that it is up to journalists, in consultation with political elites and interest groups, to set the public agenda by choosing which issues to sound the alarm about. This normative critique suggests the news media might focus public attention on the wrong things, either because they made poor decisions or because they were manipulated by political elites. Third, Bennett argues that the burglar alarm sounds almost continuously, in part because of the proliferation of internet news and twenty-four-hour cable channels, which have spurred more "look-over-the-shoulder competition between organizations that trigger uncontrollable frenzies, or, to return to the metaphor, false alarms" (133). In contrast to Bennett's normative critique, this argument suggests that the burglar alarm fails to work at all because the continual sounding of the alarm no longer generates public concern.

Although the debate over the roles of information and attention in democratic citizenship is surely far from over, the burglar alarm model is a remarkably good fit for the modern media system, in which attention and information are distinctive dimensions. Unlike the mass media era, in which sustained public attention was required to obtain and absorb campaign and public affairs information (Patterson 2002), online media transform the temporal dimensions of public affairs information, disconnecting attention from information. In an online world, whenever one's attention is caught, information on the object of attention can be acquired with relative ease. If one does not tune into a campaign until a few weeks before an election, basic biographical information or policy position information can be acquired online, even if it was published months earlier. However, catching people's attention is harder than ever before (Prior 2007; Webster 2014), making it reasonable to ask whether the burglar alarm still works—in other words, whether the news media can still focus the public agenda.

Pablo Boczkowski, Eugenia Mitchelstein, and Martin Walter (2012) test a relatively narrow version of Zaller's (2003) burglar alarm model, exploring differences between how journalists and citizens prioritize public affairs news. They find journalists place a much higher priority on public affairs information than citizens do. However, the gap between citizens' and journalists' priorities for public affairs narrows as an election nears, with both groups paying more attention to public affairs than they do at other times. The researchers interpret this as evidence the burglar alarm works, though they are concerned low audience demand for public affairs information might mean journalism chronically underproduces it. Their test suggests the news might serve monitorial citizens as Zaller hoped, by focusing public attention on an election. However by categorizing all news as "public affairs" or "not public affairs," and equating news seekers with monitorial citizens, they limit their findings. Their test is only a rough fit for the burglar alarm model's aspiration of news penetrating every corner of society and focusing public attention on an issue of public concern. Moreover, as Bennett (2003) might point out, drawing public attention to an election may not be democratically adequate because important events can happen when elections are not imminent.

Testing the Alarm

A test of the burglar alarm model truer to the richness of its theoretical origins might ask whether a narrowing news agenda (not just more focused on public affairs but on a shorter list of issues) is associated with a more focused public agenda. Rather than exploring the effects of news on viewers, it would explore the effects of news on the public, regardless of how they encountered news content, in keeping with Zaller's (2003) notion of news that permeates social spaces and cannot be avoided. Under these conditions and in this clamorous media world where public affairs information can so easily be avoided (Prior 2007), does the burglar alarm work? Can public attention be focused on a narrow range of issues, an important first step in taking collective, democratic, political action to hold public figures accountable electorally or otherwise?

We can test the burglar alarm model using the forty months of news coverage data from the Pew News Coverage Index we use to test for the similarity between news agendas in Chapter 5 and the Gallup "most important problem" question public agenda data we use to understand the history and character of the public agenda in Chapters 2 and 3.

First, we need to define what sounding the alarm would look like. Given the "less top-down . . . more distributed information system" observed by Bennett (2003, 133) and Williams and Delli Carpini (2011), the "burglar alarm" can be thought of as news consistency: the similarity of news agendas across different outlets. Tables 5.3 and 5.4 offer an intuitive illustration of what very consistent and very inconsistent news agendas look like. To measure consistency, we correlate the networks' news agendas with one another. For each month, the news agendas of each outlet (ABC, CBS, NBC, CNN, Fox News, and MSNBC) are correlated with one another to see how similar they are. Every month, there are fifteen correlations, and the average of those correlations is the "news consistency" for that month.[1] High levels of consistency between individual news outlets indicate the alarm is going off, and the more consistent the news is, the louder the alarm. This may sound like a dubious assumption, given Chapter 5's finding that news agendas across news networks tend to be fairly consistent in general. News could potentially be quite consistent across news outlets without being especially focused on a small number

---

1. The correlations are computed as Pearson's product-moment correlations. They consider the outlets as the variables and the twenty-six issues as the cases. The correlations are high when two outlets give similar levels of coverage to the same issues. Those correlations are averaged to create the news consistency measure for each month ($M = .80$, $SD = .07$, Cronbach's $\alpha = .92$).

of big issues. However, in reality, it usually does not work out that way. More consistent news agendas are strongly related to reduced news agenda diversity,[2] which makes sense when one thinks about how news works. On an average news day, although the institutional rules of journalism mean different news organizations will make relatively similar choices, there is a certain amount of flexibility about which stories get covered and how much attention each gets. If a presidential candidate holds a rally, a wildfire is still burning in a Western state, and a car company issues a recall, different networks may assign different priorities and pay different amounts of attention to those events. On a big news day, however, when a passenger jet crashes or a mass shooting occurs, there will be much less difference of opinion on what the day's most important story is, and it will dominate the news programs. The bigger the story, the more consistent the news choices are and the less diverse the news agenda tends to be. In the time frame covered by the Pew News Coverage Index, 2007 through the middle of 2012, the issue is often the economy because the index encompasses the Great Recession. However, the BP oil spill, massive earthquakes in Haiti and Japan, and the legislative fight over President Obama's Affordable Care Act also took place during this time frame.

Next, we need a way to match the public agenda to the news agenda since the twenty-six categories used to measure news agendas in the Pew data do not quite match the twenty categories used to measure the public agenda. The key conceptual problem here is that news agendas are coded by story topic, while the public agenda is coded as "problems." Christopher Wlezien (2005) points out that the "most important problem" formulation for measuring the public agenda confounds at least two dimensions of salience: the extent to which something is "important" and the extent to which it is a "problem." One place this mismatch emerges, for example, is in news coverage of election campaigns. While the campaigns may be quite salient for the public, survey respondents are unlikely to name campaigns as a most important problem. Thus, matching the news agenda to the public agenda loses some sensitivity in the coding because some categories from one data set have no parallel in the other, and, in some cases, categories must be combined to create compatible operational definitions across the two data sets. However, many categories that were very important during the time frame under study can be matched quite satisfactorily,

---

2. News consistency's correlation with the agenda diversity (H) of every news outlet is significant, sizable, and negative: ABC ($r = -.62, p < .001$), NBC ($r = -.68, p < .001$), CBS ($r = -.65, p < .001$), CNN ($r = -.60, p < .001$), MSNBC ($r = -.45, p < .01$), Fox News ($r = -.59, p < .001$), broadcast news ($r = -.70, p < .001$), cable news ($r = -.61, p < .001$), and all television news combined ($r = -.71, p < .001$).

including the economy (during the Great Recession), health (during policy debates over the Affordable Care Act), international affairs (as the Iraq War wound down), and social relations (as the movement for gay marriage gained momentum). Table 6.1 depicts how ten comparable coding categories were created across the two data sets. To help ensure we are looking at the news media's influence on the public agenda, we correlate the news agenda from one month to the public agenda from the following month (Wanta and Hu 1994), which is our measure of the agenda-setting effect. The stronger the correlation, the bigger the agenda-setting effect of news on the public.

Table 6.1. Consolidated agenda categories for news and public agendas

Consolidated categories	Gallup "most important problem"	Pew news agenda
Economy/Business/Jobs	Jobs Money General Economic	Business Economy/Economics
Welfare/Social Relations	Welfare Social Relations	Religion Race/Gender/Gay Issues Immigration Additional Domestic Affairs
Health	Health	Health/Medicine
Education	Education	Education
Environment/Technology	Environment Technology	Environment Transportation Science and Technology
Crime/Courts/Legal	Law and Order	Court/Legal System Crime
International Affairs	General International Soviet/Europe Asia Middle East Latin America/Africa	U.S. Foreign Affairs Foreign (Non-U.S.)
Terrorism	Terrorism	Domestic Terrorism
Government	Government/Political Spending	Government Agencies/Legislatures
Media	Media	Media
Excluded	Miscellaneous	Campaigns/Elections/Politics Defense/Military (Domestic) Development/Sprawl Disasters/Accidents Celebrity/Entertainment Lifestyle Sports U.S. Miscellaneous

Finally, we need to address Bennett's (2003) critique that the burglar alarm is "always" going off. From a certain perspective, he is right. The news is always drawing public attention to some subset of issues or problems as it surveils the social world, so the idea that the burglar alarm is either "on" or "off" presents some conceptual problems. While increasing news consistency might represent a "louder" alarm in our metaphor, there is also the question of how loud the alarm has to be before it provokes public response. Regression models, like the ones we have used elsewhere in this book, work well for illustrating how linear changes in one variable, like a progressively louder alarm, are related to linear changes in another variable, like public agenda diversity. However, they will not capture "tipping points" or thresholds. If the public ignores an alarm until it is "loud enough," scatterplot figures can show us what "loud enough" looks like. Our analysis uses both approaches to better understand whether and how news can focus the public agenda.

Sounding the Alarm

Although news consistency is strongly related to news agenda diversity, news consistency is not a significant predictor of public agenda diversity on its own. Instead, it works through the now-familiar ways in which the public encounters news: attention and agenda setting. Table 6.2 displays a regression equation that predicts public agenda diversity using four variables: overall news consistency, the diversity of an outlet's news agenda, public attention to that news outlet (measured by ratings),[3] and the agenda-setting effect of the news outlet. Each column represents a news outlet or a group of outlets so that we can see how these variables might function differently for different kinds of news organizations. Recall that multiple regression equations like this one let us look at the unique contribution of each predictor variable to the change in the dependent variable and that the values for each predictor are standardized so that we can compare their influence relative to each other. Bigger numbers (coefficients) mean greater influence. If the value of a predictor is positive, a higher value for that predictor is associated with a more diverse public agenda. For example, the more diverse the cable news agenda is, the more diverse the public agenda is ($\beta = .33, p < .05$). Negative values mean that a higher value for the predictor is associated with a less diverse public agenda. For example, the bigger the agenda-setting effect for cable news, the less diverse the public agenda is ($\beta = -.33, p < .05$). However, if

---

3. See Chapter 5 for an explanation of how public attention to news is measured.

Table 6.2. News agenda predictors of public agenda diversity, by outlet

	ABC	NBC	CBS	CNN	MSNBC	Fox	Broadcast	Cable	Total
Overall news consistency	−.28	−.20	−.17	.29	.09	.17	−.16	.34†	.21
News agenda diversity	−.01	.06	.06	.15	.17	.30†	.10	.33*	.32
Agenda setting	−.50**	−.56**	−.66***	−.10	−.29*	−.42**	−.62***	−.33*	−.20
Ratings	.64***	.71***	.72***	−.65***	−.60***	−.32*	.73***	−.56***	−.25
R^2	.33**	.23**	.34***	.28**	.45***	.39***	.28**	.43***	.10

Note: $N = 40$ months. "Overall news consistency" is the same variable in all models, but the other predictors are outlet-specific. "Agenda setting" is the correlation between an outlet's news agenda and the public agenda. *$p < .05$; **$p < .01$; ***$p < .001$; †approaches significance at $p < .10$.

coefficients are not statistically significant (that is, marked by one or more asterisks), the relationship could be a product of chance rather than an indicator of influence.

Looking at each in turn, it is clear that news consistency on its own does not contribute much to focusing the public agenda. Even when we look at the relationship between news consistency across all news networks and public agenda diversity, without considering other variables, the relationship is not statistically significant.[4] Table 6.2 shows that news consistency is not a significant predictor of public agenda diversity in the regression models for individual news outlets, either.[5] As we have found in earlier analyses, the diversity of the news agenda also does not have a particularly strong relationship with the diversity of the public agenda, although the results of the regression equations here do sometimes reach statistical significance. For cable news (and, marginally, for Fox News), a more diverse news agenda is associated with a more diverse public agenda. A similar relationship appears if we relate the overall television news agenda to the public agenda without taking any other variables into account.[6] However, as the regression equations show, public attention to news and agenda setting are much better predictors of the public agenda's diversity.

At this point, it may once again be useful to think about what the statistics represent in the "real world." A month with "big" news produces more consistent news and less diverse news agendas. A consistent news

---

4. $r = −.24, p = .13$.
5. In the one model where it approaches significance, its sign is positive rather than negative.
6. $r = .28, p < .05$, one-tailed.

agenda also attracts public attention,[7] and as Table 6.2 shows us, more attention to cable news tends to focus the public agenda. The results for broadcast suggest higher broadcast ratings may not have this effect, but, here again, the nature of television news as well as the way in which ratings are measured should be kept in mind. While the cable ratings in Table 6.2 are monthly, the broadcast ratings are annual, and annual ratings are much less sensitive to the ups and downs of the news cycle. Thus, the impact of particular news events, such as the stock market's collapse or the BP oil spill, on public attention to broadcast news cannot be captured with these measures. Moreover, broadcast news has traditionally served as a "headline" service, offering its audience an overview of the day's events. So, no matter how big the news day, broadcast news will almost always offer its audience coverage of several issues or problems.

Since the agenda-setting effect is tied to the frequency of an issue's coverage (McCombs and Shaw 1972; Scheufele 2000), the more consistent the news is, the larger its agenda-setting effect should be. This turns out to be the case: for every network except MSNBC, the more consistent the news is overall, the bigger an outlet's agenda-setting effects are. This is also the case when we pool outlets together: news consistency seems to make the overall agendas of cable news, broadcast news, and news in general more influential on the public agenda.[8] Table 6.2 shows us that, all else being equal, the agenda-setting effects of news are associated with a more focused public agenda for every network except CNN, whose results do not reach statistical significance. Thus, it is through the mechanisms of public attention and agenda setting that consistent news coverage reduces the diversity of the public agenda.

This relationship may seem to be at odds with the analyses in Chapter 4, which show that the growth in the news' agenda-setting effects after the Cold War was associated with a more diverse public agenda. However, those analyses do not take into account the impact of public attention to news. When we look at the analyses in Chapter 4 and focus on only those quarters where public attention as measured by cable ratings are unusually high, the broadcast news agenda's agenda-setting effect tends to focus

---

7. News consistency has a significant and positive relationship with news ratings for every news outlet individually, for every set of outlets, and for all outlets combined: CNN ($r = .60, p < .001$), MSNBC ($r = .32, p < .05$), Fox News ($r = .29, p < .05$, one-tailed), broadcast news ($r = .30, p < .05$, one-tailed), cable news ($r = .44, p < .01$), and all news ratings combined ($r = .59, p < .001$).

8. ABC ($r = .31, p < .05$, one-tailed), NBC ($r = .38, p < .05$), CBS ($r = .36, p < .05$), CNN $r = .47, p < .01$), Fox News ($r = .32, p < .05$), broadcast news ($r = .38, p < .05$), cable news ($r = .41, p < .01$), and all television news combined ($r = .41, p < .05$). The exception was MSNBC ($r = .23, p = .17$).

the public agenda.[9] By the same token, during the five years covered by the Pew News Coverage Index, if we look only at months when cable news ratings are *not* unusually high, the agenda-setting effect of the overall broadcast news agenda tends to diversify the public agenda, which is consistent with the findings in Chapter 4.[10] In other words, in the absence of a "big story," the post–Cold War television news agenda is relatively diverse and tends to emphasize issues associated with larger agenda-setting effects relative to news agendas from the Cold War era. The strength of the agenda-setting effect is related to the *content* of the news agenda and tends to fragment the public agenda. When a "big story" generates a consistent news agenda, it is the *consistency* of the news agenda that is related to the size of the agenda-setting effect, and both the high levels of attention to news and the agenda-setting effect of a consistent news agenda help focus the public's agenda.

How Loud Is Loud?

Using regression equations to look at how the news might serve as a "burglar alarm" for the public and focus public attention on particular issues makes an important assumption: that the alarm works in a linear fashion. To extend the metaphor, for every decibel the alarm grows louder, there is a corresponding increase in the public's reaction to it. But the alarm may not work this way. News is always drawing public attention to public problems, so it is possible that the public does not react until a certain threshold is reached. Because regression assumes steady increases, it cannot tell us whether there is a threshold or what that threshold might be. Creating scatterplots of the forty months of news coverage in this analysis can help us see whether there are tipping points—moments when the public reaction to the alarm grows suddenly stronger.

Since the regression equations indicate that more consistent news focuses the public agenda as it attracts more public attention, the scatterplot in Figure 6.1 shows what happens to news ratings at different levels of news consistency. The measures of broadcast news ratings are not sensitive enough to capture how the size of the audience changes in response to news events, so here we consider just the cable news ratings. Each point on the graph represents one of the forty months included in the analysis.

---

9. When cable news ratings exceed 3.5, broadcast agenda setting is negatively related with public agenda diversity, although not significantly ($r = -.23, p = .41, N = 15$).

10. When cable news ratings are less than 3.5, combined broadcast agenda setting was positively related with public agenda diversity ($r = .28, p < .10, N = 35$).

Building Consensus on Public Priorities

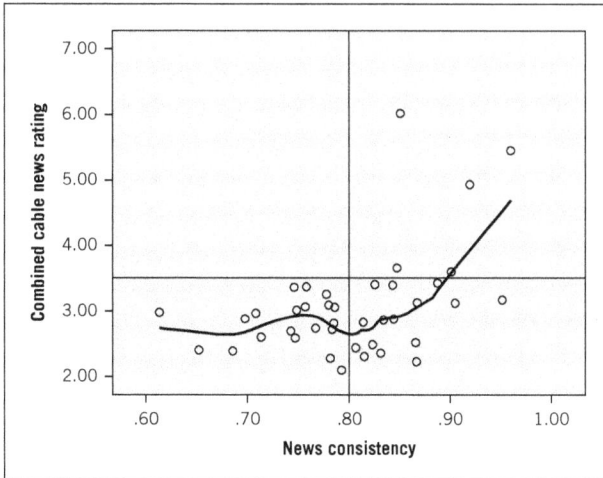

Figure 6.1. The relationship between news consistency (mean Pearson's correlation between outlet agendas) and combined cable news ratings in points, 2007–2012.

To help make the overall pattern clearer, a locally estimated scatterplot smoothing (or LOESS) regression model fit line is applied to the data points. This graph shows that attention to news does not rise steadily as news consistency increases. Instead, once news consistency is above the median level of .80, high levels of public attention to news are much more likely (though not guaranteed). This scatterplot suggests that when news consistency is more than .80, there is about a one in four chance that cable news ratings will exceed 3.5 (about 4 million households). Although high levels of news consistency do not always generate high news ratings, low levels of news consistency never do. Put another way, high levels of news consistency are a necessary but not sufficient cause of high levels of public attention to news.

Figure 6.2 applies the same kind of analysis to agenda-setting effects. Correlations show that more consistent news is associated with stronger agenda-setting effects, but not until news consistency is greater than the median. When news consistency is less than .80, the relationship between consistency and agenda setting actually appears to be negative. Once the news reaches a level of consistency of about .80, agenda-setting effects explain at least half the variance in the public agenda about half the time.[11]

Figures 6.3 and 6.4 are scatterplots examining how public attention to news and the size of the agenda-setting effect are related to the diversity

---

11. In the twenty-one months where news consistency is greater than .79, agenda-setting effects exceed .7071 (the square root of .50) more than half the time (twelve out of twenty-one).

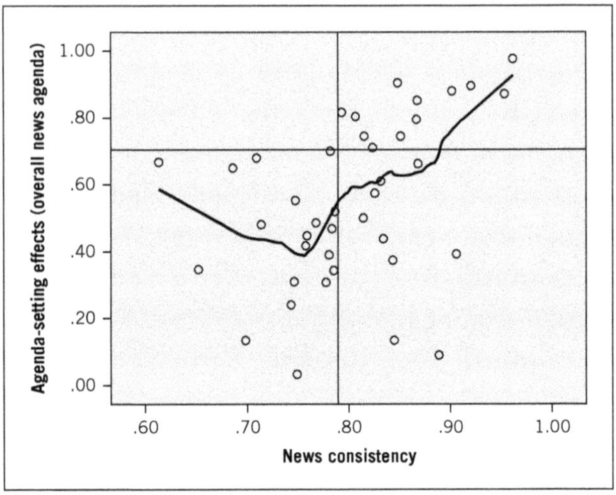

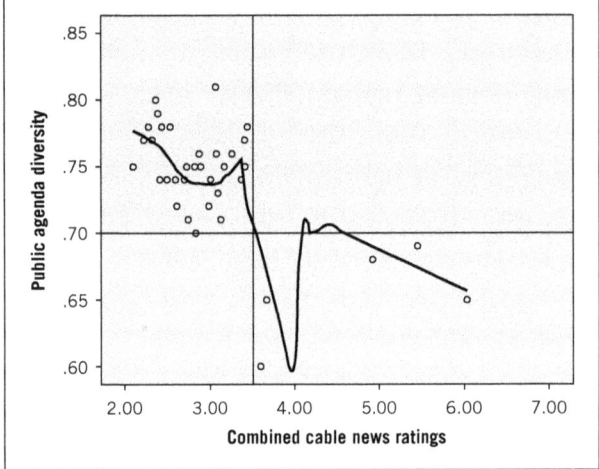

Figure 6.2. The relationship between news consistency (mean Pearson's correlation between outlet agendas) and agenda-setting effect of the overall news agenda, 2007–2012.

Figure 6.3. The relationship between combined cable news ratings in points and public agenda diversity, 2007–2012.

of the public agenda. Here, we expect to see negative relationships: more attention and agenda setting should reduce the diversity of the public agenda if the burglar alarm works. Figure 6.3 shows just how important public attention is. When cable news ratings are less than 3.5, there is no relationship between public attention and agenda diversity. Only when the cable news audience rises to more than 4 million households does public agenda diversity decline. Moreover, when the cable news audience is that big, public agenda diversity *always* declines. This suggests that for the public, the burglar alarm is either on or off; its relative volume makes little difference. This level of public attention to news is both necessary and sufficient for focusing the public agenda.

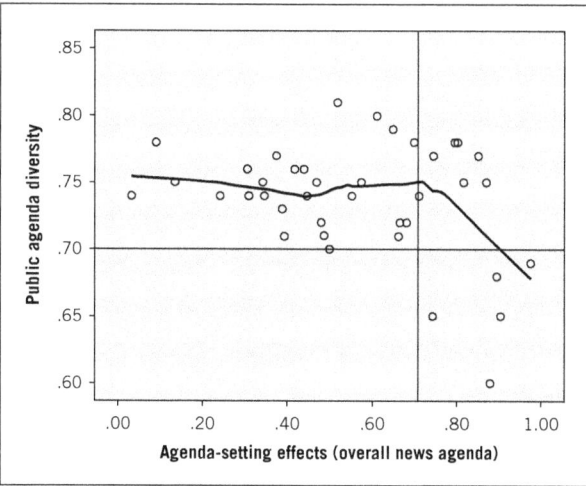

Figure 6.4. The relationship between the agenda-setting effect of the overall news agenda and public agenda diversity, 2007–2012.

Figure 6.4 illustrates the relationship between the size of the agenda-setting effect and the diversity of the public agenda. Once again, the size of the agenda-setting effect does not have much impact on the diversity of the public agenda until it gets relatively large. If the agenda-setting effect is big enough to explain about half the variance in the public agenda, there is about a fifty-fifty chance that the diversity of the public agenda will decline.

These scatterplots show that the "burglar alarm" of news consistency really does seem to work like an alarm. It does not "go off" for the public until a threshold is reached: consistency levels that are greater than the median. Moreover, the alarm function of news is not a product of consistency in itself but, rather, of the way the public uses the news. Consistent news in and of itself does not focus the public agenda on a narrower range of issues. Rather, consistent news generates higher levels of public attention to news and larger agenda-setting effects (possibly by repeating the same story many times across many sources). Unless consistency attracts attention and has an agenda-setting effect, the alarm cannot be said to be heard.

Further, the results show that the alarm is not all that reliable. High levels of news consistency do not always produce high levels of public attention or large agenda-setting effects. Strong agenda-setting effects are not always associated with a more focused public agenda, although high levels of attention to cable news always are. Even more worryingly, the months during this time frame in which the alarm has clearly sounded and the public agenda can be relied on to become more focused represent a crisis of historic proportions. The five data points in a quadrant of their own in Figures 6.2, 6.3, and 6.4 are all the same five months: September 2008 to March 2009 (October 2008 to April 2009 in terms of public agenda). These months include the climax of a presidential election and the onset of the Great Recession. It remains unclear whether the news media will generate, and the public will hear and respond to, alarms about public problems less cataclysmic than the stock market losing half its total valuation. If the news media seem unlikely to focus the public agenda, one might ask whether social reality or political leadership can do so.

Shaping the Public Agenda

For critical scholars, an inability of the news media to reliably focus the public agenda on a narrow range of issues has benefits as well as drawbacks. Virtually since the advent of mass media, scholars have worried that media misrepresent social reality in ways that benefit advertisers, politicians, and the media themselves. In a famous 1973 study, Ray Funkhouser demonstrates that news content is not linked with reality: rising seriousness of a problem is not necessarily predictive of greater coverage of that problem. He also shows that depending on how you measure it, public opinion is affected by the news agenda. In particular, the "most important problem" question seems linked to news content. The underpinnings of agenda-setting theory itself indirectly argue that the news media misrepresent reality, for if news media coverage were an accurate representation of reality, there would be no way to identify an agenda-setting effect.[12] Some view the drive for audiences and profits as the key reason for these misrepresentations. James Hamilton (1998), for instance, analyzes television violence from a market-based perspective. Others suggest that it is political elites who shape public perceptions of reality by influencing news (e.g., Bennett 1990; Hallin 1986; Kernell 2007). From a critical perspective, it might be a good thing if the power of the news media to shape public concern were to fade relative to the power of social reality to affect public concern. It might also be a good thing if political leaders were less able to direct public concern to their preferred policy agendas. In this section, we explore to what extent the news media can still override social reality in shaping public concerns and whether political leaders still seek to influence public policy by garnering public attention.

---

12. Some communication scholars would argue that it would be possible to identify an agenda-setting effect if the reality of some issues (i.e., unobtrusive issues) could only be known through the news media.

Social Reality versus Television News

Throughout the mass media era, scholars documented the mismatch between television and reality. Critics of entertainment television point out that it is too white, too young, too thin, too upper middle class, and much too violent. Some research has shown that those who watch more television believe crime is more commonplace than it is (Gerbner and Gross 1976; Romer, Jamieson, and Aday 2003). There is also evidence that news media overrepresentation of African Americans as criminals and welfare recipients shapes public opinion about crime and welfare (Dixon 2008; Gilens 1999; Valentino 1999). These misrepresentations can clearly produce negative social consequences, such as sustaining racism and discouraging support for civil liberties. But are the news media as influential as they used to be? Or has the collapse of news media gatekeeping (Williams and Delli Carpini 2011) increased the influence of social reality on public priorities?

To understand the relative power of news and social reality to shape public opinion, the nature of the issues themselves needs to be taken into account. Not all problems are equally susceptible to agenda-setting effects (Erbring, Goldenberg, and Miller 1980; Neuman 1990; Zucker 1978), and not all issues are equally susceptible to media influence. Harold Zucker, for example, argues agenda-setting effects are more pronounced for unobtrusive issues, those the public is made aware of through news media, than for obtrusive issues, those the public directly experiences. Accordingly, to see how the media's influence relative to reality's influence has evolved over time, we need to look at multiple issues.

A second challenge is how to measure reality. Joel Best (1993) makes the case that all measures of social reality are social constructions that draw attention to some of its features while ignoring others. Measures of unemployment, poverty, and other social conditions are human constructions that imperfectly capture the social reality they claim to depict. Yet Best also observes that radical relativism gets us nowhere. An external point of reference is required for meaningful communication about the reality we share.

With these considerations in mind, we select one relatively obtrusive issue and one relatively unobtrusive issue for which long-running and widely accepted, though imperfect, measures of social reality exist. The obtrusive issue is the economy, whose real state we evaluate with measures commonly used by investors, whose goal it is to make money, although they can also be used by politicians to make hay. The measures we use are: real change in gross domestic product, the inflation rate, and the unemployment rate as calculated by the federal government.[13] The unobtrusive issue is crime. Of course, crime is not a completely unobtrusive issue: people may be victims or perpetrators, or have family or friends caught up in the criminal justice system. However, crime is an issue where the media have been shown to influence public perceptions of social reality in important ways, and it is almost certainly less obtrusive than the economy. To measure the prevalence of crime, we use the FBI's annual statistics on violent crimes per one hundred thousand people.[14]

These measures have been used for many years and so can be used with the data sets in Chapter 4 to compare the relative influence of social reality and broadcast television coverage from 1968 through 2010 on public concern as measured by the Policy Agendas Project over the same time period. Public concern is measured as the proportion of responses mentioning macroeconomics (for the economy) or law/crime (for crime). Since economic data are available quarterly, we can use all 167 quarters from the television news data set to see how television news and social reality influence public concern about the economy. Because crime data are compiled annually, we examine television news and public concern in annual increments to see how reality, news, and public concern are related for this issue.

First, let us test a few assumptions. Since the economy fits the description of an obtrusive issue, television news should have less impact on public concern about it than social reality does. This turns out to be the case for the economic indicators we might expect people to experience. Both rising inflation and rising unemployment are more strongly associated with increasing public concern about the economy than is more news coverage of the economy, as Figure 6.5 demonstrates.[15] However, falling GDP, which is not something people directly experience, does not directly

---

13. Percent change in real gross domestic product from the previous quarter, seasonally adjusted, is obtained for each quarter from the Federal Reserve Bank of St. Louis (2018). Percent change in consumer prices over the same period the previous year is obtained for each quarter from the Organization for Economic Cooperation and Development (n.d.a, n.d.b), as was total unemployment as a percent of the labor force.

14. These statistics were obtained from the FBI's Uniform Crime Reporting online data tool (Federal Bureau of Investigation 2017). Property crime and murder statistics also were obtained and examined, but neither of these other statistics nor an index of all three crime indicators correlate as strongly with public concern about crime or news attention to crime as violent crime alone. Including all three indicators in a model create unacceptable collinearity.

15. Unemployment and inflation both are more strongly related to public concern than is economic news coverage (Fishers z's > 5, $p < .001$). Figure 6.5 is an observed variable path analysis model using AMOS 21. Model fit is good as indicated by a nonsignificant chi-square ($X^2 = 1.405$, $p = .236$), a comparative fit index near 1

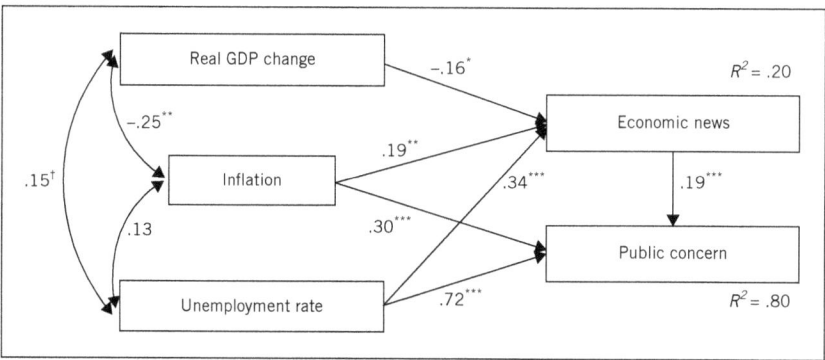

Figure 6.5. The relationships between social reality, news, and public concern about the economy, 1968–2010. *Note:* Coefficients are standardized. Curved lines represent covariances. $N = 167$ quarters. $*p < .05$; $**p < .01$; $***p < .001$; †approaches significance at $p < .10$.

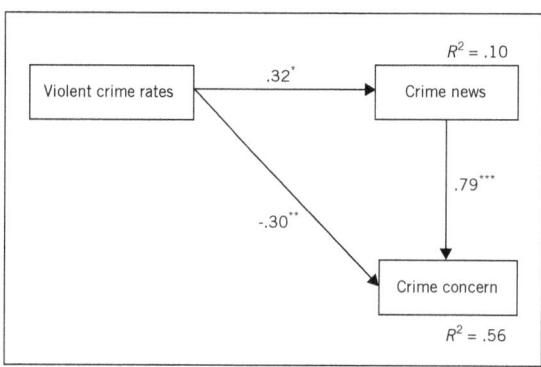

Figure 6.6. The relationships between social reality, news, and public concern about crime, 1968–2010. *Note:* Coefficients are standardized. $N = 43$ years. $*p < .05$; $**p < .01$; $***p < .001$.

influence public concern about the economy, though it is associated with more news coverage of the economy.

For our unobtrusive issue, crime, the reverse is true, as Figure 6.6 shows. More television news coverage of crime has a stronger relationship with rising public concern about crime than does the actual crime rate.[16] In fact, rising rates of violent crime are associated with less public concern about it, showing just how little reality seems to matter. Given these relationships, it may be unsurprising to learn that crime coverage is more strongly associated with public concern about crime than economic coverage is with public concern about the economy.[17]

(CFI = .999), and a root square mean error of approximation less than .08 (RMSEA = .049).

16. Fisher's $z = 7.27, p < .001$.
17. Fisher's $z = 2.17, p < .05$.

To understand how the relative influence of TV news compared to social reality may have changed as the media system evolved, we split our time frame in half—1968 through 1988 and 1989 through 2010—and reconsider the relationships thus far described. For the economy, there are no significant differences between the early time period and the later one. This suggests that the expansion of media choice and the rise of cable news have no particular effect on whether television news influences public concern about the economy. Then, as now, social reality is more likely to shape public concern than is news. From 1989 through 2010, there is no statistically significant relationship between crime rates and public concern about crime, which might be interpreted as an improvement over the earlier time period, when public concern was greater when crime rates were lower.[18] However, the relationship between more broadcast television news coverage of crime and greater public concern about crime is stronger after 1988 than it is from 1968 through 1988.[19]

Despite all the sources of information now available to the public and the technological ability to upend the news agenda via social media, none of these findings suggest social reality plays a greater role than it once did in shaping public concerns. Work by Bruce Williams and Michael Delli Carpini (2011) and Joseph Uscinski (2014) suggests this might be because the news agenda today is generated by a more collaborative process that takes into account public interests. Unable to engage in effective gatekeeping and still in search of audiences, traditional news media may adjust their news agendas to cover more extensively those issues that appear to incite public concern. However, our own analyses in Chapter 4 cannot confirm these tendencies, and the similarities between the present and the past are striking. Moreover, the apparently stronger relationship between news coverage of crime and public concern about it probably would not comfort those critical scholars who have long critiqued the news media for distracting the public from pressing social problems.

Can a President Focus the Public Agenda?

If any political leader could bring focus to be the public agenda, the president seems the most likely to have that ability. Jeffrey Cohen (2008) notes the president's unique role in "giving voice to a national interest [that] helps

---

18. $\beta = -.78, p < .001$.
19. After 1988, $\beta = .68, p < .001$; 1968 through 1988, $\beta = .42, p < .10$.

build a sense of political community . . . a counterweight to individualist impulses that often characterize American politics and culture" (207). Many media scholars studying the broadcast era demonstrated that government officials had a willing ally in the press, which commonly followed officials' lead in covering public affairs (Bennett 1990; Cook 1998; Hallin 1986; Sigal 1973), even, as Bennett showed, when government perspectives were out of sync with public opinion. The tendency of news media to personalize public affairs (Bennett 2009) gave presidents distinct advantages in shaping public opinion over other public officials representing policy-making bodies like Congress, an advantage they used by "going public" (Kernell 2007).

Despite enormous changes in the media system since these studies were published, legacy media still show signs of official influence. Recent work by Amber Boydstun (2013) reveals that policy-maker activities had a much bigger impact than reality on the amount of *New York Times* coverage of the war on terror. While actual events had a bigger impact on the *Times*' attention to the death penalty than did policy-maker actions, the effects of the latter were substantial. Both Cohen (2010) and Matthew Eshbaugh-Soha and Jeffrey Peake (2011) show that presidential public relations campaigns can influence news content.

However, research also reveals that presidential appeals to mass audiences are no longer as effective as they once were. Matthew Baum and Samuel Kernell (1999) find that in the cable era, televised presidential addresses reached smaller audiences than they did during the broadcast era, what Baum and Kernell call the "golden era of presidential television" (99). It was not because people were cynical about politics but, rather, because cable offered them greater choice (see Prior 2007). Garry Young and William Perkins (2005) demonstrated that the president's state of the union address was less influential on public concern about both foreign policy and civil rights after the golden age of televised presidential address, although state of the union addresses have never been particularly influential when it comes to economic concerns. Moreover, as audiences shrank, presidents were less able to commandeer television coverage for prime-time addresses to the nation (Kernell 2007). Not only are audiences smaller, but presidential addresses may reverberate less loudly than they once did because traditional news media pay less attention to the president than they once did (Cohen 2008; Scacco and Coe 2016). The impact of presidential addresses on public opinion was diluted further by growing political divisions in the public. The opposing partisans a president most needed to reach in order to shift public opinion could and did tune out his televised speeches (Kernell and Rice 2011).

Perhaps in response to these changes, the number of major presidential addresses has declined since the Reagan years, according to a search of the American Presidency Project database (see https://www.presidency.ucsb.edu). Brandon Rottinghaus's (2010) analysis suggests televised addresses continued to pack a punch through the Clinton years, and Eshbaugh-Soha and Peake (2011) argue that influence has continued into the twenty-first century. Nevertheless, as Robert Shapiro (2012) points out, recently televised addresses have been paired with other communicative strategies, making their independent influence difficult to sort out. Thus, available evidence shows that not only do presidents have less ability to focus public attention than they once had; they are less likely to attempt to do so by addressing the nation as a whole.

What is more, there is at least some evidence that presidents no longer seek to build a national community by directing the nation's attention to an issue. Several scholars argue that modern presidential leadership increasingly directs minor addresses at targeted audiences. Kernell (2007) notes that the number of minor presidential addresses has been growing since the Reagan years. Where Reagan averaged fewer than twenty minor addresses per year in his first three years in office, George W. Bush averaged more than forty-five each year during the first three years of his first term (122). Eshbaugh-Soha and Peake (2011), who refer to this phenomenon as "sustained attention" to issue priorities, find that it is effective in moving the public agenda, especially for issues that were not previously salient. However, other scholars find evidence suggesting that this changed practice may diversify or even polarize the public agenda instead of focusing it on a narrow range of agenda priorities. Cohen refers to the strategy as "going narrow" and suggests that its goal is not to unite the public behind the president's issue priorities: "In the new era of polarized parties and fragmented media, presidents place more emphasis on narrow groups, like their party base, interest groups, and select localities, and less on influencing national public opinion" (2010, 5). Josh Scacco and Kevin Coe (2016), in their model of the ubiquitous presidency, describe presidents reaching out to the public through multiple communication channels, consistent with the concept of making many "minor addresses," and they emphasize the breadth of subjects covered in these addresses. Daniel Kreiss's (2016) recent work on presidential campaign processes suggests that in the campaign phase as well, presidential candidates seek to personalize their messages for voters rather than to build a national community of shared concerns.

Regardless of whether presidents ever had the power to focus the public agenda, they may no longer seek to do so. As the media environment fragmented, national audiences became more difficult to convene, and national addresses became less influential. Adapting their approach to maximize their influence (Cohen 2010), presidents placed less emphasis on shared priorities and more on appeals to specific groups. As both candidate and president-elect, Donald Trump demonstrated that appealing to key factions without making an effort to unify the broader public could be an effective strategy for generating a politically useful level of public support. Thus, the question turns out to be not whether a president, as the leader most capable of influencing the American public, has the power to focus the public agenda in a fragmented media environment but, rather, whether it makes political sense for a president to try.

Conclusion

Although public attention to news media has waned over time, reality does not seem to play a larger role today in setting public priorities than it did in the mass media era. On issues where the news media influenced public perceptions in the mass media era, they still do so in the era of personalized and social media. On issues where the news media could not distract the public in the mass media era, they are still unable to do so. In line with other scholarship, this analysis shows that the public cannot be persuaded about the state of the economy but can be persuaded about violent crime. To the extent that media critics hoped that breaking the network television monopoly on news would reduce the ability of traditional news media to distract the public from real problems at hand, it does not seem to have worked out.

What has happened instead is that it has become extraordinarily difficult to focus the public agenda. Even though the public pays more attention to news in moments when the news agenda is more consistent and less attention when the news agenda is more diverse, the effects of growing public agenda diversity seem to be difficult to reverse. During the period from 2007 through the first half of 2012, the only moment that reliably reduced the diversity of the public agenda was the deepest financial crisis since the Great Depression, the scope of which became apparent in the middle of an open presidential election. In other words, nothing short of economic Armageddon was capable of increasing the focus of public concerns.

Moreover, for good or ill, the issue was one for which neither the news media nor the president seem to exert much leadership of public opinion no matter the media environment. As this chapter shows, economic reality tends to dwarf media influence. Young and Perkins (2005) and Eshbaugh-Soha and Peake (2011) find no evidence of presidential leadership of public opinion on the economy. If this is the only kind of circumstance under which the public agenda becomes more focused, it would appear that traditional opinion leaders do not have much power to reduce the diversity of public priorities in the contemporary media environment.

Recent research suggests that strategies of opinion leadership have adapted to the changed communication environment of the twenty-first century. Presidents who once commanded mass audiences through mass media have developed tactics that depend to a greater extent on communicating with smaller, more specialized audiences (Cohen 2010; Eshbaugh-Soha and Peake 2011; Kernell 2007). Aware of the public's fragmentation and polarization, they capitalize on the divisions rather than seeking to unify the public behind them, engaging in coalition building by appealing to their party bases and to issue partisans (Cohen 2010; Kernell 2007).

Kernell's (2007) analysis suggests presidential strategy has always involved this sort of tactic, noting that presidents commonly seek leverage by visiting the constituencies of legislators who are electorally vulnerable. Yet a communication environment that is made up of a welter of small audiences *instead of*, rather than *in addition to*, a mass audience represents a profoundly different opportunity for opinion leadership. Brandice Canes-Wrone's (2001) analysis of presidential leadership from the Eisenhower to Clinton administrations suggests that presidents mobilized the public when their issue positions were generally popular, leveraging a unified public to achieve their policy goals. In contrast, a strategy aimed at small partisan audiences would allow an opinion leader to divide and conquer by avoiding the public as a whole and mobilizing only favorably disposed groups.

A focused public agenda almost certainly would not allow for such a strategy. Widespread public concern about an issue would demand that leaders address that issue and thus address the public as a whole. In contrast, a diversified public agenda in which no single issue emerged from the pack of public concerns could make opinion leaders less responsive to the public as a whole. A president seeking to respond to public concerns can still use the bully pulpit on only so many occasions, and a strategic president might use it to mobilize select supportive groups and address their demands. This suggests that a diversified public agenda empowers leaders, at least in part, by giving them more latitude in choosing which issues to address. In the mass media era, the political power of opinion leadership was the power to draw public attention to an issue. In the personalized media era, the power of opinion leadership may be the power to pick and choose among a wide selection of issues on a diverse public agenda. This possibility is the focus of Chapter 7.

7

Political Responsiveness and the Public Agenda

When John McCain (R-AZ) was first elected to the U.S. House of Representatives in 1982, it was pretty clear what the public wanted him to tackle. That fall, more than half of Americans named jobs as the most important problem facing the country. Little else concerned them. By the early twenty-first century, reading the public's priorities was much more difficult. Instead of one or two issues dominating the public agenda, it now included three or four. During McCain's campaign for the Republican presidential nomination in early 2008, as the economy spiraled into recession and investment bank Bear Stearns collapsed, the public agenda included money, social relations, the economy in general, and the Middle East. Moreover, the public agenda in 2008 was actually more focused than the one that had prevailed when McCain first became Arizona's senior U.S. senator in 1995.

Faced with a fragmented public that seems to want a host of different things, how does a representative respond? More generally, how does a democratic system respond to the agenda of a fragmented public? How do political leaders react to a public that seems to want everything simultaneously yet nothing in particular?

Whether applying a delegate or a trustee model, a fragmented public agenda produces problems for representation. In the delegate model, in which representatives are expected to follow their citizens' wishes, the signals sent to representatives about what the public wants them to do become less and less clear as the public agenda becomes more diverse. Should they tackle jobs, health care, crime, or national security? In a trustee model, in which representatives are expected to act in the citizens' best interests, a fragmented public agenda that offers no clear guidance about what the public as a whole wants further enables public officials to address the problems they want to address and sidestep those they wish to avoid. In other words, it gives them the kind of agenda-setting power Peter Bachrach and Morton Baratz (1962) identify: the ability to avoid making decisions that represent a threat to their power. Either way, political leaders might be expected to be less responsive to the public as the public agenda becomes more fragmented. This chapter explores the relationships between the fragmenting public agenda and the actions of political leaders.

Do Political Leaders Respond to the Public?

Examining how the increasing fragmentation of the public agenda has affected political representation in the United States is more complicated than it looks. Some might argue that the political system does not now and never has responded to public opinion. There is a good deal of scholarly evidence that political leaders shape public opinion to fit their own needs rather than responding to the public's desires (e.g., Bennett 1990; Entman 1991; Hallin 1986; Jacobs and Shapiro 2000). Some argue that public opinion measurement processes themselves exist to tame and manage public concerns rather than identify and respond to them (e.g., Bourdieu 1979; Ginsberg 1986; Jacobs and Shapiro 2000). Furthermore, recent research suggests that presidents, at least, may feed the fragmented public agenda rather than trying to build public consensus (Cohen 2010; Kernell 2007). Of course, sometimes both the government and the public respond to what are essentially external events, such as acts of terrorism or economic downturns, although even here the ways that events are perceived can be shaped by political leadership (Entman 1991; Bennett, Lawrence, and Livingston 2007).

Others might point out that the political system should not respond to public opinion. Most people do not know much about public affairs (Converse 1964; Delli Carpini and Keeter 1996), and many have wrongheaded ideas about public policies and the circumstances that give rise to them (Edy and Risley-Baird 2016; Meirick 2016; Nyhan and Reifler 2010; Redlawsk 2002). Public concerns may be sparked by sensational events or news stories, and public reaction may be neither thoughtful nor measured.

Yet, for democracy to be meaningful, some sort of linkage between what the public wants and what the government does would seem to be required, and some scholars have found evidence that political institutions respond to public opinion (Jones and Baumgartner 2004; Stimson, MacKuen, and Erikson 1995). The key question addressed in this chapter is whether the nature of that responsiveness has changed as the character of the public agenda has changed.

What Does Responsiveness Look Like?

Political researchers have looked at two different dimensions of leaders' influence over and responsiveness to public opinion. Some measure influence and responsiveness in terms of public opinion about a particular issue or issues. Those studying presidential influence ask whether presidents are able to get the public to back their policies (e.g., Rottinghaus 2010). Those studying legislatures ask whether the policies they produce respond to the policy "mood" of the country, whether a public in a more conservative mood gets more conservative policy (Stimson, MacKuen, and Erikson 1995). This dimension is known as positional representation. However, as Morris Fiorina (2010) argues, many of the issues political campaigns and legislatures take up are not terribly important to the public. Gay marriage was a prominent issue in media and political discourse, but it did not occupy a prominent place in the public's list of most important problems. Thus, a second way to look at influence and responsiveness is in terms of whether leaders can shape the public agenda (e.g., Canes-Wrone 2001; Eshbaugh-Soha and Peake 2011) and the extent to which the public agenda matches the legislative agenda (Jones and Baumgartner 2004). Do political leaders address the issues that the public names as important, and do they influence how important people believe an issue to be? Since this book has consistently focused on the public agenda, here we examine the relationship between the public's agenda and political representation.

Where Should We Expect Political Responsiveness?

Two democratic institutions should be especially affected by the changing character of the public agenda: the president and the U.S. House of Representatives. The president is unique among public officials as the only elected leader who represents the entire nation, and many scholars examine the role of presidential address in moving public opinion. Although much of this scholarship focuses on the president's ability to lead public opinion with speeches (e.g., Canes-Wrone 2001; Kernell 2007; Rottinghaus 2010; Tulis 1987), in some respects this oversimplifies the functions of presidential addresses. Both George Edwards (2003) and Matthew Eshbaugh-Soha and Jeffrey Peake (2011) point out that presidents also respond to public opinion. While the primary purpose of some presidential addresses is to galvanize public opinion behind a policy proposal, such as President Barack Obama's 2013 speech advocating military action against the Syrian government, others are reactions to public concern, like President Jimmy Carter's famous "malaise" speech in 1979. Either way, the president's capacity to both shape and respond to public concerns by means of a national address may have been changed by the growing diversity of the public agenda.

The U.S. House, although relatively parochial in its representation of the U.S. public, should in principle be particularly responsive to public opinion for several reasons. First, its members stand for reelection more often than any other federal-level elected officials. The more insulated an institution is from electoral consequences, the less responsive it is to public opinion (Stimson, MacKuen, and Erikson 1995). Of all the national governing institutions, the Supreme Court is the least responsive to public opinion. Its members are appointed for life and do not stand for election. In the Congress, the House of Representatives, whose members stand for election every two years, is more responsive to public opinion than is the U.S. Senate, whose members come up for election every six years (Stimson, MacKuen, and Erikson 1995). Second, the House has greater institutional capacity than other governing institutions (Jones, Larsen-Price, and Wilkerson 2009). It has more members, so it can hold more hearings, consider more bills, and so on, which should make it more capable than other institutions of dealing with a fragmenting public agenda. Third, most scholarship suggests that Congress is less effective at shaping public opinion and the public agenda than the president is. Not only is the White House more ideologically unified than the Congress, the president serves as a focal point for media attention in a way that cannot be matched by the myriad leadership in the House and Senate. In looking for evidence of how political leaders have *responded* to a more diverse public agenda, the U.S. House should thus provide clearer indicators, as well as a best-case scenario, for how well political institutions might adapt.

Presidential Address: Leading and Responding to the Public Agenda

Most research on presidential addresses focuses on leadership rather than responsiveness to public opinion, and a good deal of it conflates opinion leadership and agenda leadership. Of course, shaping agendas and shaping opinions can interact with each other in complex ways. John Zaller (1998) suggests that regardless of whether Americans believed President Clinton to have had an inappropriate sexual relationship with Monica Lewinsky, they could not be convinced of the matter's importance given the robust economy. Kernell's (2007) analysis of Clinton's unsuccessful attempt at health care reform suggests large segments of the public were satisfied with their health insurance and that when opponents of the plan reminded them of this (and warned a new system would be complicated), they lost their appetite for change. Although the opponents' campaign framed the president's plan as complex and unwieldy, it also reduced the felt need for change—the public priority placed on health care reform. Health care did not cease to be perceived as a problem; it ceased to be a priority. Anthony Downs's (1972) issue attention cycle similarly suggests that issues perceived as complex and requiring sacrifice to resolve lose their priority on the public agenda, again suggesting that opinions and agendas work together in complex ways when public officials endeavor to lead public opinion.

Nevertheless, where opinion leadership and agenda leadership are conceptually separated, there is evidence that presidents try to shape the public agenda with their public addresses and are successful at doing so. Brandice Canes-Wrone (2001) suggests that in the twentieth century, presidential agenda setting on issues was both more common and more effective than presidential attempts to shape public opinion about a particular issue. Studying presidents' public appeals about the budget from the Eisenhower era through the Clinton years, she found that in only one of eighty cases did a president make a public appeal for support on an aspect of the budget on which public opinion was against him and that the appeals were generally effective. From this perspective, leading the public agenda in the mass media era amounted to raising the salience of issues on which the public supported the president. Reagan's push for deficit reduction and tax reduction provide nice examples—who would want to be deeper in debt or pay more taxes? Presidents raising the salience of crime as an issue provide another opportune example—no one is in favor of violent crime—and scholars found evidence that presidents used the news media to raise the salience of drug-related crime in the 1980s and 1990s (Reeves and Campbell 1994; Reinerman and Levine 1997).

Much less has been written about presidential address that responds to public opinion, perhaps because there are important conceptual difficulties in distinguishing speeches that shape the public agenda from those that respond to it. For one thing, presidents commonly seek to shape public opinion, even as they respond to it. In 2007, when President George W. Bush addressed the nation about the Iraq War, he responded to public concerns, but he also sought support for his plans to send in additional troops to attempt to bring the war to a close. Just as important, major presidential addresses are seldom isolated acts. Instead, they are usually elements of much larger persuasive campaigns that seek to shape public opinion. Presidents and their administrations may engage in a variety of communication activities before a major address in order to encourage a felt need for the policy the president is about to propose. Thus, by the time the major speech is given, the president may appear to be responding to public demand for policy to address an issue of concern, when, in fact, the concern itself is a product of the administration's earlier efforts. Both Bill Clinton and Barack Obama ran for president on campaign platforms that prioritized health care, and their attention to the issue meant that when they gave major addresses on health care as presidents, there was already substantial public concern about it. Their speeches appeared responsive, but they had in some respects created the demand they sought to satisfy. Much contemporary research on presidential address has considered the structure and effectiveness of these campaigns, treating major speeches as one element in a larger flow of communication.

Yet presidents remain unique among political leaders in their ability to convene and address a national audience of citizens, and major addresses remain unique in their function of responding to the concerns of the public as a whole rather than of particular interest or demographic groups. One thinks of George W. Bush addressing the nation after the 9/11 terrorist attacks, even though polling had not caught up to public concern about terrorism. One thinks, too, of Bush's address to the nation in the aftermath of Hurricane Katrina.

Distinguishing Leadership Speeches from Responsive Speeches

Because persuasion is always an element of presidential address, any evidence that presidential speeches respond to public concerns must be taken with a grain of salt, since anywhere we stop the cycle of influence to observe responsiveness is likely to be somewhat arbitrary. Still, we can say with some confidence that when presidents address an issue that is not on the public's agenda, they are leading public opinion rather than responding to it. A similarly blunt rule that when presidents address an issue that is on the public agenda, they are responding to public opinion produces some unintuitive classifications but offers some insight. It reveals different patterns for responsive speeches than for leadership speeches, suggesting a meaningful distinction, and the apparent differences are robust enough to withstand the uneven intervals between polls and presidential addresses.

To explore presidential leadership of and responsiveness to the public agenda in major public addresses, we use the poll-by-poll Gallup measures of the public's agenda (described in Chapter 3 and Appendix A) and the archive of presidential addresses from the American Presidency Project at the University of California, Santa Barbara. The main topic of each major presidential speech given from 1975 through 2014 was coded using the same categories used for the Gallup "most important problem" responses. A few speeches that were ceremonial, like Independence Day addresses, or that covered many topics, like state of the union speeches, had to be left out. Speeches on issues that garnered 10 percent or more mentions from the public as a most important problem in the last Gallup poll taken before the speech were considered responsive speeches because they addressed issues that were on the public agenda. Speeches on issues that were mentioned in fewer than 10 percent of the public responses in the last preceding Gallup poll were considered leadership speeches because they addressed issues that were not on the public agenda. This gives us 127 major presidential addresses from 1975 through 2014, sixty-six about issues that were not on the public agenda (leadership speeches) and sixty-one about issues that were (responsive speeches).

However, there are two instances in which historical events and presidential addresses are so hopelessly entangled as to make their classification as leadership or responsive speeches virtually impossible. President George W. Bush gave three speeches immediately after the September 11, 2001, terrorist attacks (September 11, September 20, and October 7). Since polling is done relatively infrequently, these speeches would be coded as leadership speeches because terrorism was not an issue on the public's agenda at the time of the attacks. Clearly, George W. Bush had no intention at the time of the attacks of leading the public to fear terrorism, and the apparently strong relationship between the speeches and rising public concern about terrorism may alter our results. Similarly, President George H.W. Bush gave a series of speeches in quick succession during the 1991 Gulf War (January 16, February 23, February 26, February 27, and March 6). Once again, the infrequency of polling overstates the effects of presidential responsive speeches on public opinion, suggesting the president responded to public concern about the war with overwhelming effectiveness, banishing their concerns almost entirely. Including these few speeches given in quick succession may alter our conclusions, so we offer estimates both with and without these eight addresses, but we prefer the more conservative approach of eliminating them as outliers. This leaves us with sixty-three leadership speeches and fifty-six responsive speeches. For more information about how the speeches were coded, see Appendix F.

Responding to the Public Agenda

If we look at major presidential speeches about issues that were not on the public's agenda, those in which the president is presumably trying to attract public attention and increase public concern, like most scholars of presidential address, we find the president's power to lead the public agenda declining over time.[1] That said, presidents did not typically increase public concern about these issues much. On average, public concern about an issue on which the president was trying to lead rose from about 2.6 percent in the last poll before the speech to about 4 percent in the first poll after the speech, which is significant but small and improved only a bit by including Bush's post-9/11 speeches. Nevertheless, the declining effectiveness could be an explanation for why presidents have made fewer major addresses over time. In the first half of our time frame, 1975 until 1994, presidents made about two major addresses per year on issues where they led the public agenda. In the second half of the time frame, from 1995 through 2014, they averaged just one.

These results line up well with what other scholars might have expected to see, but the pattern for responsive speeches is different. If we look at presidential speeches on issues about which the public was already concerned, we do not see a decline in effectiveness over time. When an issue is already on the public agenda, major presidential addresses have about the same impact on public concern in the 2010s as they did in the 1970s. Public concern stayed at about the same level after the speech as before the speech: 23.1 percent before the speech to 22.6 percent after.[2] Including the 1991 Gulf War speeches, again, makes the effect a bit larger, but the overall conclusion is much the same. Yet the frequency of major addresses responding to public concern still declines over time—from about three speeches every two years, from 1975 to 1994, to about one speech per year, from 1995 through 2014. Why?

Since the public agenda was becoming more diverse over that time frame, one possibility is that the public sent less clear signals about which issues it wanted the president to address. The more issues on the public agenda and the more diverse that agenda is, the more diluted public demand might be. In contrast, the higher the peak of public concern about a

---

1. $r = -.27, p < .05, N = 63$. This excludes the three 9/11 speeches.
2. $t(55) = .55, p = .59$, ns.

single issue, what we might call peak public concern, the greater the public demand that the president address that issue. Think, for example, about the public agenda in October 1978, when President Carter gave a major public address on the economy. More than 50 percent of responses to the "most important problem" question named inflation, the subject of the speech. Only one other issue, jobs, garnered more than 10 percent of responses, and public agenda diversity was at .57 (where 0 is the minimum and 1 is the maximum). In comparison, when President Bush gave his speech in the aftermath of Hurricane Katrina, concerns about the government and about social relations, the two categories most associated with Katrina, did not quite reach 35 percent of responses. Moreover, four issues vied for position on the public agenda: government (20.6 percent of responses), social relations (13.9 percent), money (13.5 percent), and the Middle East (12.7 percent). Public agenda diversity was at .78. Although the public's leading concern was the government's response to Katrina, that issue stands out much less clearly than inflation did in the late 1970s.

To see how the more diverse public agenda and the lower levels of peak concern relate to presidential responsiveness to the public agenda, rather than looking at the president's addresses speech by speech as we have been, we need to consider them year by year. This allows us to consider what affects (1) the number of speeches responding to issues on the public agenda that are given in a year, (2) whether the public will get a speech that responds to any issue on the public agenda during the year, and (3) whether the public will get a speech on the issue that tops the public agenda for that year. Table 7.1 offers regression models that address all three of these questions. Because the latter two models have a dependent variable that amounts to a dichotomy (whether or not such a speech was given that year), they use binomial logistic regression, which does not produce the kinds of standardized coefficients presented in other tables throughout this book. The results for all three models, then, are reported using unstandardized coefficients and their standard errors, which means that a larger coefficient does not necessarily mean a "bigger" effect. However, it does tell us which factors have a strong enough impact that their relationship with the likelihood of responsive speeches is probably not due to chance. Like other statistical models, it attempts to sort out the unique effect of each variable in the model.

The models include four variables that might be expected to be related to the number and likelihood of presidential response speeches. First, the total number of speeches given helps to control for the differences between presidents and between eras. Some presidents may be more likely to use the bully pulpit, and presidential addresses may be more common

Table 7.1. Predictors of response speeches in a year

	Number of response speeches per year		Response speech given in a year		Speech given on year's top issue	
	b	SE	b	SE	b	SE
Total speeches	.42***	.08	1.48**	.57	1.18**	.43
Mean capacity	.09	.24	1.77	1.14	.35	.77
Peak concern	.01	.02	.22*	.10	.20*	.08
Mean public agenda diversity	1.55	2.60	24.69*	12.55	34.08**	12.92
R^2	.41		.47		.44	

Note: Numbers reflect annual data for 1975–2014; $N = 40$ years. Coefficients are unstandardized. Peak concern is the highest level of public concern observed for any issue in a year. Mean capacity is average number of issues on the public agenda. The analysis for number of response speeches is linear regression, and we report the adjusted R^2. The analyses for whether a response speech was given in a year and whether the year's top issue was addressed are binomial logistic regressions, and we report the Cox and Snell R^2. Using the year's highest level of public concern before the speech was given rather than peak concern for the year does not substantively change results for the third model. $*p < .05; **p < .01; ***p < .001$.

in some eras than others. Second, capacity is the number of issues on the public's agenda. We counted the number of issues named in more than 10 percent of responses for each poll taken in a calendar year and used the average number of issues as a measure of that year's agenda capacity. Higher capacity gives more potential topics for responsive speeches but could make it harder to identify and address the issue of greatest public concern. Third, peak public concern is the highest spike in public concern for any issue in any poll taken that year. One might expect that the higher the peak, the more likely a responsive speech should be. Finally, public agenda diversity is the average of all the diversity scores for all the polls taken that year. Presumably, a more focused public agenda should demand more responsiveness.

The number of responsive speeches given in a year is affected only by the total number of speeches given (column 1). The likelihood of a responsive speech given about any issue on the public agenda in a particular year and the likelihood that a speech responds to the issue about which the public is most concerned both depend to some extent on how fragmented or focused the public agenda is. The table shows that the higher the peak level of public concern about a particular issue, the more likely the president will give a responsive speech (column 2) and that the president will give a responsive speech about that particular issue (column 3). The number of issues on the public agenda does not seem to matter, but once peak level of public concern is accounted for, the diversity of the rest of the public agenda actually improves the likelihood of both a responsive speech and a speech responding to the public's issue of greatest concern. Although this may seem strange, one should note that the relationship linking higher public agenda diversity to an increased likelihood of a responsive speech and one that addresses the issue of greatest public concern appears only after statistically controlling for the effects of peak public concern. These two variables are strongly related to each other, sharing almost half their variance. So what this model really shows is that a more diverse public agenda improves the likelihood of a speech only after the level of concern about the public's top issue is taken into account.[3] In other words, we also have to think about how agenda diversity and peak concern are related to each other.

To do this, we create a path analysis model in AMOS shown in Figure 7.1.[4] It shows that over time, the public agenda grew more diverse and peaks in public concern became less pronounced. More public agenda diversity was related to fewer total speeches. Higher peaks of public concern, more speeches, and more diversity in the public agenda all increased the likelihood of a speech addressing the public's top issue for the year. Since higher peaks of public concern make it more likely a president will respond and peak public concern declines over time, this may help explain why fewer major presidential addresses responding to public concerns are given today than were given in earlier decades. It also suggests that presidents in recent years are less likely to deliver an address about the public's most important problem than they once were. As the public's priorities become more diverse, the total number of major presidential speeches given in a year also declines, and this, too, reduces the likelihood that a president will address the issue of greatest public concern in a given year.

Like the logistic regression models, this path model shows that the direct effect of a diverse public agenda is greater likelihood that the public's top issue will be addressed in a major speech, which seems counterintuitive. However, in the larger context of the model, the pathway acquires meaning. In both models, peak public concern and public agenda diversity control for each other so that their distinct influences on presidential addresses emerge. In the absence of statistical controls, the higher the public concern about a single issue, the lower the public agenda diversity will be because of the way public agenda diversity is measured. When peak public concern is already accounted for in the model, higher levels of public

---

3. The zero-order relationship for public agenda diversity is $r = .02$ for top issues addressed, $r = -.13$ for any responsive speech, both p's $> .40$. Public agenda diversity has a strong negative relationship with peak public concern, $r = -.71, p < .001$.

4. Model fit is good as indicated by a nonsignificant chi-square ($X^2 = .040$, $df = 3, p = .998$), a comparative fit index near 1 (CFI = 1.000), and a root square mean error of approximation of less than .08 (RMSEA = .000).

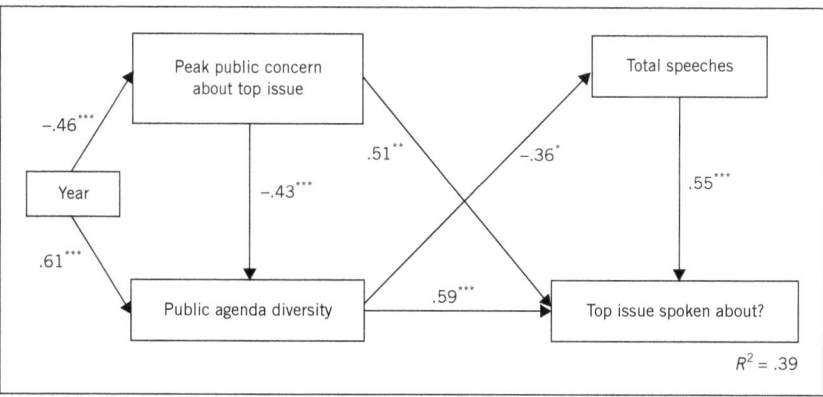

Figure 7.1. Path model predicting whether the president speaks about the public's top issue. *Note:* Standardized coefficients. $*p < .05$; $**p < .01$; $***p < .001$.

agenda diversity indicate just how much the issue of greatest public concern stands out from the other issues on the public agenda. The more that issue stands out, the greater public agenda diversity there is over the remaining issues and the more likely the president is to make a speech on that issue. Where peak public concern is lower, the public sends a less clear signal to the president. The presence of another issue (or two or three issues) that garners substantial public concern means public agenda diversity does not increase much, even after the issue of greatest concern is factored out. Signal clarity, then, is a function of both how worried people are about the issue of peak concern (peak public concern) and how much that issue stands out from the rest (public agenda diversity). Think again about the speech given by President Carter in 1978. Public concern about inflation was forty points greater than the next most important issue, and peak concern contributed substantially to the low level of public agenda diversity. Public agenda diversity on the remaining issues was about average. In other words, once Carter addressed inflation, there was not much focused public demand to address anything else.

Distracting the Public

Another intriguing aspect of presidential address as it relates to the public agenda seems worth exploring here. Scholars argue that presidents are less effective in directing the public's agenda to issues they would like to confront than they were in the "golden age" of presidential address, prior to the growth in media choice and political polarization. However, another aspect of presidential leadership might be to draw public attention away from issues one would prefer not to tackle. Some suggest, for example, that presidents attempt to deflect public attention to foreign affairs when faced with controversy at home. Four days after President Clinton addressed the nation about his relationship with Monica Lewinsky, he returned to the airwaves to announce U.S. military airstrikes in Sudan and Afghanistan. After a bruising year with a failed Supreme Court nomination and an ongoing investigation into his role in trading arms for hostages, President Ronald Reagan took to the airwaves in December to announce the results of a historic summit held with Soviet leader Mikhail Gorbachev in Washington, D.C. If distracting the public is, indeed, an aspect of presidential leadership, how has the president's ability to distract the public changed over time?

One way to find out is to consider how what we call leadership speeches affect the public agenda. If a president addresses an issue that is not on the public agenda and succeeds in increasing the level of public concern about that issue, it should also increase the diversity of the public agenda. That is, raising the salience of an issue about which the public was not previously concerned should spread public concern more evenly over more issues and increase the diversity of the public agenda. Although the ability of presidents to increase attention to a particular issue has declined over time, the effects of presidential addresses on the *diversity* of the public agenda have not. Presidential addresses that attempt to lead public opinion increase the diversity of the public agenda, and their ability to do so does not diminish over time.[5] In other words, presidents are as effective at distracting the public as they ever were, even if they are less able to direct public attention toward a particular policy issue. Once again, major presidential addresses responding to public concerns work differently. They are not associated with a change in public agenda diversity.[6]

Some Conclusions

This evidence must be treated with caution because all presidential addresses involve some degree of opinion leadership and are typically part

---

5. Average public agenda diversity increased from .66 before a leadership speech to .69 after, $t(62) = 2.39, p < .05$. Including the three post-9/11 speeches makes the increase in public agenda diversity somewhat smaller but still significant at $p < .05$, one tailed. Time had no relationship with the diversifying effect of these speeches on the public agenda, $r = -.03, p = .83, N = 63$.

6. Agenda diversity was virtually unchanged, .668 before and .666 after, $t(56) = .18, p = .85$, ns. When we include the five Gulf War speeches, public agenda diversity is still virtually unchanged. Time was unrelated to changes in public agenda diversity ($r = -.03$, ns, $N = 56$) from before the speech to after it.

of a larger communication strategy. Nevertheless, the evidence suggests that presidents have become less responsive to public concerns as the public agenda has grown more diverse. Moreover, it is a logical truism that as the public agenda has fragmented, even when presidents address the issue of greatest public concern, they are typically ignoring substantial public concerns as well, and this has become more true over time as consensus erodes about what the top issue is.

The relative rarity of major presidential addresses further complicates drawing conclusions about long-term trends. Presidential addresses are commonly driven by historic events, though not every event draws a presidential speech and some events acquire importance if the president speaks about them. As elsewhere in this book, the length of the timeline involved should help manage the effects of particular historical moments. Nevertheless, we are also stuck with the problem that the issue addressed in the speech is, to some extent, confounded with whether it leads or responds to public opinion. As one might expect, almost two-thirds of leadership speeches are given about foreign policy issues, while most responsive speeches are given about domestic and economic issues. This helps explain the relatively small increases in public concern found in connection with leadership speeches. As other chapters illustrate, it is difficult to arouse public concern about international affairs in the absence of actual military conflict. It also makes it possible that the results we see are influenced by the speech topic as well as by the changing relationship between the president and the public agenda, and the small number of speeches makes it tough to factor that out.

Although a great deal of attention has historically been paid to the special relationship between the president and the public, the complexities of this relationship make it worth considering another indicator of how changes in the public agenda may have affected democratic responsiveness. To confirm our suspicions that an increasingly diverse public agenda weakens the linkage between what the public wants and what the government does, we consider the prosaic day-to-day functions of the U.S. House of Representatives.

How Does the U.S. House of Representatives Respond to the Public Agenda?

From 1969 through 2013, the U.S. House held between one thousand and twenty-three hundred hearings per year. They are the stuff of everyday politics rather than historic occasions, and their number suggests an enormous capacity to address issues of public concern. What happens to the U.S. House's agenda of hearings when the public agenda becomes more diverse?

Considering the House's responsiveness to public priorities allows us to consider not only how the fragmentation of the public agenda affects democratic representation but also the relative impacts of fragmentation and polarization on responsiveness. While polarization in the public is not measured all that frequently, polarization in Congress is measured with every new Congress that convenes. There is some debate over what the term *polarization* actually means. Some argue that the parties' issue positions are more distant from each other than they once were. Others suggest a process of sorting in which issue positions are becoming increasingly consistent but not necessarily more distant from each other. In other words, the views of Republicans are becoming more and more consistent with those of other Republicans, but the difference in opinion between Republicans and Democrats on any particular issue may not be all that great. The measure used in the following analyses arguably captures some elements of both. However polarized the public is, Congress should be even more so because members of Congress tend to have more consistent issue positions than the public (Converse 1964). Thus, including both fragmentation of the public agenda and polarization in the U.S. House in models helps us to see the relative contribution of each of these aspects of modern American politics to the degree of fit between the issues people believe to be most important and the issues to which Congress pays attention.

In spite of increasingly rationalized gerrymandering and low rates of turnover, the U.S. House has still been shown to be quite responsive to public opinion (Jones and Baumgartner 2004). Beyond electoral vulnerability, another factor that may influence responsiveness is the activity in which the legislature is engaged. Bryan Jones and colleagues (Jones, Larsen-Price, and Wilkerson 2009) describe "institutional friction" as a process by which declining institutional capacity—a greater need for consensus in order to act—makes responsiveness progressively more difficult. For example, any member of the House can introduce a bill, but to pass major legislation requires that the bill navigate procedural hurdles, receive a yes vote from a majority of House members, be reconciled with the Senate version of the bill, and so on. The legislative agenda might more closely resemble the public agenda at lower levels of friction when party control of the House, lobbying interests, and other intervening factors do not yet exert as much influence. Jones and colleagues found that holding hearings was more responsive to public priorities than any other government activity they studied, so this is likely to be a best case scenario for governmental responsiveness to increasingly diverse public priorities.

The data collected by the Policy Agendas Project at the University of Texas, which is used in Chapter 4, was specifically designed to compare the agendas of various government institutions and of the public, so it is ideally suited for exploring how Congress responds to the fragmenting public agenda. Researchers code each agenda into the same categories, allowing for comparisons both between different government institutions and processes and between those institutions and processes and the public. In measuring the public agenda, it uses the same raw data source, the Gallup "most important problem" question, as the analysis of presidential responsiveness earlier in this chapter. However, the way the responses are coded is driven by the structure of congressional committees rather than the public's perceptions, and the data are compiled into quarters rather than poll by poll. Since there is likely to be some delay between when the public becomes concerned about an issue and when Congress takes up that issue, the analysis that follows compares the agendas at a yearly rather than a quarterly level, which seems like a fairer test of responsiveness. For more information about how these data are coded and divided into units, see Appendix G.

Evaluating Congressional Responsiveness

Bryan Jones and Frank Baumgartner, the researchers who designed the Policy Agendas Project data set, look at the relationship between the public's concerns about specific issues and the House's schedule of hearings during the period from 1946 through 1998. They find what they describe as "impressive congruence between the priorities of the public and the priorities of Congress across time" (2004, 1). When public concern about an issue increased, the proportion of hearings about that issue in the House tended to increase as well. For ten of the sixteen issues they examine (62.5 percent), when public concern went up, the proportion of House hearings rose, too. Moreover, when the public became more concerned about an issue, the House's attention to that issue was more likely to rise than was House attention to another issue. Finally, assuming the House's capacity to hold hearings is limited and that more attention to one issue would have to come at the expense of attention to another issue, Jones and Baumgartner find a number of negative correlations in their comparison of issue agendas. When the House devoted more attention to issues of public concern, it paid less attention to other issues. All of this seems to indicate House responsiveness to the public agenda.

Jones and Baumgartner's (2004) analysis covers a period largely prior to the emergence of partisan cable news, and although political polarization was under way in the House in the years toward the end of their time frame, it was not as deep as it would become. During most of the years they analyze, broadcast news was the dominant source of public affairs information. What would happen if we replicate their analysis for a time frame during which the public agenda became more fragmented and partisan divisions deepened in the House? If we use their analytic techniques on the Policy Agendas Project data covering the period from 1969 through 2013, the most recent complete year available at the time of writing, we see good news about the linkage between the U.S. House's hearing agenda and the public agenda. Table 7.2 shows the zero-order correlations between twenty issues on the public and House agendas for the period from 1969 through 2013.

Allowing for a few differences in categories (for example, immigration has become a category in recent years) and a somewhat more granular approach in our analysis as compared to theirs, we see comparable levels of responsiveness.[7] For twelve of twenty categories (60 percent), when public concern about an issue increased, so did the proportion of House hearings about that issue. These are the boxed correlations that run diagonally down the center of the table. The average of these twenty correlations is .326, which suggests significant responsiveness because it is significantly greater than zero. Moreover, this average is virtually identical to the average of Jones and Baumgartner's on-diagonal correlations.[8]

There is also evidence that public concern about an issue was still much more likely to elicit hearings about that issue (60 percent of cases, as in Table 7.2) rather than about another issue (13.4 percent of cases). This 46.6 percent difference in probabilities is similar to the 43.3 percent for Jones and Baumgartner.[9] However, their finding of a crowded congressional agenda in which attention to one issue robs attention from another does not reappear to the same extent. Where they find significant negative correlations, instances where more attention to other issues robbed

---

7. For more details on how data are categorized, see Appendix G.

8. Our mean correlation of .326 ($SD = .28$) is significantly different from 0 ($t = 5.27$, $p < .001$). The mean computed from Jones and Baumgartner's (2004) table is $M = .324$, $SD = .31$.

9. We compute the probability of a significant positive off-diagonal correlation (e.g., rising public concern about an issue is associated with rising congressional attention to something else) by dividing the number of positive off-diagonal coefficients that are significant at $p < .05$, two-tailed (fifty-one for us, forty-six for Jones and Baumgartner) by the total number of off-diagonal coefficients (380 for us, 240 for Jones and Baumgartner) rather than dividing by the total number of all coefficients as Jones and Baumgartner do. The probability of a significant off-diagonal correlation that we observe is not quite significantly lower than what Jones and Baumgartner see ($\chi^2 = 3.68$, $p = .055$).

Table 7.2. Public–congressional hearing agenda confluence

House hearing attention to issues

Public concern	Econ	CRts	Hlth	Agri	Labr	Educ	Envi	Ener	Immi	Tran	Crim	Welf	Hous	Cmrc	Def	Tech	Trad	Intl	Govt	Land
Economy	**.80**	−.35	−.18	.06	.01	−.12	−.01	**.62**	−.26	.10	−.27	.00	.29	.02	.06	−.25	.14	−.29	−.09	−.34
Civil rights	−.18	**.51**	−.54	.29	**.35**	.12	−.06	−.19	−.46	**.36**	−.20	**.50**	.18	−.34	−.11	−.24	−.04	−.43	**.61**	**.37**
Health	−.42	−.11	**.50**	−.17	−.23	.02	**.51**	−.36	.25	−.39	.15	−.33	−.04	.27	−.10	**.33**	.28	.25	−.31	−.12
Agriculture	.19	.07	−.09	**.33**	.12	−.05	−.23	.23	−.12	.11	−.12	.19	.22	−.28	−.09	−.21	**.36**	−.21	.00	.13
Labor	.05	.15	−.19	−.12	−.13	−.40	−.28	.17	−.20	**.34**	−.15	.06	−.07	−.02	.16	−.36	−.34	.09	**.30**	.08
Education	−.54	−.23	**.40**	−.25	−.18	.29	−.03	−.39	**.34**	−.23	**.30**	−.30	−.50	.14	−.29	**.71**	−.21	**.57**	−.16	.10
Environment	−.37	.22	**.31**	−.10	−.07	.15	**.40**	−.27	−.19	−.03	.01	−.05	−.01	−.03	−.08	−.08	.00	.00	−.08	**.29**
Energy	**.33**	−.05	−.18	.04	−.06	−.21	−.26	**.71**	−.06	.13	−.24	.09	−.01	−.10	.14	−.24	−.17	−.16	.10	−.25
Immigration	−.28	.08	.15	−.56	−.43	−.26	−.23	−.17	**.65**	−.13	.06	−.63	−.53	.59	**.56**	.15	−.35	**.62**	−.15	−.41
Transport	**.30**	−.10	−.20	.07	.07	−.10	−.05	**.51**	−.11	.12	−.18	.09	.04	−.22	−.10	−.09	.08	−.17	.10	−.09
Crime	−.47	−.12	.06	.07	.02	.22	−.12	−.36	.06	−.13	.13	.04	−.25	−.16	−.38	**.38**	−.25	.25	.28	**.44**
Welfare	−.45	−.06	**.34**	−.12	−.04	.12	.26	−.48	**.34**	−.38	.28	−.14	−.24	.10	−.37	**.38**	.17	**.43**	−.14	.10
Housing	.00	.29	−.44	.26	**.30**	.04	−.17	.05	−.46	.23	−.34	**.54**	.24	−.34	−.04	−.44	−.19	−.41	**.61**	**.38**
Commerce	−.15	.09	.11	−.60	−.32	−.22	−.11	−.18	**.35**	−.12	.13	−.52	−.39	**.64**	**.63**	.02	−.37	**.45**	−.26	−.32
Defense	−.23	**.49**	−.13	.05	.16	.04	−.23	−.38	.09	.18	.24	.21	.01	−.06	**.30**	−.28	−.15	−.07	.08	.19
Technology	−.33	−.03	**.37**	−.40	−.30	.08	−.13	−.22	**.54**	−.05	**.33**	−.41	−.50	**.45**	.27	**.45**	−.48	**.46**	−.37	−.23
Trade	−.22	−.01	**.43**	.12	.12	.17	**.60**	−.31	.22	−.39	.15	−.12	.04	.07	−.24	.28	**.53**	.04	−.44	−.10
International	−.07	−.10	.04	−.07	−.14	.21	−.06	.09	.12	.15	.07	−.07	−.21	.10	−.16	.23	.11	.12	−.06	−.10
Government	−.07	−.25	−.06	−.46	−.42	−.34	−.43	.27	.08	.13	−.30	−.50	−.55	**.31**	**.36**	.16	−.50	**.48**	.15	−.10
Public land	.26	−.12	−.20	.09	.07	−.08	−.05	**.48**	−.10	.11	−.16	.07	.03	−.22	−.09	−.08	.07	−.16	.11	−.08

Note: Numbers are correlation coefficients between the percentage of Gallup responses naming an issue as the most important facing the country and the percentage of hearings allotted to an issue. Numbers reflect annual data, 1969–2013; $N = 45$ years. Bold denotes a correlation that is significant at $p < .05$; on-diagonal issues at $p < .05$, one-tailed. Italics denote a correlation that approaches significance at $p < .10$.

an issue of attention, in about 28 percent of cases in the period from 1946 through 1998, it happens in less than 17 percent of cases from 1969 through 2013. Even as the public agenda may have greater capacity than scholars once thought, the congressional agenda may as well. The smaller number of tradeoffs could also be a sign of declining congressional responsiveness: Since it has been much less common in recent years for one or a few issues to dominate the public agenda, the House has been less likely to divert attention from its own pursuits to respond to public concern.

Evidence of Declining Responsiveness in U.S. House Hearings

Issues of chronic public concern or acute public concern—those at or near the top of the public agenda—were not much affected by the fragmentation of public priorities. However, we do see signs that the more diverse public agenda began to eat away at congressional responsiveness to a few more marginal issues, those toward the middle or bottom of the public's list of priorities, like energy and technology. For those issues, greater public concern was a weaker predictor of congressional attention to that issue when the public agenda was more diverse.[10]

We also can look at congressional responsiveness overall rather than issue by issue by considering the strength of the relationship between the public agenda as a whole and the congressional agenda of hearings as a whole. Regardless of whether the public is sending less clear signals or is less capable of demanding action, we would expect when the public agenda is more diverse, the correlation between the public and House agendas would be weaker.

We should perhaps begin by acknowledging that the fit between the congressional agenda and the public agenda is never all that good, and it has gotten worse over time. From 1969 through 1991, the first half of the time frame covered by the data, the public agenda explained about 6 percent of variation in the House hearings agenda. From 1992 through 2013,

---

10. Using a PROCESS (Hayes 2013) moderation analysis, we see that this is the case for energy ($b = -1.10$, $SE = .61$, $p = .04$, one-tailed), domestic commerce ($b = -14.62$, $SE = 6.18$, $p = .02$), and technology ($b = -29.06$, $SE = 11.67$, $p = .02$). Two other issues have similar negative interactions that fall just short of significance: labor ($b = -4.22$, $SE = 2.59$, $p = .11$) and the environment ($b = -3.66$, $SE = 2.46$, $p = .15$). Including the latter two issues, the expected moderation effect of public agenda diversity is not significant for sixteen of the twenty issues, and the effect is positive for one issue, agriculture ($b = 18.16$, $SE = 6.41$, $p = .007$). For a discussion of this analysis, see Appendix G.

the second half, explained variation dropped to 2 percent.[11] Moreover, the congressional agenda itself is stunningly diverse. We measure diversity in the House's agenda of hearings the same way we measure public agenda diversity (see Appendix B), and like the public agenda diversity measure, the measure for Congress varies from 0 (a very focused agenda) to 1 (a very diverse agenda). When measure with the Policy Agendas Project data, the average diversity for the House hearings agenda in a given year is .93 compared to an average level of public agenda diversity at .56.[12] This is partly a function of the way the Policy Agendas Project data is coded. Since its code categories are based on congressional committee structures, every category receives at least some congressional attention, whereas some of them receive no attention from the public. One way to think of this is to say that Congress has "housekeeping" to do, whether the public is interested in it or not, and it points up the fact that it is neither necessary nor desirable for the congressional agenda and the public agenda to match perfectly.

The question of how much correspondence there *should* be between the public's agenda and Congress's agenda is a normative one. Empirically, it is more useful to consider how diversity in the public's agenda affects the number of hearings and the degree of agenda correspondence. In creating regression models to look at this relationship, we include measures of partisan polarization and the number of days the House spends in session, along with the degree of diversity in the public agenda, to assess the unique effects of public fragmentation on representation processes.[13] The patterns emerge more clearly in these models when the prior year's public agenda diversity is used to predict the current year's degree of agenda correspondence, an approach that has the added benefit of aiding causal inference. To measure the degree of correspondence between the agendas, we compare the public agenda to the House hearings agenda each year.[14] When the match is good, we should see issues rising and falling together on the two agendas. Table 7.3 shows these analyses. The first column, la-

---

11. This is based on squaring the average Pearson's correlation (mean r for 1969–1991 = .25, mean r for 1992–2013 = .14) between the issue agendas of the public and the House; that is, the degree of similarity between the relative levels of concern or attention across all issues in a given year. For more on how this correlation is computed, see Appendix G.

12. Recall that the policy-oriented coding structure of the Policy Agendas Project leads to lower estimates of public agenda diversity than the coding system we adapted from McCombs and Zhu 1995. For a comparison, see Figure 4.1.

13. For more information about these measures, see Appendix G.

14. This measure of correspondence is a Pearson's correlation. For more details, see Appendix G.

Table 7.3. Correspondence between public agenda and House of Representatives agenda

	r	β
Legislative days	−.03	−.01
House polarization	−.19	−.33*
Prior H-20	−.04	.08
Public concern: defense	.56***	.54***
Prior H-20 × defense	.51***	.29*
Adjusted R^2		.51***

Note: Numbers reflect annual data, 1969–2013; $N = 45$ years. The first column shows zero-order correlations; the second shows standardized regression coefficients. Significance indicated by *$p < .05$; **$p < .01$; ***$p < .001$.

beled *r*, shows the zero-order correlations between the predictors and the fit between the public and House agendas. The second column, labeled β, shows standardized multiple regression coefficients that measure the unique contribution of each of the predictors to explain the match between the agendas.

The relationship between the amount of diversity in the public agenda in one year and the degree of correspondence between the public agenda and the House hearings agenda in the following year is complex. In zero-order correlation, none of the variables—number of days in session, House polarization, and public agenda diversity—improves the match between the public agenda and the House agenda. This apparent lack of relationship between public agenda diversity and agenda correspondence was largely the result of three exceptional years: the Iraq War years of 2005 through 2007, when public concern about defense was high and the public agenda was very diverse. When those years are excluded, a more diverse public agenda does result in a weaker match between the public's agenda and the House's, as we had expected.[15] Moreover, most years when House responsiveness was high were years when public concern about defense was also high, which suggests high public concern about defense could override the tendency of public agenda diversity to reduce responsiveness. This implies that public agenda diversity may have different effects on agenda correspondence, depending on whether public concern about defense was low or high. This type of relationship, known as an interaction effect, is included as a predictor in the regression model, as is public concern about defense. Essentially, the interaction effect measures to what extent the effect of public agenda diversity on the match between

15. $r = −.27, p < .05$, one-tailed.

the public agenda and the House agenda depends on what the public is worried about.

With all of the predictors in place, the model in Table 7.3 explores how fragmentation of the public agenda compares with other potential explanations of congressional responsiveness. It shows that how many days the House was in session does not predict the degree of correspondence between the House hearings agenda and the public agenda—even if Congress were to meet for more days, the model suggests, the match between the agendas would not improve. Next, the degree of polarization in Congress does contribute to the quality of the fit between the agendas. A more politically polarized House is less responsive to the public agenda. Public agenda diversity on its own does not seem to predict a better match between the agendas, but when it interacts with concern about defense it becomes a strong predictor. Finally, when the public is more worried about defense issues, as they might be in wartime, the match between the public agenda and the House agenda improves.

The regression model reveals that the degree of diversity in the public agenda and the issue that drives that diversity matter as much as polarization does in explaining how well the House agenda matches the public's. This means that fragmentation of the public agenda produces unique challenges for democratic leaders responding to public opinion. Figure 7.2 depicts the interaction. When public concern about defense is high, a diverse public agenda in the previous year is associated with a slightly better fit between the House hearings agenda and the public agenda in the following year. However, if the public is less concerned about defense, the more diverse public agenda is linked with a considerably worse fit between the House and public agendas the following year. The recent spate of U.S. wars may have camouflaged the declining congruence between the public agenda and the House agenda as the public's priorities have become more diffuse. Moreover, since the House is chronically concerned about defense as an issue, to some extent the agenda congruence that is associated with higher levels of public concern about defense is a result of the public's agenda coming to match the House's rather than the other way around.

Conclusion

The analyses in this chapter must be treated with some caution. Presidential addresses have a complex relationship with public opinion, and the substantive effect of public agenda diversity on the relationship between public priorities and U.S. House hearings is fairly small. Nevertheless, both analyses reveal that fragmentation of the public's priorities produces

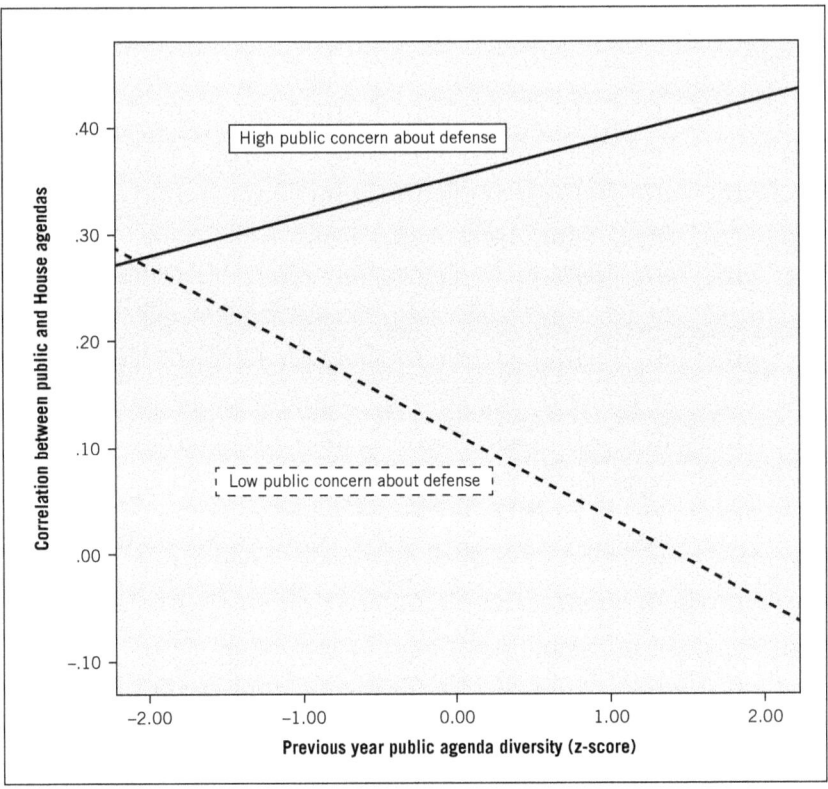

Figure 7.2. Predicted values of public/House agenda match and the interaction of lagged public agenda diversity and public concern about defense, 1969–2013. *Note:* High and low concern about defense are 1 standard deviation above and below its mean.

problems for democratic representation above and beyond the partisan polarization it may facilitate. When public priorities are more diverse, democratic political institutions are less likely to respond to them. One could, of course, argue that the government ought not to slavishly follow public opinion, which is sometimes volatile and commonly ill-informed. However, regardless of how much attention one thinks the government *should* pay to the public's agenda of concerns, the results show that when the list of concerns is more diverse, the government pays less attention to them.

In the U.S. House of Representatives, unless there is a war on, the more diverse the public agenda becomes, the worse the fit between the issues the public is concerned about and the issues about which the House holds hearings. No matter how many days the chamber meets or how deep its partisan divides, a fragmented public agenda carries less weight than a public agenda that is more focused. This occurs even at the level of public hearings, before logrolling or lobbying or partisan control become major factors in explaining the fate of public policies, and it happens even in the national legislative body with the greatest capacity to deal with a long list of public concerns. Indeed, some of the evidence suggests that the longer the list of public concerns, the fewer hearings the House holds.

When no particular issue stands out from the crowd of issues on the public agenda, presidents are less likely to address the issue that most concerns the public or, indeed, to respond to any issue on the public agenda. Of course, a good deal of recent research suggests that this is no longer the goal of presidents, who commonly speak to specific partisan and issue audiences as they attempt to marshal support from various factions or to respond to the concerns of specific constituencies. The evidence offered in this chapter suggests that the public as a whole, increasingly divided as it is, is not as well represented as these subgroups and perhaps cannot be. Major presidential addresses tend to be historic occasions, and, especially in a cacophonous media environment, a president may need to hoard the sense of occasion that accompanies a national address. If such speeches must be rare to remain meaningful, the sheer number of issues that today vie nearly equally on the public agenda mean that a national presidential address will leave a great deal of public demand for presidential response unsatisfied.

The results presented here also suggest, though they cannot confirm, another troubling change in the relationship between the public and its representatives. During the mass media era, what was sometimes called the golden age of presidential television, many scholars argued that a key source of political power was the ability to shape public opinion. Leaders, particularly presidents, could focus public attention on the issues they wanted to take up (e.g., Canes-Wrone 2001) and possibly even shape public perspectives on an issue (Bennett 1990; Hallin 1986; Kernell 2007). Some have suggested that this power has waned in the post-broadcast era, as partisan political actors preach to their respective choirs rather than persuading opponents or agnostics, and many citizens tune out altogether (Baum and Kernell 1999; Kernell and Rice 2011; Young and Perkins 2005).

Yet, as the public agenda became more diverse, a new kind of power became possible: choice. When a single issue dominates the public agenda by drawing considerable public concern, representatives who want to appear responsive need to address that issue. If half of the public names inflation as the most important issue, a responsive government should take up inflation and should probably expect considerable public outcry if it does not. In contrast, if three or four issues vie for the top of the public agenda, political leaders can choose among them. If jobs, the economy, the Middle East, and health care are all nearly tied in the level of concern they attract on the public agenda, a political actor has more choice about which one to tackle and may face fewer penalties for not addressing any of them but, rather, striking out in a different direction. In other words, they can craft a political agenda that avoids issues threatening to their power by ignoring rather than by setting the public agenda.

We see at least two hints of this in the data analyzed in this chapter. First, as the public agenda has become more diverse, the U.S. House has made fewer tradeoffs between the issues it had been pursuing and issues about which the public is concerned. This could, of course, be attributed to slight differences in measurement between this analysis and that of Bryan Jones and Frank Baumgartner (2004), or it could be that the capacity of the House to hold hearings has increased over time so that tradeoffs are rarer. Nevertheless, the combination of declining responsiveness and declining tradeoffs suggests that the House has been freer to choose its issues and less guided by public concerns. Second, although the ability of presidents to direct public attention to the issues of their choice seems to have declined, their ability to distract the public by further diversifying its agenda has not. This suggests that perhaps the power of the president to shape public opinion, rather than waning, has changed. By diluting the public agenda, presidents may be able to pursue whatever issues they wish, whereas a more focused public might demand that they respond to a particular policy issue.

Political actors may have used the opportunity presented by a diverse public agenda to pursue their own ends or satisfy particular constituencies. Or institutions may simply have been overwhelmed by the long, undifferentiated list of public priorities. Either way, the fragmented public agenda has frayed the democratic relationship between the public and the government.

8

What Happened to *Us*?

> When our government is spoken of as some menacing, threatening foreign entity, it ignores the fact that in our democracy, government is us. We, the people.
>
> —PRESIDENT BARACK OBAMA, commencement address at the University of Michigan, May 1, 2010

Over the course of the later twentieth century and into the twenty-first, the public agenda has become more and more fragmented. Although there have been one or two historical fluctuations in this trend, in general, the individual citizen concerns that make up the public agenda have become more and more different from each other. Perhaps it is no wonder that we no longer see the government as an extension of us—perhaps we no longer recognize an *us*. Perhaps we no longer see common causes among the welter of particularistic interests. Perhaps the term *public agenda* has become a misnomer, suggesting an entity, *the public*, which no longer exists.

Some would argue that this is as it should be—that there were always multiple publics with different issue agendas whose concerns went unrecognized when "the public" was perceived as a single entity. Yet the data do not suggest that these "publics" always existed but rather that the "general public," which shared common concerns in the middle of the twentieth century, fragmented into what some might see as multiple "publics" with diverse concerns. The shared priorities that give force to majority opinions in democratic contexts have dwindled.

This fragmentation of public concern is a phenomenon distinct from the political polarization about which so many political leaders, pundits, scholars, and journalists have expressed alarm. Not only has the public become increasingly divided about how the government should respond to a particular issue, such as LGBTQ rights or health care—the hallmark of polarization. The public has become increasingly divided about which problems the government should address, in other words, fragmented. The problems produced by each are different. Polarization on particular policies may grind government to a halt, sometimes literally, as in the case of the fight over raising the debt ceiling. When polarized government does produce policy because one party has a clear legislative majority, that policy stands a good chance of being more extreme than the majority of people would prefer. Fragmentation, however, can lead to policies that serve the few rather than the many because no general public exists to stand opposed to specific interests. It can allow government institutions to ignore public concerns because no public problem receives a level of public concern sufficient to require that government address it. It can also, as Barack Obama notes in his commencement speech (quoted in the epigraph), lead to a government estranged from its people, and a people who are estranged from one another, because they fail to recognize the common challenges that bind them together.

It would be a mistake to think that the media environment is solely responsible for the fragmentation of the public agenda during the late twentieth and early twenty-first centuries. Many other social changes have undoubtedly contributed. The end of the Cold War may have made the threat of human annihilation less salient for people, enabling them to shift their focus to other, more diverse public problems, although the newer global threat of terrorism does not seem to have encouraged Americans to refocus their concerns to the same degree. Some scholars suggest that political leaders no longer seek to unify the public in support of their candidacy or their policies (Cohen 2010; Kreiss 2016), which could be either a cause or an effect in the contemporary media environment: either national leaders no longer seek to unify the public and, thus, no unified public emerges, or the degree of fragmentation defies national leaders' ability to unify the public and so they no longer attempt to do so. Most likely, both patterns are at play. Morris Fiorina (2010), Robert Putnam (2000), and Theda Skocpol (2003) note the decline of the kinds of broad-based organizations prominent during the mid-twentieth century. Labor unions, and service clubs, such as the Kiwanis or Elks clubs, which once served as umbrella organizations for a diversity of concerns and interests and so might have served to focus the public, have seen their memberships and activity levels decline. Newer organizations with much narrower interests, such as Amnesty International (begun in 1961) or the recently politicized National Rifle Association (transformed in 1977), have proliferated, as Fiorina observes, and also require less engagement from their members, as Skocpol notes. Yet, if these scholars are correct, fewer people today are active in clubs and organizations that advocate for social change, so it is hard to see how this explosion of narrow advocacy groups could explain the growing diversity of the public's issue agenda unless the media played a role.

The relationships we document reveal the role of the news media in the fragmentation of the public agenda, but they also upend much of the conventional wisdom about how this process works. Cable news channels do not promote distinctive issue agendas, and the agenda-setting influence of broadcast news has not faded. Instead, once the Cold War ended and the competition for audience attention intensified in the expanding media universe, the news agenda itself changed. Issues that were more likely to provoke public concern received more attention from news outlets. International issues, which were both expensive to cover and unlikely to arouse much concern in the public were replaced by crime, terrorism, and health care, all of which were quick to spark public anxiety. Although this did not increase the diversity of the news agenda, which had always been relatively broad as it surveyed the social world for citizens, it fragmented the public agenda as more concerns appeared on the public's list of issue priorities. The expansion of media choices did not put an end to a shared public forum for identifying public problems. Instead, it turns out that a shared public forum does not necessarily produce consensus on the most important issue.

Occasionally, this process has been interrupted by historical events. Public concern about the economy has typically resulted in a more focused public agenda, and the Great Recession of 2007–2009 sharply reduced the diversity of the public agenda for the first time in decades, even though the Iraq War still competed with the nation's economic troubles on the public agenda. However, the increased focus of public concerns did not last, and, by 2014, the public agenda was, once again, on a steep trajectory of increasing diversity. The terrorist attacks of September 11, 2001, slowed the fragmentation of the public agenda briefly, but they did little to focus it. It is not clear that either media or political leaders can still bring focus to the public agenda, although, for some issues, the public may be more influenced by media than by social reality.

The evidence suggests it takes extreme events to increase the level of public consensus about issue priorities, but it also suggests that patterns of public attention to news mean the public's issue agenda is not as diverse as it might be. It seems likely that everyday news agendas have come to devote more attention to issues that spark public concern, in part as a response to flagging public attention, and therefore make for a more fragmented public agenda. Yet those periods of typical news with the greatest potential to drive public agenda fragmentation are precisely the days when the public is paying the least attention to news. The moments when the public pays the most attention to news are periods of national crisis, the kinds of events when the news media's agenda is more focused and less likely than the everyday agenda to promote diversity in the public agenda. Oddly, this implies that if people paid more attention to news than they do, public consensus on issue priorities would be at a lower ebb than it is.

In general, while there is evidence that expanding media choice is related to a more diverse public agenda, supporting the *falling apart* explanation of public agenda diversity, the evidence for the *driven apart* argument is more compelling. News media cues present the public with a wider array of public problems, introducing citizens to a world beyond personal experience, and in doing so, news promotes a more diverse public agenda to the extent that its content sparks public concern. Attention to news tends to focus the public agenda at least in part because it rises in moments of crisis, when the news agenda is more focused.

The fragmented public agenda has changed the relationship between the public and the government as well. Well-intentioned legislators faced with a list of public concerns longer than Santa's gift list, with many issues given virtually equivalent priorities, may struggle to figure out where to start. The sheer diversity of public concerns may overwhelm the ability of governmental institutions to respond to public opinion. In addition, the signals from the public about what it wants government to prioritize become less and less clear as the public agenda becomes more and more diverse. Presidents may not be as effectively signaled to give national addresses about a public concern and, thus, become less responsive to public concern. They may, as several scholars have suggested, "lean into" the fragmentation by appealing to favored groups rather than to the public as a whole (Cohen 2010; Kernell 2007). Moreover, while their ability to lead the public has been undermined, their ability to distract the public by adding still more issues to the list of public concerns has not. For their part, legislative institutions may take the opportunity presented by a diverse public agenda to pursue their own priorities while giving short shrift to the public's. Even institutions and legislative processes with enormous capacity pay less attention to a more fragmented public agenda. Thus, the media system that some hoped would liberate the public agenda from the influence of political elites may have liberated political elites from the public agenda instead. As Peter Bachrach and Morton Baratz (1962) suggest, hyperpartisan polarized political debate masks the ability of political actors to avoid issues that matter to the public when there is little consensus on a public agenda.

Democratic Governance and the Diverse Public Agenda

The fragmentation of the public's issue agenda has consequences for democracy and for the role of public opinion in democracy. First, fragmentation may liberate political leaders to take up issues as they choose. Political leaders may take the opportunity presented by an unfocused public agenda to advance their own pet issues or attend to the concerns of groups likely to be essential to their reelection. In several of President Donald Trump's earliest forays into policy making, he kept promises he made to his base, but he was not responsive to the concerns of the general public. A poll taken by the Harvard T. H. Chan School of Public Health (Politico and T. H. Chan School of Public Health 2017) reveals that many issue priorities of Trump voters were not shared by the public more generally. Ninety percent of Trump voters saw illegal immigration as an important problem, while 40 percent of the public did not see it as much of a problem at all. Thus, while more than three-quarters of Trump voters wanted aggressive action on illegal immigration in the first hundred days of the Trump presidency, for most Americans, it was not a priority. Similarly, while 85 percent of Trump supporters wanted the administration to prioritize repealing and replacing Obamacare, only 44 percent of the country did.

Martin Gilens and Benjamin Page (2014) offer evidence of a broader trend in policy making: public policy better reflects the wishes of the economic elite than of the general public. Given the importance of money to political success, this kind of responsiveness makes political sense, but it also suggests that public policy is less responsive to the public will, perhaps because the public will is much more difficult to discern and much easier to circumvent. Of course, this pattern in policy making is not novel. E. E. Schattschneider noted in 1975 that the "heavenly chorus of public opinion sings with a strong upper class accent" (35–36). He meant by this that organized interests are much more capable of shaping public policy than is the general public. Yet fragmentation may play a unique role in subverting policy responsiveness and enhancing the power of interest groups. The public would seem to be an even less effective counterweight against such organized interests to the extent that no general public interest can be identified.

It may also be the case that polarization in legislatures and fragmentation in the public feed each other. Polarization makes it hard to reach decisions in the absence of supermajorities. When the public agenda is highly focused on a single issue, it may encourage legislators to work toward the passage of legislation even from their disparate, entrenched positions. For example, a major recession or a government shutdown can provoke a great deal of public wrath that may encourage legislators to work it out, even when neither side is capable of imposing its will. When the public agenda is fragmented, it is surely tempting to respond to gridlock by simply taking up another issue that seems just about as important on the public agenda. Rather than working to resolve a broken immigration policy, why not move on to address a broken health care system when you get stuck?

From the public's perspective, the more fragmented public agenda may have contributed to changed public assessments of government. In light of the diversity of the public's issue agenda, many contemporary public complaints about government performance make much more sense. Complaints that the government pays attention to the wrong issues reference a fragmented agenda—"Why in the world is the government devoting all that time and attention to health care when the real problem is the lack of good jobs?" Moreover, when people complain that government fails to pay much attention to the issues they care most about, they are almost certainly right. With more issues on the public agenda and with public concern spread over them more evenly, a government with a limited legislative capacity devotes relatively less attention to the concerns of relatively more people. Apparently, contradictory complaints that government overregulates yet fails to respond to public concerns also seem to echo a fragmented public agenda—"Why in the world does the government impose all these regulations on how you do your hiring and what kinds of safety equipment you have to have and how you dispose of waste but does not do anything about improving public education?" If government makes policies in places where many people perceive a low-level problem or no problem at all but does not do much to address the particular concern that tops their lists, such a complaint would resonate. Yet, if the public agenda is highly diverse, most people would experience this paradox of overregulation and lack of attention at the same time. These may not be problems of positional representation—the complaint need not be that the policies fail to align with public preferences about what should be done. Rather, the complaints are about where policy making is needed, that the government "does nothing" to address the public's concerns.

Recognizing that the public is fragmented also offers some insight into the demand for more localized governance. Of course, for much of the twentieth century, the demand for "states' rights" was a veiled appeal to maintain racial inequalities in some parts of the country. That tradition surely continues as particular communities balk at the expansion of civil rights to racial and sexual minorities. However, local-level movements toward legalizing marijuana and raising the minimum wage reveal the broader implications of localized governing. For a fragmented public, it may be more appealing because it is seen as more likely to deal with "our" problems rather than "other people's" problems. Average Oklahomans, who were not much affected by the collapse of housing prices during the 2008 credit crisis, could not figure out why the federal government spent so much time, energy, and money addressing the breakdown of the mortgage industry. Most Americans were delighted when the price of oil began to collapse in 2014, but, for Oklahomans, it meant a serious state budget crisis about which the rest of the nation seemed unaware. Social problems are often local and regional, and to the extent that a generalized public has given way to a fragmented one, a demand to address community problems may no longer be the equivalent of a demand to address the problems of the public as a whole. The fragmented public agenda, then, may be one reason for the wave of public discontent with a government that seems unresponsive to it.

A Public of Publics? Majorities, Minorities, and Power

The fragmented public agenda may also be part of a larger transformation in which public opinion majorities became less and less important in U.S. politics. From the founding of the republic, there has always been debate over the role public opinion majorities should play in governance, and that role has been dynamic. The twentieth century was rife with lessons about the dangers of majority public opinion, particularly toward minority communities such as European Jews and African Americans, and many political processes in the late twentieth and early twenty-first centuries became more and more insulated from majority opinion. Early twentieth century social justice movements fought to reduce economic inequality and, thus, benefited from the majority status of workers compared to owners. In the later twentieth century, social justice movements fought for equality of respect for ethnic, racial, sexual, and religious minorities, and majority public opinion was an important element of the discrimination they struggled against. The Supreme Court, rather than the legislature or the public, became the site where battles for recognition of minority rights were waged (Meyer and Boutcher 2007). Other political processes came to be insulated from majority opinion as well. Increasingly rationalized redistricting produced legislators who were insulated from voters because their districts were overloaded with voters from a single party, many to such an extent that candidates ran unopposed. Campaign finance laws proved inadequate to stem the growing preeminence of wealthy donors over average voters. Legislatures, and sometimes the public itself, instituted legislative processes that required supermajorities to pass legislation and, so, indirectly, created systems of minority rule. For example, Proposition 13, passed by California voters in 1978, requires a two-thirds majority vote in the state legislature to increase taxes. In Oklahoma, increasing taxes requires a three-quarters legislative majority after the passage of State Question 640 in 1992.

As the political power of majorities declined, the rise of identity politics and the struggle for respect of differences threw into sharp relief the unique problems faced by different social groups. Political researchers identified different groups as having different agendas (e.g., Cavari 2017). In this sense, not only did the character of the public agenda change but our way of thinking about it changed. Majority opinion was now something to be resisted rather than heeded. The idea of the general public seemed disrespectful of the many intergroup differences, even though, as we have seen, government responsiveness to minority groups does not necessarily (or even typically) mean addressing the needs of the oppressed. Indeed, it may mean that to those who have, more shall be given (Gilens and Page 2014).

The move from serving a general public to acknowledging numerous publics undercut the traditional power of public opinion in democracy, for while the power of an interest group may lie in its wealth or its commitment, the power of the public resides in its numbers. Any one citizen's vote is unlikely to be the vote that decides an election outcome, but together the public elects its representatives. Holding public officials accountable commonly requires mass public attention and condemnation; without it, abuses of power may continue. Demanding legislative change virtually requires that the public act in large numbers, and a united public can be a counterweight to the demands of powerful (as well as powerless) minority interest groups. Changes in the political system and changes in the media system have helped to fragment the public so that meaningful majorities are less likely and less powerful. Without the ability to perceive common interests, without a shared understanding of the most important problems of the day, it is difficult for the general public to make itself heard in mass democracy at all (Schattschneider 1975). In the wake of Donald Trump's election to the presidency, many pundits have doubled down on the idea that majority public opinion cannot be trusted, that a hostile, populist public elected a dangerously unstable and unqualified president. Yet, if majority public opinion had decided the election, Trump would not be president: 3 million more voters cast ballots for Hillary Clinton than for Trump. It was only in the Electoral College, an institution designed to protect against the excesses of majority public opinion, that Trump prevailed.

All of this suggests that new opportunities for exercising political power emerged in a saturated communication environment. In the twentieth century, political power was tied to the ability to influence mass opinion (and particularly the public's agenda of priorities) via mass media. The propaganda and demagoguery of two world wars, the Cold War, countless smaller conflicts, and several genocides made the dangers of elites' manipulation of the mass media and the public very apparent. As the publicly available media choices grew, many worried this power would be enhanced by a polarized media environment in which leaders could mobilize their ideological supporters. Others believed the power to influence had been undermined for the same reason: leaders could reach only those who already supported them. Yet, if the public is fragmented, power may emerge not in influencing public opinion to produce majority support but, rather, in leveraging the vacuum created by divisions within the public. Distracting the public by adding more issues to its already long list of priorities and addressing those specific groups most likely to be supportive via the specialized media they use enables leaders to pursue their own agendas without regard for the general public, which, in some senses, no longer exists. At the end of the day, the power to shape the public agenda is just that: power. It can be bent to uses both evil and good, and the lack of a sense of common cause in the public generates its own problems. As Senator Elizabeth Warren pointed out at the Democratic National Convention in July 2016, if poor and working-class communities cannot see past their racial, ethnic, or religious differences, they cannot band together to fight their shared economic disadvantages. Democracy requires not just citizens but a public.

Appendix A

Coding the "Most Important Problem" Question

Using the iPoll database, we identified 254 instances from 1975 through 2014 when Gallup pollers asked the "most important problem" question with this wording: "What do you think is the most important problem facing this country today?" All are included in our data set.

We adapted Max McCombs and Jian-Hua Zhu's (1995) eighteen categories to recode responses but found we needed two additional broad categories to capture changes in public life after 1995. First, we added "Media" as a broad category to capture responses that the media were the most important problem facing the country. Second, we added "Terrorism" as a broad category. When McCombs and Zhu initially developed their coding scheme, terrorism was a subcategory of "Law and Order." The national security implications of the September 11 attacks may very well have changed the conceptualization of terrorism for both policy makers and citizens. To avoid methodological problems arising from the concept's evolving meaning, we reclassified it as a main category rather than a subcategory. Details of the coding categories and key coding rules (such as the changing meaning of references to Afghanistan) follow.

Two coders converted the Gallup response coding into the twenty broader categories. Next to each response category coded by Gallup is the percentage of respondents giving that answer, and coders input this value into the relevant broader category and summed total percentage of responses for each of these broad categories. Where Gallup reported a response category as including less than 1 percent of responses (signified by an asterisk), coders entered .5 into the relevant broader category. Although our coders assigned each of Gallup's code categories to one and only one of our broader categories, overall totals for Gallup's coding of each poll typically exceed 100 percent because some respondents gave more than one response to the question. A few polls have overall totals of less than 100 percent.

Intercoder reliability was tested on a random sample of thirty-nine Gallup polls (16.3 percent of the total). Krippendorff's alpha for the coders' ratio-level totals for each of the twenty categories ranged from .78 to 1.0, with a mean of .93 (SD = .07). To ensure that any coding error would not be confounded with time, one coder coded all data from odd-numbered months (e.g., January, March, May), while the other coded even-numbered months (e.g., February, April, June). Alphas for each of the twenty broad categories are shown in the list that follows.

Most Important Problem Codes

1. Jobs (Krippendorff's α = 1.00)
Unemployment
Unemployment/jobs
Unemployment/depression
Unemployment/recession
Unemployment recession/depression
Recession
Trade deficit
Foreign trade/trade deficit
Labor/unions/strike
Imports/loss of American jobs

2. Money (Krippendorff's α = .96)
Inflation
Cost of living
Inflation/cost of living
Food prices
Fuel/oil prices
Gasoline price
Gap between rich and poor
Housing cost
Housing shortage
Corporate corruption
Interest rates
Lack of money
Savings and loans
Taxes
Taxes/cost of living
Wages
Wage issues

3. Spending (Krippendorff's α = .78)
Federal budget/deficit/national debt
Government spending
Government spending too much for space
Military spending
Social spending
Reagan budget cuts
Military budget cuts
Military downsizing
Lack of military defense

4. Welfare (Krippendorff's α = .83)
Welfare
Social security/welfare
Shortages of welfare
Too much welfare
Cuts in spending for social programs/welfare
"Fairness" issue: government policies favor rich

5. General Economic (Krippendorff's α = .998)
General economic
Economy in general
Other economy (when "general economy" is present)
Farms

6. General Int'l Issues (Krippendorff's α = .88)
General international problems/foreign relations/foreign policy
Foreign aid/focus overseas
General war/peace/arms race/arms talks
Defense/military/national security
Fear of war
War
War/peace

Peace/war/atomic bomb
Peace/war/nuclear war/China/Russia
Disarmament/nuclear disarmament
Nuclear testing/arms race
Future of United Nations
Preparedness of navy and army
Atomic bomb, hydrogen bomb
Failure of summit conference/arms talk/arms negotiation
Second-rate nation prestige

7. Soviet/Europe (Krippendorff's $\alpha = 1.00$)
Afghanistan war/Russian invasion
Soviet
Relations/communications with Russia
Russia/threat of war with
Kosovo/Serbia/Yugoslavia/Milosevic
Bosnia
Russia/break up of Soviet Union

8. Asia (Krippendorff's $\alpha = 1.00$)
Vietnam
Korea
Southeast Asia
China/Asia/Formosa/Far East
Situation in North Korea
Situation with China

9. Mideast (Krippendorff's $\alpha = .96$)
Gulf
Saddam Hussein
Middle East/Persian Gulf crisis
Iranian situation
War/conflict in the Middle East
Situation in Iraq
War in Afghanistan
Iraq/Persian Gulf crisis
Iraq/Kuwait/Middle East crisis/Persian Gulf crisis
Kuwait/Iraq/Middle East crisis/the war
Kuwait/Iraq/Middle East crisis/the war/Saddam Hussein

10. Latin America/Africa (Krippendorff's $\alpha = .79$)
Central America
Africa/Congo
Somalia
Iran/Contra
Haiti

11. Law and Order (Krippendorff's $\alpha = .99$)
Spying/espionage
CIA/FBI
Crime/law and order/riots
Lenient judicial system
Supreme court
Drugs
Gun control
School shootings
Child abuse
Crime
Crime/violence
Guns laws too weak
Availability of guns
Judges, criminal justice system/lawyers
Judicial system/courts/laws

12. Health (Krippendorff's $\alpha = .96$)
Health care for the elderly
Health care
Number of people without health care
AIDS
Alcoholism
Cost of health care/health insurance
Care for the elderly/health insurance
Cancer/diseases
Poor health care/hospitals
Medicare

13. Environment (Krippendorff's $\alpha = 1.00$)
Environment
Water shortages
Nuclear power plant accidents
Water/air pollution
Environment/pollution

14. **Education** (Krippendorff's α = .85)
    Education
    Education costs/quality/tuition/credits
    Youth
    Education/poor education/access to education

15. **Government/Political** (Krippendorff's α = .87)
    Government leadership
    Political corruption
    Watergate
    Nixon
    Distrust in government
    Apathy
    Moral
    American public's desire to get something for nothing
    Religion
    Religion and politics
    School prayer
    Racial/civil rights
    Protest/demonstrations
    Abortion/pro and con
    Women's rights
    National unity
    General unrest
    Dissatisfaction with government
    Big government
    Gay rights issues/gay marriage
    Natural disaster response/relief efforts/funding
    Elections/election reform/election year
    Lewinsky controversy
    Parental rights taken away
    Political corruption/abuse of power
        Dissatisfaction with government/congress/politicians/poor leadership/corruption/abuse of power
    Government/president/Congress/politicians
    Judicial system

16. **Social Relations** (Krippendorff's α = .91)
    Slums/urban renewal
    Poverty/homeless
    Food shortages
    Population explosion
    Immigration
    Refugee problems
    Aliens
    Communication/lack of/generation gap
    Family problems/child rearing
    Family problems/child rearing/parental discipline/alcoholism
    Housing/slums/urban renewal/dying cities
    Busing
    Teens' problems/employment/need for recreation
    Ethics/moral/religious/family decline/dishonesty
    Lack of respect for each other
    Care for the elderly
    Children's behavior/way they are raised
    Race relations/racism
    Youth/teen pregnancy

17. **Technology** (Krippendorff's α = .91)
    Energy
    Energy crisis
    Space
    Technology
    Transportation
    Mass transportation
    Automation
    NASA
    Advancement of computers/technology
    Y2K
    Lack of energy resources

18. **Terrorism** (Krippendorff's α = .92)
    Terrorism
    Feeling of fear in this country

Terrorism/hijacking
Terrorism/hostages

19. Media (Krippendorff's α = 1.00)
The media

20. Miscellaneous (Krippendorff's α = .94)
Miscellaneous (general)
Miscellaneous (domestic)
Miscellaneous (foreign)
Others (please indicate in the coding sheet)/undesignated

Coding Guidelines

References to Afghanistan prior to 1995 are coded under "Soviet Union/Europe." During and after 1995, Afghanistan is coded under "Mideast."

References to Iran between November 1979 and July 1981 are coded under "Terrorism." Otherwise, Iran is coded under "Mideast."

Iran/Contra is coded under "Latin America/Africa."

The subcategory "Care for the elderly" without any mention of health is coded under "Social Relations."

If a Gallup category contains elements that fit multiple issue categories in our coding scheme, the first and/or most general response is used to categorize it. (For example, "Excessive government spending: Government spending too much for space, military, government spending too much for social programs, big government" belongs under "Spending" because it first refers to government spending.)

Appendix B

Computing Diversity and Volatility
in the Public Agenda

Agenda Diversity

Previous research (Chaffee and Wilson 1977; Culbertson 1992; McCombs and Zhu 1995) has quantified agenda diversity with the Shannon index of entropy, also known as the H statistic (Shannon and Weaver 1949). The formula is as follows:

$$H = -\sum_{i=1}^{k} P_i(\log_2 P_i)$$

In the notation, P_i is the percentage (expressed as a decimal between 0 and 1) of responses naming the ith issue on an agenda of k issues. Each percentage is multiplied by its base-2 logarithm—like Max McCombs and Jian-Hua Zhu (1995), we use the natural log rather than the base-2 log for ease of computation—and then summed. Because the log of values less than 1 are negative, the sum is then multiplied by –1.

As McCombs and Zhu note, the main contributors to H in this formula are the equality of the percentages (indicating greater agenda diversity and less concentration of public attention on certain issues) and k, the number of issues. Like McCombs and Zhu, we essentially hold k constant by coding the range of issues into a set number of larger categories; thus, the main determinants of H are how evenly public attention is divided among issues and the summed total number of responses. When public concern is distributed more evenly across more issues, the value of H is higher, indicating greater agenda diversity. The theoretical minimum of H is 0, when all responses name the same issue. The theoretical maximum depends on the number of responses and, in our sample, ranges from 2.68 to 4.80. Like McCombs and Zhu (1995), we standardize H for ease of interpretation and comparison between polls so that it ranges from 0 (all public attention focused on a single issue) to 1 (public attention evenly divided across all issue categories). Our refinement is to standardize by dividing each poll's H statistic by its theoretical maximum, which avoids inflating H for polls with a high total. If we assume a total of 100, the approach McCombs and Zhu (1995) use, the theoretical maximum would be 2.996. This would result if every one of the twenty issue categories had been named in 5 percent of responses.

Agenda Volatility

When agendas have high issue volatility, issues stay on the agenda for a shorter period. We chart the time in months from when an issue rises to at least 10 percent of responses as the most important problem to when it drops to less than that threshold. We also calculate a survival statistic to estimate, for each poll, the probability that an issue would have survived on the agenda over a specific time period: four to six months. In both these general approaches, we follow McCombs and Zhu (1995), although we differ in our calculation of the survival statistic. The Kaplan-Meier survival function (Kaplan and Meier 1958) is as follows:

$$P(t) = \prod_{t_j < t} \frac{n'_j}{n_j}$$

In the formula, the number of cases (issues) under observation at the beginning of a time interval from t_{j-1} to t_j is represented as n_j, and n_j' is the number of cases (issues) surviving (on the agenda) at t_j. The value of this survival statistic can vary from 0 (a 0 probability, if all previous issues dropped off the agenda) to 1 (100 percent probability if all previous issues stayed on the agenda). To make the statistic more intuitive and more conceptually and directionally consistent with the notion of volatility, our variable is not likelihood of survival but rather the likelihood of mortality, of dropping off the agenda, or $1 - P(t)$.

McCombs and Zhu (1995, 504) modify the Kaplan-Meier formula to calculate their survival statistic as follows:

$$S(t) = \prod_{t_i < t} (1 - \frac{n_i}{N_i})$$

In this modified formula, the number of issues dropping off the agenda at time t_i is n_i. The total number of issues on the agenda at time t_i is N_i. The problematic change is that the denominator is not the number of issues under observation at the *beginning* of the interval, so n_i/N_i is not properly a proportion of issues that dropped off the previous agenda. Because the number of issues that drop is not necessarily constrained by N_i, it is possible to have negative values of the statistic, where the number of issues that drop off the agenda is greater than the number of issues on the current agenda. These problems make the resulting statistic difficult to interpret. Thus, we prefer the unmodified Kaplan-Meier formula. But as the product notation indicates, the formula was intended to examine the product of a series of survival probabilities at different times. Where our data differ from a typical survival data set is that (1) our cases are issues, not patients, and (2) issues, unlike patients, can come back after mortality. Since it does not make sense to multiply survival probabilities over time, we confine ourselves to examining one interval at a time.

Since the statistic estimates the likelihood of survival, and the longer the time frame the less likely something survives, we explore how likely one of our twenty issues was to drop off the public agenda in four to six months. More than 90 percent of the 254 "most important problem" polls taken from 1975 through 2014 had a poll with the question asked in the preceding four to six months. Only twenty-seven polls had to be dropped from the volatility analysis. This approach also solves the problem of more frequent polling in more recent time periods distorting the findings.

Appendix C

Measuring Agenda-Setting and Alternate Time Series Models

Measuring Agenda Setting

Previous research on agenda setting has used either Pearson's r, which correlates the actual levels of news coverage and public concern in the two agendas as ratio-level data, or more commonly Spearman's rank correlation coefficient, or rho(ρ), which correlates the rank order of issues in the two agendas as ordinal-level data (first, second, third, and so on). These measures usually produce fairly similar results, and there are merits to both, but we prefer Pearson's correlation for both computational and methodological reasons. On the computation side, it is fairly straightforward to write syntax that calculates Pearson's r for each quarter from the following formula:

$$r = \frac{N\sum xy - (\sum x)(\sum y)}{\sqrt{[N\sum x^2 - (\sum x)^2][N\sum y^2 - (\sum y)^2]}}$$

Note that x is news coverage and y is public concern for each of $N = 19$ issues (the Other category is not included). But before computing Spearman's ρ, coverage and concern for each issue have to be ranked from 1 to 19 for each of the 167 quarters, which is not straightforward. From a methodological perspective, Pearson's r allows for using more meaningful data. We think it matters how much more or less coverage one issue gets than another, and Pearson's considers this, while Spearman's cannot. Similarly, we do not want to make too much of the relative rankings of the issues in the bottom half of the agenda, which differ on average by only a percentage point or two.

In Table 4.1, we explore issue-level agenda setting—that is, the correlation over time between coverage of a given issue and public concern about that issue. In the third column of Table 4.3, the correlation we report is a correlation with a correlation—that is, between coverage of a given issue and the overall strength of the agenda-setting effect, which itself is the correlation between the news and public agendas as computed from this formula.

Time Series Analysis: Alternate Models and Diagnostics

Elsewhere in this book, we use linear multiple regression rather than time series analysis, in part because Gallup polls are taken with irregular time intervals, which violates a basic assumption of time series analysis. In Chapter 4, we use Policy Agendas Project data with quarterly intervals, which raises the possibility of time series analysis as an alternate approach. Time series analysis considers prior levels of the dependent variable in predicting its subsequent levels. Dynamic regression (or ARIMAX modeling) may also include differenced dependent variables and moving averages, as well as independent variables.

In Table C.1, for agenda setting, and Table C.2, for public agenda diversity, we present the original linear regression models from Table 4.3 (Model 1 in each case) alongside three alternate models. These tables also include the relevant diagnostics for the models. Model 1 presents one element of time series analysis, an autoregressive (or lagged) version of the dependent variable as a predictor. This is because Durbin-Watson diagnostic tests for these models without the lagged variables suggest first-order autoregression is present ($d = 1.074$ for agenda setting, $d = .783$ for public agenda diversity, both outside the critical values of 1.5 to 2.5).

Notice that the dependent variable in Models 2 through 4 actually represents change in the dependent variable from one quarter to the next. This is done to address another violation of a time series analysis assumption: that the means and standard deviations of the dependent variable remain stationary rather than changing or trending over time. This cannot be said for either public agenda diversity or agenda setting. The usual diagnostic for stationarity is the Augmented Dickey-Fuller (ADF) test, in which a nonsignificant result indicates nonstationary data; this is the case for both agenda setting (Dickey-Fuller $= -2.60$, lag order $= 5, p = .32$) and public agenda diversity (Dickey-Fuller $= -2.33$, lag order $= 5, p = .44$). We include time as a predictor in our regressions to control for any linear trend, but this does not guarantee stationarity. The standard remedy is differencing, creating a change score by subtracting the previous level of the dependent variable from its subsequent level. We find that first-order differencing of these dependent variables makes them stationary, as shown by ADF tests (for agenda setting, Dickey-Fuller $= -7.91$, lag order $= 5, p < .01$; for public agenda diversity, Dickey-Fuller $= -7.08$, lag order $= 5, p < .01$). That is, the changes in the dependent variables from one interval to the next are relatively stable over time. Time ceases to be a meaningful predictor for detrended data, so it is excluded in Models 2 through 4 that use a differenced dependent variable.

Model 2 in both tables uses the change from the previous quarter as the dependent variable and drops time as a predictor. The results are similar, but Durbin-Watson tests suggest that both models need the lagged difference as a predictor (differenced agenda setting, $d = 2.607$; differenced public agenda diversity, $d = 2.613$, both greater than 2.5). Model 3 makes the recommended change. The results, again, are similar, but model evaluation statistics suggest that Model 3 compares unfavorably with Model 1 in explaining variance (as shown by R^2) and minimizing prediction errors (as shown by residual standard errors) and serial

Table C.1. Original and alternate models for predicting agenda setting

	Model 1: agenda setting	Model 2: change in agenda setting	Model 3: change in agenda setting	Model 4: change in agenda setting
AR1	.349***		−.364***	
	(.053)		(.069)	
MA1				−.614***
				(.074)
Time	−.0007			
	(.0011)			
Macroeconomics	.018***	.016***	.018***	.018***
	(.002)	(.003)	(.003)	(.002)
Health	.003	−.001	−.002	.006
	(.005)	(.007)	(.006)	(.005)
Law and crime	.007***	.007**	.009***	.011***
	(.002)	(.002)	(.002)	(.002)
Defense	.007***	.0022†	.003**	.005***
	(.001)	(.0013)	(.001)	(.001)
International affairs	−.006***	−.0018	−.0020†	−.006***
	(.001)	(.0012)	(.0011)	(.001)
News agenda diversity	−.155**	−.137*	−.133*	−.130***
	(.050)	(.069)	(.064)	(.041)
Constant	1.848	.068	.026	
	(2.136)	(.117)	(.109)	
Adjusted R^2	.68***	.144***	.271***	
Residual SE	.131	.183	.170	.118
AICc	−662.21	−553.49	−574.40	−225.60
Serial correlation test	22.06*	16.43†	46.60***	2.26

Note: Coefficients are unstandardized. Standard errors are in parentheses. AR1: prior level of the dependent variable. MA1: moving average of prior values of the dependent variable. In Model 4, an ARIMAX model, all variables are differenced, there is no constant, and R^2 is not computed. Base $N = 167$, with losses for lags and differences. Serial correlation test is Breusch-Godfrey tests for Models 1 to 3 and Box-Ljung test for Model 4. *$p < .05$; **$p < .01$; ***$p < .001$; †approaches significance at $p < .10$.

correlation (as shown by Breusch-Godfrey tests for linear regression and Box-Ljung tests for ARIMAX models). Lower information criteria measures (as shown by corrected Akaike's Information Criterion values) are preferred, and Model 3 fares worse on that score, as well.

Model 4 in each table is an ARIMAX model rather than a linear regression model. This incorporates not just an autoregressive (AR) term and a differenced dependent variable but allows for a moving average (MA) term. We use the auto.arima function in Rob Hyndman and Yeasmin Khandakar's (2008) "forecast" package for R, which automatically diagnoses and chooses an ARIMAX model. This yields ARIMAX models for agenda setting and public agenda diversity that have one autoregressive lag, one first-order difference, and one moving average

Table C.2. Original and alternate models for predicting public agenda diversity

	Model 1: public agenda diversity	Model 2: change in public agenda diversity	Model 3: change in public agenda diversity	Model 4: change in public agenda diversity
AR1	.622***		−.363***	.426***
	(.057)		(.075)	(.150)
MA1				−.822***
				(.104)
Time	.001†			
	(.0006)			
Macroeconomics	−.005***	−.0033*	−.004**	−.006***
	(.001)	(.0015)	(.0015)	(.001)
Health	.001	.003	.001	.001
	(.003)	(.003)	(.003)	(.003)
Law and crime	−.0005	−.0004	−.001	−.001
	(.001)	(.0011)	(.0006)	(.001)
Defense	−.001†	−.0012†	−.0009	−.0012*
	(.0006)	(.0006)	(.0006)	(.0006)
International affairs	.0005	.0009	.0006	.0012*
	(.0005)	(.0006)	(.0005)	(.0006)
News agenda diversity	.026	.020	.045	.017
	(.026)	(.029)	(.028)	(.025)
Agenda setting r	.156***	.091*	.078*	.178***
	(.038)	(.041)	(.038)	(.044)
Constant	−1.949†	.050	−.074	
	(1.162)	(.052)	(.049)	
Adjusted R^2	.689***	.013	.135***	
Residual SE	.068	.076	.071	.067
AICc	−886.25	−848.98	−869.91	−412.15
Serial correlation test	13.85	31.73***	23.06*	6.89†

Note: Coefficients are unstandardized. Standard errors are in parentheses. AR1: prior level of the dependent variable. MA1: moving average of prior values of the dependent variable. In Model 4, an ARIMAX model, all variables are differenced, there is no constant, and R^2 is not computed. Base $N = 167$, with losses for lags and differences. Serial correlation test is Breusch-Godfrey tests for Models 1 to 3 and Box-Ljung test for Model 4. *$p < .05$; **$p < .01$; ***$p < .001$; †approaches significance at $p < .10$.

term (1,1,1). This model takes the step of differencing the independent variables as well. These models, again, had very similar results to Model 1. The main difference is that in the public agenda diversity Model 4, defense coverage reaches conventional significance as a negative predictor, and international coverage becomes a significant positive predictor. Information criteria are not directly comparable between the linear and regression and ARIMAX models, but we see improvements to residual standard errors. Serial correlation disappears in the agenda-setting Model 4 and only approaches significance in the public agenda diversity Model 4.

A lack of significant serial correlation suggests that the regression is not spurious. We achieve this in Model 1 for public agenda diversity, but only the ARIMAX lets us do so for agenda setting.

Regardless of the model we use, we get essentially the same results as in Table 4.3. This strengthens the level of confidence in our findings.

Appendix D

Collecting Data on the Media System and Using Ridge Regression

Collecting Data on the Media System

Media Choice

Media choice is an index that represents the standardized mean of three variables, each of which is an indicator of the level of choice in the media environment: percentage of homes with cable and alternate delivery systems (ADSs), number of channels available in the average household, and percentage of homes with internet access (M = −.11, SD = .98, α = .96). What follows is a description of how data for each component variable were obtained.

- **Cable penetration.** Nielsen media research began annual measurement of the percentage of television households that were "basic cable subscribers" in 1977 (TV History, n.d.), and these figures are used to measure the expansion of nonbroadcast television through 1991. For 1992 through 1996, annual data are used from the FCC's (1997) third Video Competition Report, which includes data for cable and seven ADSs, as these services were becoming more widespread. Quarterly measures of wired cable and ADS penetration as a percentage of television households from the Television Bureau of Advertisers (n.d.) are used for 1997 through 2014.

- **Average number of channels.** From 1995 to 2014, the Federal Communications Commission has annually compiled the average number of channels available in a cable "expanded basic service" package (FCC 2014). From 1985 until 1995, Nielsen compiled data on the "number of channels available in the average U.S. home" ("Average U.S. House" 2007). The data for 1975 (7.4 channels, used for 1975–1979) and 1980 (10.2 channels, used for 1980–1985) comes from Compaine and Gomery

(2000). The FCC generated an index to account for a change in the way it counted channels in 2009; the index uses 1995 as a base year and 2009 as a transition year, allowing for comparability in change over time. This index is extended backward to include our earlier data sources.

- **Home internet access.** Data for the percentage of American adults with broadband or dial-up internet access at home come from Pew Research Center's Internet and American Life Project surveys since 2000 (Zickuhr and Smith 2013). For the years 1990 through 1999, data for percentage of American adults with internet access come from the World Bank (n.d.).

Since there are no meaningful data for home internet access prior to 1990, the media choice variable before that time is an average of the z scores for cable/ADS and number of channels. An alternate version of the media choice variable that treats home internet access as 0 percent prior to 1990 correlates highly with the original version of media choice ($r = .995$) and has very similar relationships with public agenda diversity.

Broadcast News Ratings

Annual ratings data for broadcast network news from 1980 through 2014 are available from the Pew Research Center (2015a). News ratings data for 1976 (also used for 1975) and 1977 through1978 (also used for 1979) are obtained from various issues of the industry publication *Broadcasting and Cable* (previously *Broadcasting*).

Cable News Ratings

Each cable network's rating is considered a separate independent variable (CNN, MSNBC, Fox). CNN first appeared in 1980. MSNBC and Fox both launched in 1996. Quarterly ratings data for prime-time CNN programming are available from 1988 through 1996 from *Broadcasting and Cable*. Monthly prime-time viewership measures for each of the three cable news networks, from 1997 through 2014, were obtained from the Pew Research Center (e.g., Pew Research Center 2005). To convert viewership to ratings points, we use estimates of the total number of television households. Data for 1997 through 2006 came from TV by the Numbers (Gorman 2007), an online source for number-driven media analysis. Estimates after 2006 come directly from Nielsen (e.g., Nielsen 2013).

Facebook

Facebook first appeared in 2004. Its adoption is measured in millions of active users by means of a report from the Associated Press that relies on data from Facebook, Inc., for information covering 2004 through 2007 (measured at uneven intervals, but measured at least once a year). Beginning with the third quarter of 2008 (but missing data from the fourth quarter of that year), data are retrieved from Statista (2018), a leading online statistics portal. Although the Associated

Press report is less detailed than that of Statista for the years 2008 through 2014, where both include data for the same time frame, the reports are consistent. Number of active users within the United States is unavailable; these measures are for worldwide use. However, we have no reason to imagine the rate of Facebook adoption and use in the United States is substantially different from the rate of adoption and use worldwide.

Using Ridge Regression

This analysis uses ridge regression because, without it, one or more predictors would need to be excluded. Typically, the best solution for a multiple regression equation is found by minimizing the sum of the squared errors—the total differences between each predicted Y and its actual value, squaring each difference so that negative errors do not cancel out positive errors. This is called ordinary least-squares regression, or OLS. This gives *unbiased* estimates of the coefficients of the predictors. However, when predictors are highly correlated with one another, as is the case here, the predictors' coefficients can be quite unstable; small changes in the data can lead to large changes in the coefficients. Collinearity for our data is very high. One measure of collinearity is the variance inflation factor (VIF), which should not exceed 5 or 10; for our full model, it is 26.95. In such a case, a *biased* estimator can give more stable coefficients, although they tend to underestimate the true values of the coefficients in the population. This is what ridge regression does. Instead of minimizing the sum of the squared errors alone, it minimizes that sum, plus a term, the ridge parameter K, that is proportional to the sum of the squared coefficients. The ridge parameter is included in the bottom row of Table 5.2. In ridge regression, principal components analysis often is used to prioritize the predictors so that the coefficients of weaker predictors are underestimated most (Cule and De Iorio 2012). The R package used here was lmridge, version 1.0 (Imdadullah and Aslam 2018).

Appendix E

Analyzing the Pew Excellence in Journalism News Coverage Index

The data comparing news agendas across networks come from the Pew Excellence in Journalism News Coverage Index, which content-analyzed tens of thousands of individual news stories from January 2007 through May 2012 (Pew Research Center 2012). This study uses data on broadcast news (ABC, NBC, and CBS) and cable news (CNN, MSNBC, and Fox News). The broadcast sample includes the first half hour of one or two of the three morning news programs (e.g., *Good Morning America*) and the entirety of two of the three evening news programs each weekday. The cable sample includes two thirty-minute daytime segments (rotated each weekday across the cable networks) and one to two thirty-minute segments of "programming from 5 P.M. to 10 P.M. that was focused on general news events of the day" (Pew Research Center 2011).

Pew coders placed news stories into one of twenty-six issue categories: government agencies/legislatures, campaigns/elections/politics, defense/military (domestic), court/legal system, crime, domestic terrorism, business, economy/economics, environment, development/sprawl, transportation, education, religion, health/medicine, science and technology, race/gender/gay issues, immigration, additional domestic affairs, disasters/accidents, celebrity/entertainment, lifestyle, sports, media, U.S. miscellaneous, U.S. foreign affairs, and foreign (non-U.S.). Pew coders reported 78 percent raw agreement on story issue (Pew Research Center 2011).

We initially sampled a constructed year (thirteen months) from this data set, choosing every fifth month (to avoid periodicity effects), with a randomly selected starting point of February 2007. To lend subsequent analyses more power, we added previously unselected odd-numbered months for a total sample of forty months. This gave us a respectable but not overpowered number of stories for each month (n's ranged from 800 to 1,100).

For each month of coverage we selected, we ran chi-square tests of independence to see to what extent distributions of stories across issues were contingent upon news outlets. The counts of stories in each issue for each outlet were saved to a separate data set so that correlations could be run on the agendas of the news outlets. We report Cramer's V, a strength of association measure that can be used with any chi-square test of independence, regardless of number of cells. These separate data sets were then transposed, making *issues* the variables and *outlets* the cases, so that a diversity score, the H statistic, could be computed for each outlet's issue agenda for that month. We analyzed each month separately to see how agendas related and differed at given points in time and to give us internal replication. We also compared the means of the monthly correlations and diversity statistics. Note that we did not transform our Pearson's correlations using Fisher's (1958) r' before computing their means, so we may have slightly underestimated the magnitudes of the mean correlations we found (Corey, Dunlap, and Burke 1998).

The H statistic and how it is computed are described in Appendix B. The number of issues varied slightly from month to month between twenty-four and twenty-six issues, but the main determinant of H is how evenly news attention is divided among issues. The theoretical maximum of H—which would be reached if there were an equal number of stories for each of twenty-six issues—would be 3.26. As in Appendix B, we divided by this theoretical maximum so that our standardized H varies between 0 (no diversity) and 1 (maximum diversity).

Appendix F

Coding Major Presidential Addresses

Major presidential speeches were obtained from the American Presidency Project at the University of California, Santa Barbara (see https://www.presidency.ucsb.edu). Speeches listed there as major addresses to the nation or addresses to joint sessions of Congress from 1975 through 2014 were selected for a total of 143 speeches. Two data sets were created: one in which the speech was the unit of analysis and one in which the year ($N = 40$) was.

Coding

Speech Topic

One researcher read the speeches and wrote a brief description of the main issue or issues. Another researcher then coded the main issue, if one could be discerned, into one of the twenty categories for the Gallup "most important problem" question (see Appendix A for details). In seventeen instances, a main issue could not be identified—such as President Jimmy Carter's "report to the nation" in February 1977, which covered energy, the economy, jobs, taxes, welfare, government, and international issues. That left 127 presidential speeches in which a main issue could be identified. The two researchers independently coded 10 percent (thirteen) of these 127 speeches and achieved satisfactory intercoder reliability on issue category (Cohen's kappa = .81).

Leadership versus Responsive Speeches

A decision rule was adopted to classify addresses as either leadership or responsive speeches. If the speech addressed an issue that was already on the public agenda—that is, if 10 percent of Gallup responses in the last poll taken before the speech named the issue the most important facing the country (McCombs and

Zhu 1995; Neuman 1990)—it was considered responsive, an attempt to respond to public concern. If the speech raised an issue that was not on the public agenda, it was considered a leadership speech, an attempt to exercise issue leadership and increase concern about the issue.

Measures

Public Concern

Public concern about the main issue of the speech was taken from Gallup data and recorded for the last poll before the speech and the first poll after the speech. It represented the percentage of responses naming that issue as the most important facing the country. The change in concern from before the speech to after was calculated for each speech. For the annual data set, we also identified the peak level of public concern about any issue that arose during each year.

Public Agenda Diversity

See Appendix B for a discussion of this calculation.

Public Agenda Capacity

Using the same metric that decided whether an issue was on the agenda—that is, 10 percent of Gallup responses in a poll named the issue the most important facing the country—we computed the mean number of issues on the agenda for each year.

Appendix G

Public Agenda and House Hearings Data of the Policy Agendas Project

The public agenda and House hearings data we use here, like the public agenda data we use in Chapter 4, come from the Policy Agendas Project. The House hearings data were compiled from annual volumes published by the Congressional Information Service and the ProQuest Congressional database. According to the project codebook, "The hearings included are those of committees, subcommittees, task forces, panels and commissions, and the joint committees of Congress" (Policy Agendas Project 2015). Data on the public agenda comes from responses to the Gallup open-ended question "What do you think is the most important problem facing this country today?" Results are compiled quarterly.

The great advantage of these data is that they are coded using the same categories across institutions (such as the House and Senate), political processes (such as hearings held and laws passed), and public opinion. As we note in Chapter 4, the code categories are largely driven by the Congressional committee structure, which privileges legislators' view of the social world over the public's. Although the data used in Chapter 4 contain only nineteen categories (which align with the broadcast news agenda data when those data were collected), the Policy Agendas Project subsequently updated its coding scheme to include immigration as a separate category. The updated twenty-category data set is used in this chapter.

In comparing the categories in our issue-by-issue analysis with that of Bryan Jones and Frank Baumgartner (2004), we use all twenty categories. Jones and Baumgartner use sixteen. This is because of three differences: First, they use the older coding scheme (the same one we use in Chapter 4), which puts immigration under labor. Second, they combine defense and international affairs. Finally, they omit two categories (government operations and public lands) that they consider "housekeeping"—that is, routine government business. In computing our overall correlation between public and House agendas, we omit the same two categories.

Data spanning the years 1969 through 2013 are used because they comport with the time frame of the book and, when the data were downloaded, these were the years for which information was available. In earlier years, a sizable proportion of hearings was unpublished for a number of reasons, including executive sessions, national security, or the committee chair's whim. As of this writing, supplemental publications have released these data for the House only up through 1958. From 1959 through 1972, the Policy Agendas Project considers the problem of underreported hearings data "acute." In assessing the House hearing agenda, we focus on the proportion (rather than the raw number) of each year's hearings that addresses each issue. This allows more equitable comparisons of attention across years, but there remains a possibility that the proportion of House attention to national security or other issues is underrepresented for 1969 through 1972.

PROCESS Moderation Analyses

To assess the potential moderating effect of public agenda diversity on the relationship between public concern about an issue and House hearings on that issue, we use Andrew Hayes's (2013) PROCESS macro in SPSS and employ Model 1, classic moderation. We first center the public concern and agenda diversity variables to avoid excessive collinearity with the interaction term, which represents the moderation effect. We find modest evidence that, for some issues that are usually no higher than the middle of the public agenda, public concern becomes a weaker predictor of Congressional hearings when public agenda diversity is greater.

Overall Correlation between Public and House Agendas

As our dependent variable in Column 2 of Table 7.3 and in Figure 7.2, we compute the Pearson's correlation between the relative levels of public concern and House hearing attention across all issues in each year. We exclude two issues, government and public lands, because these are considered "housekeeping" by Jones and Baumgartner (2004), and including them leads to a skewed variable (skewness $z = 2.60, p < .01$). The resulting variable, computed with an eighteen-issue agenda, is strongly related to the agenda correlation for the full agenda ($r = .86, p < .001$), but it is not skewed (skewness $z = .86$, ns).

Measuring House Days in Session and Polarization

In Table 7.3, our data for days the House of Representatives worked each year comes from the House website (U.S. House of Representatives, n.d.) and is "the total days Congress recorded as a working parliamentary day." Our measure of political polarization in the House of Representatives is based on DW-NOMINATE, a widely used measure of legislative behavior and ideological location developed by Keith Poole and Howard Rosenthal (2007) and made available on their website Voteview. DW-NOMINATE (short for dynamic weighted nominal three-step estimation) allows for comparisons over time within a given chamber. It is made up of two dimensions, but we focus on the first, which is the liberal-conservative ideological spectrum on a scale from −1 (very liberal) to 1 (very conservative). Specifically, our measure calculates the distance between the median ideological locations of the Republican and Democratic delegations for each Congress.

References

Aday, S. 2010. "Chasing the Bad News: An Analysis of 2005 Iraq and Afghanistan War Coverage on NBC and Fox News Channel." *Journal of Communication* 60 (1): 144–164.
Aday, S., S. Livingston, and M. Hebert. 2005. "Embedding the Truth: A Cross-Cultural Analysis of Objectivity and Television Coverage of the Iraq War." *Harvard International Journal of Press/Politics* 10 (1): 3–21.
Althaus, S. L. 2003. *Collective Preferences in Democratic Politics: Opinion Surveys and the Will of the People*. New York: Cambridge University Press.
Althaus, S. L., J. A. Edy, and P. Phalen. 2002. "Using the Vanderbilt Television Abstracts to Track Broadcast News Content: Possibilities and Pitfalls." *Journal of Broadcasting and Electronic Media* 46 (3): 473–492.
Althaus, S. L., and D. Tewksbury. 2002. "Agenda Setting and the 'New' News: Patterns of Issue Importance among Readers of the Paper and Online Versions of the *New York Times*." *Communication Research* 29 (2): 180–207.
Anderson, C. W. 2013. *Rebuilding the News: Metropolitan Journalism in the Digital Age*. Philadelphia: Temple University Press.
Arceneaux, K., and M. Johnson. 2013. *Changing Minds or Changing Channels? Partisan News in an Age of Choice*. Chicago: University of Chicago Press.
Arceneaux, K., M. Johnson, and C. Murphy. 2012. "Polarized Political Communication, Oppositional Media Hostility, and Selective Exposure." *Journal of Politics* 74:174–186.
"Average U.S. House Now Receives a Record 104.2 TV Channels, According to Nielsen." 2007. *eHomeUpgrade*, March 22. Available at http://www.ehomeupgrade.com/2007/03/22/average-us-home-now-receives-a-record-1042-tv-channels-according-to-nielsen.
Bachrach, P., and M. S. Baratz. 1962. "The Two Faces of Power." *American Political Science Review* 56 (4): 947–952.
Bagdikian, B. 2004. *The New Media Monopoly*. Boston: Beacon Press.

Bartels, L. M. 1996. "Uninformed Votes: Information Effects in Presidential Elections." *American Journal of Political Science* 40:194–230.
Baum, M. A. 2002. "Sex, Lies, and War: How Soft News Brings Foreign Policy to the Inattentive Public." *American Political Science Review* 96:91–110.
Baum, M. A., and S. Kernell. 1999. "Has Cable Ended the Golden Age of Presidential Television?" *American Political Science Review* 93 (1): 99–114.
Baym, G. 2009. *From Cronkite to Colbert: The Evolution of Broadcast News*. Boulder, CO: Paradigm.
Behr, R. L., and S. Iyengar. 1985. "Television News, Real-World Cues, and Changes in the Public Agenda." *Public Opinion Quarterly* 49 (1): 38–57.
Bennett, W. L. 1990. "Toward a Theory of Press-State Relations." *Journal of Communication* 40:103–125.
———. 2003. "The Burglar Alarm That Just Keeps Ringing: A Response to Zaller." *Political Communication* 20:131–138.
———. 2009. *News: The Politics of Illusion*. 9th ed. New York: Pearson Longman.
Bennett, W. L., and S. Iyengar. 2008. "A New Era of Minimal Effects? The Changing Foundations of Political Communication." *Journal of Communication* 58 (4): 707–731.
Bennett, W. L., R. G. Lawrence, and S. Livingston. 2007. *When the Press Fails: Political Power and the News Media from Iraq to Katrina*. Chicago: University of Chicago Press.
Benoit, W. L., K. A. Stein, and G. J. Hansen. 2005. "New York Times Coverage of Presidential Campaigns." *Journalism and Mass Communication Quarterly* 82 (2): 356–376.
Berelson, B. R., P. F. Lazarsfeld, and W. N. McPhee. 1954. *Voting: A Study of Opinion Formation in a Presidential Campaign*. Chicago: University of Chicago Press.
Best, J. 1993. "But Seriously Folks: The Limitations of the Strict Constructionist Interpretations of Social Problems." In *Reconsidering Social Constructionism: Debates in Social Problems Theory*, edited by J. A. Holstein and G. Miller, 129–147. New York: Aldine de Gruyter.
Boczkowski, P. J., E. Mitchelstein, and M. Walter. 2012. "When Burglar Alarms Sound, Do Monitorial Citizens Pay Attention to Them? The Online News Choices of Journalists and Consumers during and after the 2008 U.S. Election Cycle." *Political Communication* 29:347–366.
Bourdieu, P. 1979. "Public Opinion Does Not Exist." In *Communication and Class Struggle*, vol. 1, edited by A. Mattelart and S. Siegelaub, 124–130. New York: International General.
Boydstun, A. E. 2013. *Making the News: Politics, the Media, and Agenda Setting*. Chicago: University of Chicago Press.
Boyle, T. P. 2001. "Intermedia Agenda Setting in the 1996 Presidential Election." *Journalism and Mass Communication Quarterly* 78 (1): 26–44.
Brosius, H.-B., and H. M. Kepplinger. 1992. "Linear and Nonlinear Models of Agenda-Setting in Television." *Journal of Broadcasting and Electronic Media* 36:5–23.
Calhoun, C. J. 1992. *Habermas and the Public Sphere*. Cambridge, MA: MIT Press.
Canes-Wrone, B. 2001. "The President's Legislative Influence from Public Appeals." *American Journal of Political Science* 45 (2): 313–329.
Carey, J. W. 1987. "The Press and Public Discourse." *Center Magazine* 20 (2): 4–16.

———. 1989. *Communication as Culture: Essays on Media and Society*. New York: Unwin Hyman.
Cavari, A. 2017. *The Party Politics of Presidential Rhetoric*. New York: Cambridge University Press.
Chaffee, S. H., and M. J. Metzger. 2001. "The End of Mass Communication?" *Mass Communication and Society* 4 (4): 365–379.
Chaffee, S. H., and D. G. Wilson. 1977. "Media Rich, Media Poor: Two Studies of Diversity in Agenda-Holding." *Journalism Quarterly* 54 (3): 466–476.
Chiang, C. 1995. *Bridging and Closing the Gap of Our Society: Social Function of Media Agenda Setting*. Master's thesis, University of Texas, Austin.
Coe, K., D. Tewksbury, B. J. Bond, K. L. Drogos, R. W. Porter, A. Yahn, and Y. Zhang. 2008. "Hostile News: Partisan Use, and Perceptions of News Programming." *Journal of Communication* 58 (2): 201–219.
Cohen, B. C. 1963. *The Press and Foreign Policy*. Princeton, NJ: Princeton University Press.
Cohen, J. E. 2008. *The Presidency in the Era of 24-Hour News*. Princeton, NJ: Princeton University Press.
———. 2010. *Going Local: Presidential Leadership in the Post-broadcast Age*. New York: Cambridge University Press.
Coleman, R., and M. E. McCombs. 2007. "The Young and Agenda-less? Exploring Age Related Differences in Agenda Setting on the Youngest Generation, Baby Boomers, and the Civic Generation." *Journalism and Mass Communication Quarterly* 84 (3): 495–508.
Collins, S. 2011. "Japan Earthquake and Tsunami Coverage Drives Huge Traffic Gains for CNN and Fox News." *Los Angeles Times*, March 11. Available at http://latimesblogs.latimes.com/showtracker/2011/03/japan-earthquake-and-tsunami-coverage-drives-huge-traffic-gains-for-cnn-and-fox-news-.html.
Compaine, B. M., and D. Gomery. 2000. *Who Owns the Media?* 3rd ed. Mahwah, NJ: Erlbaum.
Converse, P. E. 1964. "The Nature of Belief Systems in Mass Publics." In *Ideology and Discontent*, edited by D. Apter, 206–261. New York: Free Press.
———. 1990. "Popular Representation and the Distribution of Information." In *Information and Democratic Processes*, edited by J. A. Ferejohn and J. H. Kuklinski, 369–388. Urbana: University of Illinois Press.
Cook, T. E. 1998. *Governing with the News: The News Media as a Social Institution*. Chicago: University of Chicago Press.
Corey, D. M., W. P. Dunlap, and M. J. Burke. 1998. "Averaging Correlations: Expected Values and Bias in Combined Pearson rs and Fisher's z Transformations." *Journal of General Psychology* 125 (3): 245–261.
Culbertson, H. M. 1992. "Measuring Agenda Diversity in an Elastic Medium: Candidate Position Papers." *Journalism Quarterly* 69:938–946.
Cule, E., and M. De Iorio. 2012. "A Semi-automatic Method to Guide the Choice of Ridge Parameter in Ridge Regression." Available at https://arxiv.org/pdf/1205.0686.pdf.
Dalton, R. J., P. A. Beck, R. Huckfeldt, and W. Koetzle. 1998. "A Test of Media-Centered Agenda Setting: Newspaper Content and Public Interests in a Presidential Election." *Political Communication* 15 (4): 463–481.

DellaVigna, S., and E. Kaplan. 2007. "The Fox News Effect: Media Bias and Voting." *Quarterly Journal of Economics* 122:1187–1234.

Delli Carpini, M. X., and S. Keeter. 1996. *What Americans Know about Politics and Why It Matters.* New Haven, CT: Yale University Press.

Demers, D. P., D. Craff, Y. H. Choi, and B. M. Pessin. 1989. "Issue Obtrusiveness and the Agenda-Setting Effects of National Network News." *Communication Research* 16 (6): 793–812.

Dixon, T. L. 2008. "Crime News and Racialized Beliefs: Understanding the Relationship between Local News Viewing and Perceptions of African Americans and Crime." *Journal of Communication* 58 (1): 106–125.

Douglas, G. H. 2001. *The Early Days of Radio Broadcasting.* Jefferson, NC: McFarland.

Downs, A. 1957. *An Economic Theory of Democracy.* New York: Harper and Row.

———. 1972. "Up and Down with Ecology: The Issue Attention Cycle." *Public Interest*, Summer, 38–50.

Druckman, J. N. 2004. "Political Preference Formation: Competition, Deliberation, and the (Ir)Relevance of Framing Effects." *American Political Science Review* 98:671–686.

Edelman, M. 1988. *Constructing the Political Spectacle.* Chicago: University of Chicago Press.

Edwards, G. C. 2003. *On Deaf Ears: The Limits of the Bully Pulpit.* New Haven, CT: Yale University Press.

Edy, J. A., and P. C. Meirick. 2007. "Wanted, Dead or Alive: Media Frames, Frame Adoption, and Support for the War in Afghanistan." *Journal of Communication* 54:119–141.

Edy, J. A., and E. E. Risley-Baird. 2016. "Rumor Communities: The Social Dimensions of Internet Political Misperceptions." *Social Science Quarterly* 97 (3): 588–602.

Entman, R. M. 1989. *Democracy without Citizens.* New York: Oxford University Press.

———. 1991. "Framing U.S. Coverage of International News: Contrasts in Narratives of the KAL and Iran Air Incidents." *Journal of Communication* 41:6–27.

———. 2012. *Scandal and Silence: Media Responses to Presidential Misconduct.* Cambridge, UK: Polity.

Erbring, L., E. N. Goldenberg, and A. H. Miller. 1980. "Front Page News and Real World Cues: A New Look at Agenda Setting by the Media." *American Journal of Political Science* 24 (1): 16–49.

Eshbaugh-Soha, M., and J. S. Peake. 2011. *Breaking through the Noise: Presidential Leadership, Public Opinion, and the News Media.* Stanford, CA: Stanford University Press.

Ettema, J. S., and T. L. Glasser. 1998. *Custodians of Conscience: Investigative Journalism and Public Virtue.* New York: Columbia University Press.

Farnsworth, S. J., and R. S. Lichter. 2010. *The Nightly News Nightmare: Media Coverage of U.S. Presidential Elections, 1988–2008.* Lanham, MD: Rowman and Littlefield.

Federal Bureau of Investigation. 2017. "Estimated Crime in the United States—Total." Available at https://www.ucrdatatool.gov/Search/Crime/State/StatebyState.cfm.

Federal Communications Commission. 1997. "Annual Assessment of the Status of Competition in the Market for the Delivery of Video Programming." Available at http://transition.fcc.gov/Bureaus/Cable/Reports/fcc96496.txt.

———. 2014. "Report on Cable Industry Prices." Available at http://transition.fcc.gov/Daily_Releases/Daily_Business/2014/db0516/DA-14-672A1.pdf.

Federal Reserve Bank of St. Louis. 2018. "Real Gross Domestic Product." Available at https://fred.stlouisfed.org/series/A191RL1Q225SBEA.

Fennessey, J., and R. D'Amico. 1980. "Collinearity, Ridge Regression, and Investigator Judgment." *Sociological Methods Research* 8:309–330.

Fiorina, M. 2010. *Disconnect: The Breakdown of Representation in American Politics.* Norman: University of Oklahoma Press.

Fisher, R. A. 1958. *Statistical Methods for Research Workers.* 13th ed. Edinburgh: Oliver and Boyd.

Freedman, J. L., and D. O. Sears. 1965. "Selective Exposure." In *Advances in Experimental Social Psychology*, vol. 2, edited by L. Berkowitz, 58–98. San Diego, CA: Academic Press.

Frey, D., and R. A. Wicklund. 1978. "A Clarification of Selective Exposure: The Impact of Choice." *Journal of Experimental Social Psychology* 14:132–139.

Fryer, R. G., P. S. Heaton, S. D. Levitt, and K. M. Murphy. 2013. "Measuring Crack Cocaine and Its Impact." *Economic Inquiry* 51 (3): 1651–1681.

Funkhouser, G. R. 1973. "The Issues of the Sixties: An Exploratory Study in the Dynamics of Public Opinion." *Public Opinion Quarterly* 37 (1): 62–75.

Garrett, R. K. 2009. "Politically Motivated Reinforcement Seeking: Reframing the Selective Exposure Debate." *Journal of Communication* 59:676–699.

Garrow, D. J. 1978. *Protest at Selma: Martin Luther King Jr., and the Voting Rights Act of 1965.* New Haven: CT: Yale University Press.

Gerbner, G., and L. Gross. 1976. "Living with Television: The Violence Profile." *Journal of Communication* 26 (2): 172–194.

Gilens, M. 1999. *Why Americans Hate Welfare: Race, Media, and the Politics of Antipoverty Policy.* Chicago: University of Chicago Press.

Gilens, M., and B. I. Page. 2014. "Testing Theories of American Politics: Elites, Interest Groups, and Average Citizens." *Perspectives on Politics* 12 (3): 564–581.

Ginsberg, B. 1986. *The Captive Public: How Mass Opinion Promotes State Power.* New York: Basic Books.

Gorman, B. 2007. "U.S. Television Households by Season." Previously available at http://tvbythenumbers.zap2it.com/2007/08/28/us-television-households-by-season/273.

Groeling, T. 2008. "Who's the Fairest of Them All? An Empirical Test for Partisan Bias on ABC, CBS, NBC, and Fox News." *Presidential Studies Quarterly* 38 (4): 631–657.

Groseclose, T., and J. Milyo. 2005. "A Measure of Media Bias." *Quarterly Journal of Economics* 120:191–237.

Hallin, D. C. 1986. *The "Uncensored War": The Media and Vietnam.* Oxford: Oxford University Press.

Hamilton, J. T. 1998. *Channeling Violence: The Economic Market for Violent Television Programming.* Princeton, NJ: Princeton University Press.

Hayes, A. F. 2013. *Introduction to Mediation, Moderation, and Conditional Process Analysis: A Regression-Based Approach.* New York: Guilford Press.

Heim, K. 2013. "Framing the 2008 Iowa Democratic Caucuses: Political Blogs and Second-Level Intermedia Agenda Setting." *Journalism and Mass Communication Quarterly* 90 (3): 500–519.

Herbst, S. 1993. *Numbered Voices: How Opinion Polling Has Shaped American Politics.* Chicago: University of Chicago Press.

Herman, E. S., and N. Chomsky. 1988. *Manufacturing Consent: The Political Economy of the Mass Media.* New York: Pantheon.

Huckfeldt, R., and J. Sprague. 1987. "Networks in Context: The Social Flow of Political Information." *American Political Science Review* 81:1197–1216.

Hyndman, R. J., and Y. Khandakar. 2008. "Automatic Time Series Modeling: The Forecast Package for R." *Journal of Statistical Software* 27 (3): 1–22.

ICPSR (Interuniversity Consortium for Political and Social Research). n.d. "Campaign Strategies." Available at http://www.icpsr.umich.edu/icpsrweb/instructors/setups/notes/strats.jsp (accessed September 11, 2018).

Imdadullah, M., and M. Aslam. 2018. "lmridge: Linear Ridge Regression with Ridge Penalty and Ridge Statistics." R package, version 1.0. Available at https://cran.r-project.org/web/packages/lmridge/index.html.

Iyengar, S. 1987. "Television News and Citizens' Explanations of National Issues." *American Political Science Review* 81:815–832.

Iyengar, S., and K. S. Hahn. 2009. "Red Media, Blue Media: Evidence of Ideological Selectivity in Media Use." *Journal of Communication* 59:19–39.

Jacobs, L. R., and R. Y. Shapiro. 1995. "Presidential Manipulation of Polls and Public Opinion: The Nixon Administration and the Pollsters." *Political Science Quarterly* 110 (4): 519–538.

———. 2000. *Politicians Don't Pander: Political Manipulation and the Loss of Democratic Responsiveness.* Chicago: University of Chicago Press.

Jones, B. D., and F. R. Baumgartner. 2004. "Representation and Agenda Setting." *Policy Studies Journal* 32 (1): 1–24.

Jones, B. D., H. Larsen-Price, and J. Wilkerson. 2009. "Representation and American Governing Institutions." *Journal of Politics* 71 (1): 277–290.

Journalism.org. 2005. "Prime Time Cable News Viewership, 1997 to 2004." Available at http://web.archive.org/web/20080109145125/ http://stateofthemedia.org/2005/chartland.asp?id=224.

Jurkowitz, M., P. Hitlin, A. Mitchell, L. Santhanam, S. Adams, M. Anderson, and N. Vogt. 2013. "The Changing TV News Landscape." In *The State of the News Media, 2013*, edited by Pew Research Center. Washington, DC: Pew Research Center. Available at http://assets.pewresearch.org.s3.amazonaws.com/files/journalism/State-of-the-News-Media-Report-2013-FINAL.pdf.

Kaplan, E. L., and P. Meier. 1958. "Nonparametric Estimation from Incomplete Observations." *Journal of the American Statistical Association* 53 (282): 457–481.

Katz, E. 1996. "And Deliver Us from Segmentation." *Annals of the American Academy of Political and Social Science* 546:22–33.

Katz, E., and D. Dayan. 1988. "Articulating Consensus: The Ritual and Rhetoric of Media Events." In *Durkheimian Sociology: Cultural Studies*, edited by J. Alexander, 161–186. Cambridge: Cambridge University Press.

Kernell, S. 2007. *Going Public: New Strategies of Presidential Leadership.* 4th ed. Washington, DC: CQ Press.

Kernell, S., and L. L. Rice. 2011. "Cable and the Partisan Polarization of the President's Audience." *Presidential Studies Quarterly* 41 (4): 693–711.

Kreiss, D. 2016. *Prototype Politics: Technology-Intensive Campaigning and the Data of Democracy*. New York: Oxford University Press.

Lasswell, H. 1948. "The Structure and Function of Communication in Society." In *The Communication of Ideas*, edited by L. Bryson, 37–51. New York: Harper.

Lawrence, R. G. 2000. *The Politics of Force: Media and the Construction of Police Brutality*. Berkeley: University of California Press.

Lazarsfeld, P. F., and R. K. Merton. 1948. "Mass Communication, Popular Taste, and Organized Social Action." In *The Communication of Ideas*, edited by L. Bryson, 95–118. New York: Institute for Religious and Social Studies.

Leccese, M. 2009. "Online Information Source of Political Blogs." *Journalism and Mass Communication Quarterly* 86:578–593.

Lee, J. K. 2007. "The Effect of the Internet on Homogeneity of the Media Agenda: A Test of the Fragmentation Thesis." *Journalism and Mass Communication Quarterly* 84 (4): 745–760.

Lee, J. K., and R. Coleman. 2014. "Testing Generational, Life Cycle, and Period Effects of Age on Agenda Setting." *Mass Communication and Society* 17 (3): 3–25.

Levendusky, M. 2013. *How Partisan Media Polarize America*. Chicago: University of Chicago Press.

Lim, J. 2006. "A Cross-Lagged Analysis of Agenda Setting among Online News Media." *Journalism and Mass Communication Quarterly* 83 (2): 288–312.

Lippmann, W. 1922. *Public Opinion*. New York: Macmillan.

Lopez-Escobar, E., J. P. Llamas, and M. McCombs. 1998. "Agenda Setting and Community Consensus: First and Second Level Effects." *International Journal of Public Opinion Research* 10 (4): 335–348.

Lopez-Escobar, E., J. P. Llamas, M. McCombs, and F. Rey. 1998. "Two Levels of Agenda among Advertising and News in the 1995 Spanish Elections." *Political Communication* 15 (2): 222–238.

Lukes, S. 1974. *Power: A Radical View*. London: Macmillan.

McChesney, R. W., and J. Nichols. 2010. *The Death and Life of American Journalism: The Media Revolution That Will Begin the World Again*. Philadelphia: Nation Books.

McCombs, M. 1997. "Building Consensus: The News Media's Agenda Setting Role." *Political Communication* 14:433–443.

———. 2004. *Setting the Agenda: The Mass Media and Public Opinion*. 2nd ed. Cambridge, UK: Polity Press.

McCombs, M., J. P. Llamas, E. Lopez-Escobar, and F. Rey. 1997. "Candidate Images in Spanish Elections: Second-Level Agenda-Setting Effects." *Journalism and Mass Communication Quarterly* 74:703–717.

McCombs, M., and D. Shaw. 1972. "The Agenda Setting Function of the Mass Media." *Public Opinion Quarterly* 36 (2): 176–187.

McCombs, M. E., and D. Weaver. 1985. "Toward a Merger of Gratifications and Agenda-Setting Research." In *Media Gratifications Research: Current Perspectives*, edited by K. E. Rosengren, L. A. Wenner, and P. Palmgreen, 95–108. Beverly Hills, CA: Sage.

McCombs, M., and J.-H. Zhu. 1995. "Capacity, Diversity, and Volatility of the Public Agenda: Trends from 1954–1994." *Public Opinion Quarterly* 59:495–525.

Meirick, P. C. 2016. "Motivated Reasoning, Accuracy, and Updating in Perceptions of Bush's Legacy." *Social Science Quarterly* 97 (3): 699–713.

Meraz, S. 2011. "Using Time Series Analysis to Measure Intermedia Agenda Setting Influence in Traditional Media and Political Blog Networks." *Journalism and Mass Communication Quarterly* 88 (1): 176–194.
Meyer, D., and S. Boutcher. 2007. "Signals and Spillover: Brown v. Board of Education and Other Social Movements." *Perspectives on Politics* 5 (1): 81–93.
Morgan, M., and J. Shanahan. 1997. "Two Decades of Cultivation Research: An Appraisal and Meta-Analysis." *Communication Yearbook* 20:1–45.
Mullainathan, S., and A. Shleifer. 2005. "The Market for News." *American Economic Review* 95:1031–1053.
Neuman, W. R. 1990. "The Threshold of Public Attention." *Public Opinion Quarterly* 54:159–176.
———. 1991. *The Future of the Mass Audience*. Cambridge: Cambridge University Press.
Newport, F. 2014. "Economy, Government Top Election Issues for Both Parties: Differ Most Widely on Climate Change, Deficit." Gallup, October 9. Available at http://www.gallup.com/poll/178133/economy-government-top-election-issues-parties.aspx.
Nielsen. 2013. "Nielsen Estimates 115.6 Million TV Homes in the U.S., up 1.2%." Available at http://www.nielsen.com/us/en/insights/news/2013/nielsen-estimates-115-6-million-tv-homes-in-the-u-s---up-1-2-.html.
———. 2014. "Changing Channels: Americans View Just 17 Channels Despite Record Number to Choose From." Available at http://www.nielsen.com/us/en/insights/news/2014/changing-channels-americans-view-just-17-channels-despite-record-number-to-choose-from.html.
Nyhan, B., and J. Reifler. 2010. "When Corrections Fail: The Persistence of Political Misperceptions." *Political Behavior* 32:303–330.
Organization for Economic Cooperation and Development. n.d.a. "Inflation (CPI)." Available at https://data.oecd.org/price/inflation-cpi.htm (accessed December 13, 2018).
———. n.d.b. "Unemployment Rate." Available at https://data.oecd.org/unemp/unemployment-rate.htm (accessed December 13, 2018).
Page, B. I., and R. Y. Shapiro. 1992. *The Rational Public: Fifty Years of Trends in Americans' Policy Preferences*. Chicago: University of Chicago Press.
Pariser, E. 2011. *The Filter Bubble: How the New Personalized Web Is Changing What We Read and How We Think*. New York: Penguin.
Patterson, T. E. 1993. *Out of Order*. New York: Knopf.
———. 2002. *The Vanishing Voter*. New York: Knopf.
Perrin, A. 2015. "Social Media Usage: 2005–2015." Pew Research Center, October 8. Available at http://www.pewinternet.org/2015/10/08/social-networking-usage-2005-2015.
Peter, J., and C. H. de Vreese. 2003. "Agenda-Rich, Agenda Poor: A Cross-Sectional Comparative Investigation of Nominal and Thematic Public Agenda Diversity." *International Journal of Public Opinion Research* 15 (1): 44–64.
Peters, J. D. 1995. "Historical Tensions in the Concept of Public Opinion." In *Public Opinion and the Communication of Consent*, edited by T. L. Glasser and C. T. Salmon, 3–32. New York: Guilford.
Petrocik, J. R. 1995. "Issue Ownership in Presidential Elections, with a 1980 Case Study." *American Journal of Political Science* 40:825–850.

Pew Research Center. 2010. "How News Happens." Available at http://www.journalism.org/2010/01/11/how-news-happens.
———. 2011. "News Coverage Index Methodology." Available at http://www.journalism.org/news_index_methodology/99.
———. 2012. "2007–2012 News Coverage Index Data Sets." Available at http://www.journalism.org/datasets/pages/2.
———. 2015a. "Network TV: Evening News Ratings over Time." Available at http://www.journalism.org/chart/network-tv-evening-news-ratings-over-time.
———. 2015b. "State of the News Media, 2015." Available at http://www.journalism.org/category/publications/state-of-the-media/pages/5.
———. 2018. "Social Media Fact Sheet." Available at http://www.pewinternet.org/fact-sheets/social-networking-fact-sheet.
Policy Agendas Project. 2015. "Congressional Hearings Data Codebook." Previously available at https://www.comparativeagendas.net/files/committee-codebook.
Politico and T. H. Chan School of Public Health. 2017. "Americans' Views on Domestic Priorities for President Trump's First 100 Days." Available at http://www.politico.com/f/?id=00000159-a9ec-d7fb-a5df-eded0c390000.
Poole, K. T., and H. Rosenthal. 2007. *Ideology and Congress*. London: Routledge.
Popkin, S. L. 1991. *The Reasoning Voter: Communication and Persuasion in Presidential Campaigns*. Chicago: University of Chicago Press.
Prior, M. 2003. "Any Good News in Soft News? The Impact of Soft News Preference on Political Knowledge." *Political Communication* 20:149–171.
———. 2007. *Post Broadcast Democracy: How Media Choice Increases Inequality in Political Involvement and Polarizes Elections*. Cambridge: Cambridge University Press.
Protess, D., F. Cook, T. Curtin, M. Gordon, D. Leff, M. McCombs, and P. Miller. 1987. "The Impact of Investigative Reporting on Public Opinion and Policymaking Targeting Toxic Waste." *Public Opinion Quarterly* 51 (2): 166–185.
Putnam, R. D. 2000. *Bowling Alone: The Collapse and Revival of American Community*. New York: Simon and Schuster.
Quandt, T. 2012. "What's Left of Trust in a Network Society? An Evolutionary Model and Critical Discussion of Trust and Societal Communication." *European Journal of Communication* 27 (1): 7–21.
Redlawsk, D. P. 2002. "Hot Cognition or Cool Consideration? Testing the Effects of Motivated Reasoning on Political Decision Making." *Journal of Politics* 64 (4): 1021–1044.
Reeves, J. L., and R. Campbell. 1994. *Cracked Coverage: Television News, the Anti-Cocaine Crusade, and the Reagan Legacy*. Durham, NC: Duke University Press.
Reinerman, C., and H. G. Levine. 1997. *Crack in America: Demon Drugs and Social Justice*. Berkeley: University of California Press.
Romer, D., K. H. Jamieson, and S. Aday. 2003. "Are We Being Mugged by Local News? Television News and the Cultivation of Fear of Crime." *Journal of Communication* 53 (1): 88–104.
Rottinghaus, B. 2010. *The Provisional Pulpit: Modern Presidential Leadership of Public Opinion*. College Station: Texas A&M University Press.
Ryfe, D. M. 2006. "Guest Editor's Introduction: New Institutionalism and the News." *Political Communication* 23:135–144.

———. 2012. *Can Journalism Survive? An Inside Look at America's Newsrooms.* Cambridge, UK: Polity Press.

Scacco, J. M., and K. Coe. 2016. "The Ubiquitous Presidency: Toward a New Paradigm for Studying Presidential Communication." *International Journal of Communication* 10:2014–2037.

Schattschneider, E. E. 1975. *The Semisovereign People: A Realist's View of Democracy in America.* Hinsdale, IL: Dryden Press.

Scheufele, D. A. 2000. "Agenda-Setting, Priming, and Framing Revisited: Another Look at Cognitive Effects of Political Communication." *Mass Communication and Society* 3 (2–3): 297–318.

Schudson, M. 1998. *The Good Citizen: A History of American Civic Life.* New York: Free Press.

———. 2007. "Citizens, Consumers, and the Good Society." *Annals of the American Academy of Political and Social Science* 611 (1): 236–249.

———. 2015. *The Rise of the Right to Know: Politics and the Culture of Transparency, 1945–1975.* Cambridge, MA: Harvard University Press.

Shannon, C. E., and W. Weaver. 1949. *The Mathematical Theory of Communication.* Urbana: University of Illinois Press.

Shapiro, R. Y. 2012. "Review of *Breaking through the Noise: Presidential Leadership, Public Opinion, and the News Media.*" *Political Science Quarterly* 127 (3): 381–483.

Shaw, D., and B. J. Hamm. 1997. "Agendas for a Public Union or for Private Communities? How Individuals Are Using Media to Reshape Society." In *Communication and Democracy: Exploring the Intellectual Frontiers of Agenda Setting Theory*, edited by M. E. McCombs, D. L. Shaw, and D. Weaver, 209–230. Mahwah, NJ: Lawrence Erlbaum.

Shaw, D., and S. E. Martin. 1992. "The Function of Mass Media Agenda Setting." *Journalism Quarterly* 69 (4): 902–920.

Shaw, D. L., and M. McCombs. 1977. *The Emergence of American Political Issues.* St. Paul, MN: West.

Sigal, L. V. 1973. *Reporters and Officials: The Organization and Politics of Newsmaking.* Lexington, MA: D. C. Heath.

Skocpol, T. 2003. *Diminished Democracy: From Membership to Management in American Civic Life.* Norman: University of Oklahoma Press.

Smith, T. W. 1980. "America's Most Important Problem: A Trend Analysis, 1946–1976." *Public Opinion Quarterly* 44:164–180.

———. 1985. "America's Most Important Problems, Part 1: National and International." *Public Opinion Quarterly* 49 (2): 264–274.

Sparrow, B. H. 1999. *Uncertain Guardians: The News Media as a Political Institution.* Baltimore: Johns Hopkins University Press.

Spector, M., and J. I. Kitsuse. 2001. *Constructing Social Problems.* New Brunswick, NJ: Transaction.

Statista. 2018. "Number of Monthly Active Facebook Users Worldwide as of 2nd Quarter 2018 (in Millions)." Available at http://www.statista.com/statistics/264810/number-of-monthly-active-facebook-users-worldwide.

Stimson, J. A., M. B., MacKuen, and R. S. Erikson. 1995. "Dynamic Representation." *American Political Science Review* 89 (3): 543–565.

Stroud, N. J. 2011. *Niche News: The Politics of News Choice.* New York: Oxford University Press.

Sunstein, C. 2007. *Republic 2.0*. Princeton, NJ: Princeton University Press.
———. 2009. *Going to Extremes: How Like Minds Unite and Divide*. New York: Oxford University Press.
Takeshita, T. 2005. "Current Critical Problems in Agenda-Setting Research." *International Journal of Public Opinion Research* 18 (1): 275–296.
Tan, Y., and D. H. Weaver. 2013. "Agenda Diversity and Agenda Setting: What Are the Trends over Time?" *Journalism Studies* 14 (6): 773–789.
Television Bureau of Advertising. n.d. "National ADS, Wired-Cable and Broadcast Only Household Penetration Trends." Available at https://www.tvb.org/Public/Research/CompetitiveMedia/CableADS/NationalADS,Wired-CableBroadcastOnlyHouseholdPenetrationTrends.aspx (accessed December 14, 2018).
Tichenor, P. J., G. A. Donohue, and C. N. Olien. 1970. "Mass Media Flow and Differential Growth in Knowledge." *Public Opinion Quarterly* 34:159–170.
Trott, B. 2015. "U.S. Appeals Ruling on Size of BP Oil Spill." *Reuters*, March 14. Available at http://www.reuters.com/article/2015/03/14/us-bp-trial-appeal-idUSKBN0MA0QB20150314.
Tuchman, G. 1973. "Making News by Doing Work: Routinizing the Unexpected." *American Journal of Sociology* 79 (1): 110–131.
Tulis, J. K. 1987. *The Rhetorical Presidency*. Princeton, NJ: Princeton University Press.
Turow, J. 1997. *Breaking Up America: Advertisers and the New Media World*. Chicago: University of Chicago Press.
TV History. n.d. "U.S. Households with Cable Television, 1977–99." Available at http://www.tvhistory.tv/Cable_Households_77-99.JPG (accessed September 14, 2018).
Uscinski, J. E. 2014. *The People's News: Media, Politics, and the Demands of Capitalism*. New York: New York University Press.
U.S. House of Representatives. n.d. "List of All Sessions." Available at http://history.house.gov/Institution/Session-Dates/All (accessed April 2, 2017).
Valentino, N. A. 1999. "Crime News and the Priming of Racial Attitudes during Evaluations of the President." *Public Opinion Quarterly* 63 (3): 293–320.
Vliegenthart, R., and S. Walgrave. 2008. "The Contingency of Intermedia Agenda Setting: A Longitudinal Study in Belgium." *Journalism and Mass Communication Quarterly* 85 (4): 860–877.
Wanta, W., and Y. Hu. 1993. "The Agenda-Setting Effects of International News Coverage: An Examination of Differing News Frames." *International Journal of Public Opinion Research* 5 (3): 250–264.
———. 1994. "Time-Lag Differences in the Agenda Setting Process: An Examination of Five News Media." *International Journal of Public Opinion Research* 5:225–240.
Weaver, D., D. Graber, M. McCombs, and C. H. Eyal. 1981. *Media Agenda-Setting in a Presidential Election: Issues, Images, and Interests*. New York: Praeger.
Webster, J. G. 2014. *The Marketplace of Attention: How Audiences Take Shape in the Digital Age*. Boston: MIT Press.
Williams, B. A., and M. X. Delli Carpini. 2011. *After Broadcast News: Media Regimes, Democracy, and the New Information Environment*. New York: Cambridge University Press.

Winter, J. P., C. Eyal, and A. Rogers. 1982. "Issue-Specific Agenda Setting: The Whole as Less than the Sum of the Parts." *Canadian Journal of Communication* 8:1–10.

Wlezien, C. 2005. "On the Salience of Political Issues: The Problem with 'Most Important Problem.'" *Electoral Studies* 24:555–579.

World Bank. n.d. "Individuals Using the Internet (% of Population)." Available at https://data.worldbank.org/indicator/IT.NET.USER.ZS?locations=US (accessed December 14, 2018).

Young, G., and W. B. Perkins. 2005. "Presidential Rhetoric, the Public Agenda, and the End of Presidential Television's 'Golden Age.'" *Journal of Politics* 67 (4): 1190–1205.

Zaller, J. 1992. *The Nature and Origins of Mass Opinion*. New York: Cambridge University Press.

———. 1998. "Monica Lewinsky's Contribution to Political Science." *PS: Political Science and Politics* 31 (2): 182–189.

———. 2003. "A New Standard of News Quality: Burglar Alarms for the Monitorial Citizen." *Political Communication* 20:109–130.

Zelizer, B. 1992. *Covering the Body: The Kennedy Assassination, the Media, and the Shaping of Collective Memory*. Chicago: University of Chicago Press.

Zhu, J.-H. 1992. "Issue Competition and Attention Distraction: A Zero-Sum Theory of Agenda Setting." *Journalism Quarterly* 69 (4): 825–836.

Zickuhr, K., and A. Smith. 2013. "Home Broadband, 2013." Pew Research Center, August 26. Available at http://www.pewinternet.org/2013/08/26/home-broadband-2013.

Zucker, H. G. 1978. "The Variable Nature of News Media Influence." In *Communication Yearbook No. 2*, edited by B. D. Ruben, 225–245. New Brunswick, NJ: Transaction.

Index

Abu Ghraib, 8, 48, 152
Affordable Care Act, 2, 56, 155, 156
agenda setting: and aspects of issues, 8, 12, 58, 77, 79; change over time in, 90–91, 98–100; intermedia, 132; issue-level, 20–21, 100–101, 164–168; issue coverage and, 93–95, 102–109, 220–221; measurement of, 98, 219; news agenda diversity and, 105–109, 220–221; news consistency and, 159–163; and political power, 5–7, 84, 178; and public agenda diversity, 10, 62–63, 105–109, 113–115, 143–144, 157–160, 163, 220, 222; and public consensus, 6, 88–93; second-level, 8, 12, 58, 77, 79
agriculture, 97, 101, 103, 191–192
Althaus, Scott, 122, 151
Anthony, Casey, 41
Arceneaux, Kevin, 118
Asia: coding of, 77, 156, 211; as most important problem, 46, 48

Bachrach, Peter, 6, 7, 84, 175, 202
banking and commerce, 97, 101, 103, 191
Baratz, Morton, 6, 7, 84, 175, 202
Bartels, Larry, 151
Baum, Matthew, 117, 169
Baumgartner, Frank, 95n, 189, 190, 198, 233, 234

Bennett, Lance, 9, 64, 152, 153, 154, 157, 169
Bennett, William, 40
Best, Joel, 165
Boczkowski, Pablo, 118, 123, 153
Boydstun, Amber, 110, 111, 169
Boyle, Thomas, 132
broadcast news: agenda diversity of coverage on, 138–139, 158–159; agenda setting of, 15–16, 91–93, 96, 98–109, 113–115, 143–147, 158–159, 167–168, 201; as era of media, 66–68, 86–88, 100, 117, 131, 169; capacity of, 62–63, 88; issue agendas of, 16, 101–107, 140–141; and news agenda diversity, 16, 103–109, 131–134, 138–139, 158–159; and public agenda diversity, 15, 103–109, 113–115, 123–130, 143–147, 158–159; as a public forum, 4, 89; ratings of, 89, 123, 143–147; similarity of issue agendas of, 134–138
Bush, George H. W., 43, 180; and economic issues, 27, 32–34; and government/political issues, 55, 57; and law and crime, 36, 40–41, 75–76, 149
Bush, George W., 37–38, 43; addresses from, 170, 178–180; and economic issues, 26–27, 31–32, 34–35; and government/political issues, 55–56, 67;

Bush, George W. (*continued*)
    and the Middle East, 49, 52, 59, 178; and terrorism, 51–52, 179–180

cable news: agenda diversity of coverage on, 131–132, 135–136, 138–139, 155, 157–158; agenda setting of, 158–163; attention to, 16, 127–130, 145, 158–162, 226; capacity of, 63, 131; as competitor for broadcast news, 110–111; emergence of, 121–122; as era of news, 126; issue agendas of, 15–16, 135–136, 140–142, 145, 229; and news agenda diversity overall, 132, 141; partisanship of, 89, 121–122; and public agenda diversity, 15–16, 117, 127–130, 128, 140–142, 145–147, 157–163; punditry on, 63, 141; similarity of issue agendas of, 15–16, 115, 137–138, 155, 201. *See also* CNN; Fox News; MSNBC; partisan news
cable television: and increased choice, 3, 5, 8, 89, 116, 119–120, 169; as era of media, 66–67, 132, 169; measures of cable penetration and choice, 225–226. *See also* cable news; media choice
Canes-Wrone, Brandice, 172, 178
capacity: of democratic institutions, 15–16, 85, 177, 187–189, 192, 197–198, 202, 204; individual cognitive, 62, 64, 83, 92; measures of, 70–72; of news media, 62–64, 83, 88, 91; of public agenda, 15, 62–64, 83–84; of public agenda over time, 15, 69–73, 83; and diversity and volatility, 69, 82–83; and presidential responsiveness, 177, 183. *See also* issue competition
Carter, Jimmy, 39, 43, 47, 54; addresses from, 59, 75, 177, 182, 186, 231; and economic issues, 25–27, 59, 75, 149, 182, 186
Chaffee, Steve, 90
civil rights, 126, 204; agenda setting and, 101, 103; coding of, 77, 97, 212; House responsiveness on, 191; as most important problem, 42, 59, 66; presidential leadership on, 169
Clinton, Bill, 38, 41; addresses from, 178–179, 186; and economic issues, 27, 31–32, 34; and government shutdown, 57–58; and health care reform, 36–37, 178–179; and impeachment over Lewinsky scandal, 55, 67, 93, 142, 178

CNN: agenda diversity of coverage on, 139, 155, 158; agenda setting of, 158–159; emergence of, 121–122; as era of media, 100, 111; issue agendas of, 136, 140–141, 145; and public agenda diversity, 16, 124–126, 128–129, 142, 146, 158–159; ratings of, 124–126, 158–159, 226; similarity of issue agendas of, 137–138, 155. *See also* cable news
Coe, Kevin, 170
Cohen, Jeffrey, 168, 169, 170
Cold War: and coding of foreign affairs issues, 46–47; as historical era, 65–66, 68; and public agenda diversity, 84, 104–105, 109–110, 112, 160, 200–201
Coleman, Renita, 90, 91
Colorado movie theater shooting, 41
Columbine High School shootings, 36, 41, 44
community development and housing, 97, 101, 103, 191
consensus: and agenda setting, 6, 15, 88, 91–93, 113, 148; erosion of, 3, 14, 90; function of news as building, 63–64, 91–92, 121–122, 147–148, 152, 201–202; implications of decline of, 10, 13–14; media choice and, 63–64, 121; nature of, 113, 147; presidents and, 175, 187. *See also* fragmentation
Converse, Philip, 150
crime: and agenda setting, 101–109, 166–168, 221; coding of, 97, 156, 211, 229; coverage of, 102–103, 107–108, 165–168, 201, 229; House responsiveness on, 191; presidential opinion leadership on, 149, 178; and public agenda diversity, 103–109, 113–114, 222. *See also* law and order

Delli Carpini, Michael, 9, 67, 118, 142, 150, 154, 168
democracy: changing importance of majorities in, 85, 203, 206; fragmentation and, 1–5, 174, 187–188, 195–199, 203; government responsiveness and, 13–14, 16, 84, 174–176, 187–188, 195–198, 203; informed citizens and, 150–154; role of mass media in, 5–10, 87–88, 112, 207. *See also* responsiveness, democratic
domestic issues, 35–36, 109, 187; coding of, 77–78, 133, 156, 229

Downs, Anthony, 150, 178
"driven apart" theory: and public agenda, 14, 113–115, 125–129, 144–147, 202; as explanation for public agenda fragmentation, 10, 12–13, 64, 115–118, 130–131. *See also* agenda setting; partisan news

economic issues: and agenda setting, 101–109, 166–168, 220–221; coding of, 23, 77, 96–97, 133, 156, 210; coverage of, 101–103, 166–168, as most important problem, 24–35, 75–77; and public agenda diversity, 77–79, 103–109, 220–222; and presidential speeches, 187
economy, as most important problem, 75–77, 150. *See also* economic issues
Edelman, Murray, 45
education: and agenda setting, 101, 103; coding of, 77, 97, 133, 156, 212, 229; House responsiveness on, 191; as most important issue, 35–36, 38; national levels of, and character of public agenda, 69–70, 83; and public agenda diversity, 103
Edwards, George, 176
elite-driven public concern, 20–21, 59–61, 75; about domestic issues, 36–38; about economic issues, 24–27, 30–35; about foreign affairs issues, 45–47; about government/political issues, 52–57; about law and order, 30–42; about social relations, 44–45; about terrorism, 50–52. *See also* event-driven public concern
entertainment: as a category of news, 133; as competing with news for audiences, 7, 9, 64, 89, 110, 116, 117, 121; criticism of representations in, 165. *See also* "fallen apart" theory
Entman, Robert, 57
environment: and agenda setting, 101, 103; coding of, 77, 97, 156, 211, 229; House responsiveness on, 191, 192n; as most important problem, 38; and public agenda diversity, 103
Eshbaugh-Soha, Matthew, 169, 170, 172
event-driven public concern, 20–21, 38, 58–61, 75; about economic issues, 24–31; about foreign affairs issues, 45–49; about government/political

issues, 52–57; about law and order, 39–42; about social relations, 42–45; about terrorism, 50–52. *See also* elite-driven public concern

Facebook, 66, 89, 118; measuring adoption of, 226–227; and public agenda diversity, 122–125, 128–129. *See also* social media
"fallen apart" theory: and public agenda, 14, 113–115, 123–125, 127, 144–146, 202; as explanation for public agenda fragmentation, 10, 12–14, 64, 116–117, 121. *See also* entertainment; media choice
Fiorina, Morris, 176, 200
Fisher, Ronald, 230
Ford, Gerald, 53, 73
foreign affairs, 19, 45–46, 59, 110; coding of, 133, 156, 229. *See also* general international issues
Fox News: agenda diversity of coverage on, 139, 155, 158; agenda setting of, 158–159; emergence of, 122; issue agendas of, 135–136, 140–142, 145; and news agenda diversity overall, 131–132, 141; and partisan news era, 66, 100; and public agenda diversity, 16, 117, 124–125, 128, 142, 145–146, 158–159; ratings of, 124–125, 158–159, 226; similarity of issue agendas of, 137–138, 155. *See also* cable news; partisan news
fragmentation, 61–62; agenda setting and, 91, 115, 148, 160; history and, 93, 201; issue coverage and, 102–103, 113, 115, 140–143, 160; media environment and, 10–11, 13, 69, 89–90, 116–117, 128–129, 200–202; partisan news and, 64, 145–147; and political power, 8–10, 16, 170–171, 205–207; and responsiveness, 16–17, 84, 174–175, 183, 187–190, 192–198, 202–205; versus polarization, 2–4, 12, 58, 199–200. *See also* "driven apart" theory; "fallen apart" theory; public agenda diversity
Funkhouser, G. Ray, 164

Gallup "most important problem" question: coding of open-ended responses, 22–23, 29n, 48, 51, 58–59, 71, 76; frequency of polls, 21, 76, 80; as a

Gallup "most important problem" question (*continued*)
  measure of public agenda, 11–12, 21–23, 76; multiple responses to, 22–23, 70, 72; partisan differences in, 132; Policy Agendas Project use of, 95–98, 189; recoding into categories, 22–23, 77; timing of polls with regard to events, 26, 50–51, 180. *See also under specific issues*
Garrett, Kelly, 118
general economic issues, 25, 28, 33–35, 65–68; coding of, 77, 156, 210. *See also* economic issues
general international issues: and agenda setting, 94–95, 103–105, 107–108, 221; coding of, 58, 77–78, 97, 156, 210; coverage of, 102–103, 109, 113; House responsiveness on, 191; as most important problem, 46–48, 50–51, 66–68, and news agenda diversity, 103; presidential leadership on, 187; and public agenda diversity, 104–109, 113, 222
Gilens, Martin, 203
government operations: and agenda setting, 101, 103; House responsiveness on, 191; and public agenda diversity, 103
government/political issues: coding of 77, 133, 156, 212; as most important problem, 52–58, 67, 142, 182, 204–205
Great Recession: and concern about economic issues, 23–25, 30, 35, 58, 155–156, 201; and public agenda diversity, 74–75, 77–79, 84, 127–129, 201

Hahn, Kyu, 64, 117
Hamilton, James, 164
Hamm, Bradley, 90, 148
Hayes, Andrew, 234
health: and agenda setting, 101–103, 220–221; coding of, 77, 97, 133, 156, 211, 229, 231, 233; coverage of, 103–104; House responsiveness on, 191; as most important issue, 36–38, 60, 68, 81; presidential attention to, 177–178; and public agenda diversity, 103–109, 220–222
Hu, Yu-Wei, 94
Hurricane Katrina, 26, 142, 152, 179, 182; and concern about government, 52–53, 55–57, 59
Hyndman, Rob, 221

inflation: as measure of social reality, 165–166; obtrusiveness of, 16, 20, 24, 68; and public agenda diversity, 75, 149; and public concern about economy, 166–167. *See also* economy, as most important problem; money, as most important problem
interest groups, 2, 14, 17, 90, 152, 170, 203, 206
international affairs. *See* general international issues
issue competition, 60, 62, 80, 82, 84. *See also* capacity; volatility
Iyengar, Shanto, 9, 64, 117

Jacobs, Lawrence, 84
Johnson, Martin, 118
jobs, 1, 10, 12; and public agenda diversity, 75–76, 79; concern about, during historical and media eras, 68, 75–76; elite influence on concern about, 35, 68; as most important issue, 27–30, 33, 58, 81, 174
Jones, Bryan, 95n, 188, 189, 190, 198, 233, 234

Katz, Elihu, 6, 9, 89, 148, 152
Keeter, Scott, 150
Kennedy, John F., 5, 93, 248
Kernell, Samuel, 84, 169, 170, 172, 178
Khandakar, Yeasmin, 221
Kreiss, Daniel, 170

labor, 97, 101, 103, 191, 200, 210, 233. *See also* jobs
lagged variables, 193–196, 220–223
Lasswell, Harold, 152
Latin America/Africa: coding of, 77, 156, 211, 213; as most important problem, 46, 48
law and order: coding of, 45, 77, 97, 133, 156, 209, 211; as most important problem, 36, 39–42, 45, 76, 149. *See also* crime
Lawrence, Regina, 20, 84
Lazarsfeld, Paul, 87
Lee, Jae Kook, 90, 91
Levendusky, Matthew, 117
Levine, Harry, 40
Lippmann, Walter, 18, 59, 87, 92
Long Island Rail Road massacre, 41

Index

macroeconomics. *See* economic issues
Martin, Shannon, 92
Martin, Trayvon, 41, 44
mass audience, 8, 10, 85, 90, 169, 172
McCombs, Max: on changes in public agenda, 22, 68, 69, 70, 71, 80; on competition for public agenda, 62, 80, 82, 83; data categories of, 95, 209, 215, 216; on news media's agenda-setting effects, 6, 87, 91, 92, 117, 148, 152
media choice: expansion of, 63, 83; measurement of, 225–226; and public agenda diversity, 9–10, 63–64, 112–126, 129, 201–202. *See also* entertainment
Merton, Robert, 87
Metzger, Miriam, 90
Middle East: coding of, 22, 58, 156, 211; coverage of, 145; as most important problem, 46, 48–49, 68, 149
Mitchelstein, Eugenia, 153
money, as most important problem, 24–27, 149, 182, 185. *See also* inflation
most important problem. *See* Gallup "most important problem" question; *specific issues*
MSNBC: agenda diversity of coverage on, 139, 155, 158; agenda setting of, 158–159; emergence of, 122; issue agendas of, 135–136, 140–142, 145; and news agenda diversity overall, 132, 141; and partisan news era, 66, 100; and public agenda diversity, 16, 117, 124–125, 128, 141–142, 145–146, 158–159; ratings of, 124–125, 158–159, 226; similarity of issue agendas of, 137–138, 155. *See also* cable news; partisan news

Neuman, Russell, 20, 63, 71
newspapers, 4, 63, 86, 87, 91
news agenda diversity, 102–103, 138–139; and agenda setting, 105–110, 221; and public agenda diversity, 105–110, 158, 222; and news consistency, 154–155
news consistency, 154–155, 157–163
Nielsen, 116, 122, 225, 226

Obama, Barack, 81, 177; and economic issues, 27–28, 30, 32, 35, 75–76; farewell address of, 1–4; and government/political issues, 56–58, 67, 199–200; and health, 36–37, 155, 179; and social relations, 43–44

Obamacare, 2, 37, 203. *See also* Affordable Care Act
obtrusiveness, 20–21, 23, 59; of domestic issues, 35–36, 38–39, 42; of economic issues, 24–25, 27, 31, 33–35; of foreign affairs, 45, 49; of government/political issues, 52; and news coverage effects on concern, 164n, 165–167
Oklahoma City bombing, 41, 49, 50, 58
Organization for Economic Cooperation and Development, 166n13

Page, Benjamin, 151, 152, 203
partisan news, 9, 90, 129, 142; as era of media, 66–68, 100, 111; issue agendas of, 130–132, 140–141, 145–146; and media as problem, 23; and polarization, 11, 117, 118, 189; and public agenda diversity, 64, 117, 121–122, 125, 128, 130, 141, 146
Peake, Jeffrey, 169, 170, 172, 177
Perkins, Williams, 169, 172
Pew Research Center, 10, 63, 90, 118, 123, 133, 226, 229
polarization: among elites, 84, 188–189, 193–196, 203; and opinion leadership, 170, 172, 185; partisan news and, 117–118, 122, 128, 130, 207; versus fragmentation, 2–4, 12, 58, 199–200
Policy Agendas Project, 95–98, 143, 166, 189, 190, 193, 220, 233–235
political power: agenda setting and, 6–8, 83–84, 149; public agenda diversity and, 10–11, 16, 85, 173, 197, 206–207; role of media in, 3–5, 14
Poole, Keith, 234
Popkin, Samuel, 20, 151
Prior, Markus, 63, 88, 116–117, 123, 150
public agenda diversity: agenda setting and, 105–109, 143–144, 157–160, 163, 222; change in, over time, 74, 77–78, 97, 124; and democratic responsiveness, 16–17, 84, 172–175, 183–190, 192–198, 202–205; issue coverage and, 14, 103–109, 113, 141–142, 222; measurement of, 73–74, 77, 96–97, 215–216; media choice and, 117, 123–125; news agenda diversity and, 130–131, 222; news ratings and, 127–129, 143–144, 157–160, 162; and presidential speeches, 179–186. *See also* fragmentation

public forum, 3–7, 9–10, 14, 88–90, 113, 201
public lands and water management, 96–97, 101, 103, 191, 233–234
Putnam, Robert, 200

Ramsey, JonBenét, 41
Reagan, Ronald, 40, 43, 81; addresses from, 170, 178, 186; and economic issues, 25–28, 30–33, 66, 77, 178; and international issues, 47, 186
Reinerman, Craig, 40
responsiveness, democratic: decline in, 84, 192; versus opinion leadership, 179, 186, 231–232; and public agenda diversity, 16–17, 84, 172–175, 183–190, 192–198, 202–205; as shown in House hearing agenda, 187–198; as shown in presidential speeches, 179–185
Rosenthal, Howard, 234
Rottinghaus, Brandon, 170

Sandy Hook Elementary School shooting, 42
Scacco, Josh, 170
Schattschneider, Elmer, 203
Schudson, Michael, 151, 152
selective exposure, 9, 10, 64, 116, 117, 132
September 11 attacks, 19, 65; and concern about terrorism, 49–52, 58, 75, 78–79, 84, 149, 201; presidential speeches after, 179–181, 186n5. *See also* terrorism; War on Terror
Shapiro, Robert, 84, 151, 152, 170
Shaw, Donald, 6, 87, 90, 92, 148
Skocpol, Theda, 200
Smith, Tom, 15, 19, 22, 23, 53, 59, 70, 71, 76, 77
social media: adoption of, 122–123; as disruptor of agenda setting, 168, 171; as era of media, 66–68, 127; and media choice, 63–64, 89, 118; and public agenda diversity, 123, 127–129. *See also* Facebook; media choice
social relations: coding of, 77, 156, 212; as most important problem, 36, 42–45, 66, 68
social welfare. *See* welfare
Soviet Union/Europe: coding of, 77, 156, 211, 213; concern about, 46–48. *See also* Cold War; general international issues

space and science, 36, 39, 97, 101, 103, 210, 212. *See also* technology
spending, 25, 31–33, 58–59, 79; coding of, 77, 156, 210, 213
Statista, 226, 227
Stroud, Natalie (Talia), 64, 117, 132
Sunstein, Cass, 64

T. H. Chan School of Public Health, 203
Takeshita, Toshio, 63
Tan, Yue, 90
taxes, 24, 26–27, 32, 96, 206, 210. *See also* money, as most important problem
technology: coding of, 77, 97, 133, 156, 212; House responsiveness on, 191–192; as most important problem, 36, 38–39
terrorism: and agenda setting, 19, 105, 113–114, 201; coding of, 22, 58, 77–78, 97, 133, 156, 209, 212–213; coverage of, 140, 142; as most important problem, 48–52, 75, 149; obtrusiveness of, 20; presidential speeches about, 175, 179–181, 186n5; and public agenda diversity, 75, 77–78, 102, 200. *See also* September 11 attacks; War on Terror
Television Bureau of Advertising, 225
trade, 27, 97, 101, 103, 191, 210
transportation, 97, 101, 103, 156, 191, 212, 229
Trump, Donald, 2, 171, 203, 206, 207, 245

U.S. House of Representatives, 16, 174, 176–177, 187–195, 196–198, 234
Uscinski, Joseph, 95, 96, 97, 110, 112, 168

Virginia Tech shootings, 41, 42
volatility, 69–71, 80–85, 110–112, 215–217

Walter, Martin, 118, 153
Wanta, Wayne, 94
War on Terror, 51–52; and agenda setting, 105, 169; as historical era, 65–66, 68. *See also* September 11 attacks; terrorism
Warren, Elizabeth, 1, 2, 207
Weaver, David, 90
Webster, James, 63, 83, 112, 117, 118, 123
welfare: and agenda setting, 101, 103; coding of, 77, 97, 156, 210, 231; coverage of, 103, 165; House responsiveness on,

191; as most important issue, 24–25, 31, 60; and public agenda diversity, 103
Williams, Bruce, 9, 63, 67, 118, 142, 154, 168
Wlezien, Christopher, 103, 112, 155
World Bank, 120, 226

Young, Garry, 169, 172

Zaller, John, 57, 152, 153, 154, 177
Zhu, Jian-Hua, 22, 62, 69, 70, 71, 80, 82, 83, 96, 209, 215, 216
Zucker, Harold, 165

Jill A. Edy is an Associate Professor of Communication at the University of Oklahoma. She is the author of *Troubled Pasts: News and the Collective Memory of Social Unrest* (Temple).

Patrick C. Meirick is an Associate Professor of Communication and Director of the Political Communication Center at the University of Oklahoma.

www.ingramcontent.com/pod-product-compliance
Lightning Source LLC
Chambersburg PA
CBHW061254230426
43665CB00027B/2939